Presented to

JOSEPH CHRISTOFI

FOR

POETRY

W.H.STUBBS
Education Officer
Inner London Education Authority

DECEMBER 1983

TREVOR FRANCIS

anatomy of a £1 million player

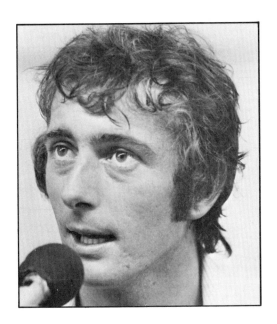

For Roy and Phyllis in gratitude,
Helen and Matthew as a chronicle

TREVOR FRANCIS

anatomy of a £1 million player

ROB HUGHES
WITH TREVOR FRANCIS

WORLD'S WORK LTD

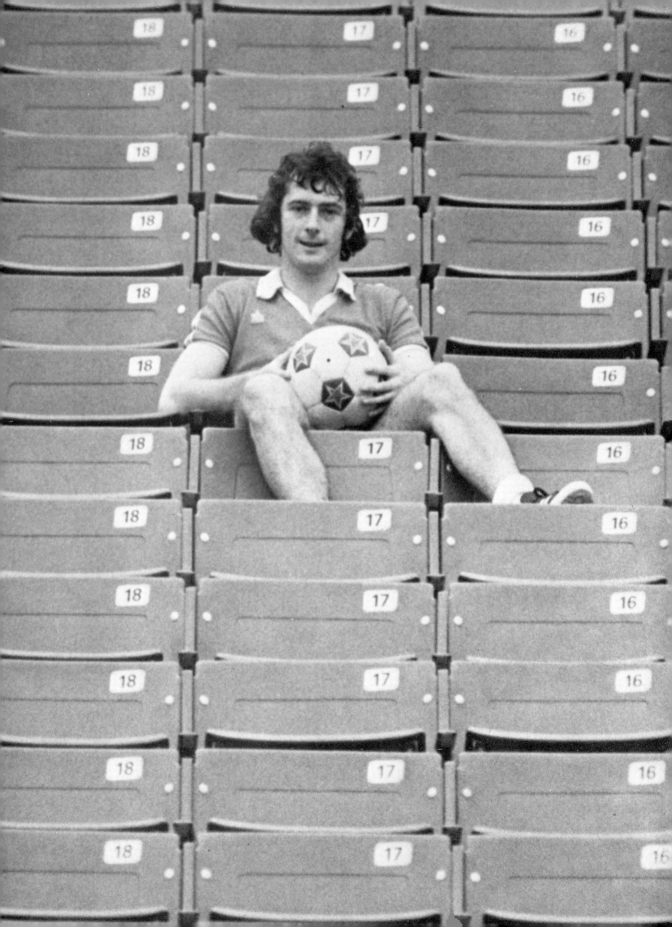

ACKNOWLEDGMENTS

The primary acknowledgment has to be to John Lovesey, whose idea the book is, whose enthusiasm and editorial stamina pushed it to conclusion. As Sports Editor of *The Sunday Times*, apparently unable to tolerate a writer's idleness during the paper's prolonged absence, John conceived The Anatomy of a £1 million Footballer two days before Trevor Francis headed the only goal of the 1979 European Cup Final. Spurred by that omen, as the book's editor he galvanised and guided – author, photographers, designer and artists – until demands and deadlines were met, more often than not during breakfasts supplied by Christine Lovesey.

Out in the world of Trevor Francis, people from Plymouth to Birmingham and from Nottingham to Detroit, unstintingly gave of their time, knowledge and opinions, none more so than the Francis family in Plymouth and Trevor's wife, Helen, who coped with the intrusion around the same time as producing baby Matthew. The grass roots of a footballer's life were articulately recalled by schoolmasters Fred Uglow, Jim Liddicoat and Bert Worrall and by Kevin Griffin who shared the goal-scoring exploits of Francis's schooldays.

Next came the scouts who pursued the boy, chiefly Ellis Stuttard of Plymouth Argyle and Don Dorman of Birmingham City, followed by the managers who gave Trevor the opportunity and us the chance to discuss at length even controversial aspects – Freddie Goodwin about Birmingham City, Brian Clough and Peter Taylor about Nottingham Forest, and Ken Furphy about Detroit Express.

There were others in football only too willing to give their impressions, including players Kenny Burns, Eddie Colquhoun, John Hollins, Frank McLintock and John Wile, and valued observers such as Bill Shankly and Jackie Milburn. There were people who helped us delve into specialist areas: the doctors, who included the Birmingham surgeon whose skill helped Francis through a serious injury in 1974; the trainer and physiotherapist George Dalton; midlands athletics coach Charles Taylor; former Olympic sprinter Ron Jones; and dance instructor Len Heppell. Michael Overs, a Birmingham City supporter loaned me a copious diary that was a useful guide to nine years at Birmingham; Steve Unger and Roger Faulkner assisted me greatly in Detroit; police constable Alan Cooper and musician Jeff Lynne, two close friends of Trevor, supplied me with anecdotes the subject's modesty forbade; and business agent Dennis Roach sketched in the commercial background.

Finally, there was a house in St. Albans where Jenny Hughes somehow invested two small boys, Michael and Christopher, with a growing vocabulary which did not, after a time, begin every sentence with the words Trevor Francis.

Rob Hughes
April 1980

Photographs by Gerry Cranham

Designed by Margaret Smith

CONTENTS

Key to introductory picture gallery
and picture credits—pages 168–9

I
MARGIN
FOR ERROR

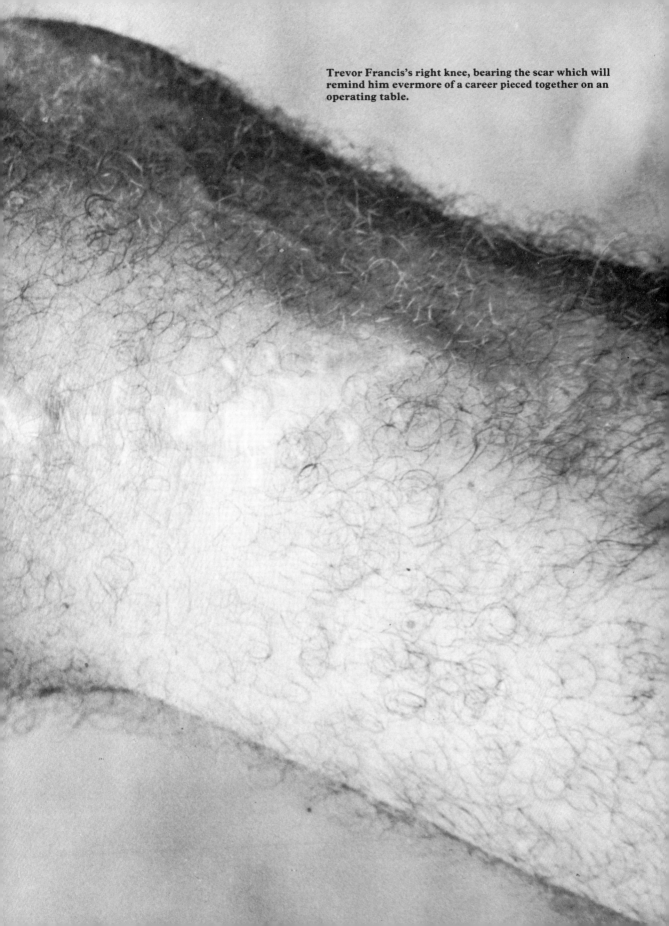

Trevor Francis's right knee, bearing the scar which will remind him evermore of a career pieced together on an operating table.

They had called Roy Francis at the gasworks, told him Trevor was having an operation. Right now.

Back at the house on Plymouth's Pennycross council estate, Phyllis Francis was left with her cigarettes to smoke, with a meal to cook that nobody would eat, with her nerves for once as tense as Roy's. It should have been a week of celebration; everything had been laid on for that first England cap at Wembley, the fulfilment of boyhood dreams, of a family's obsession. Instead they had six days of waiting – waiting and worrying as their son was carted from Sheffield to Birmingham, and from Birmingham to Leeds and Leeds to London, then back to Birmingham. One specialist after another examined the injury until, after the fifth assessment, came the decision to operate immediately.

So now, as Trevor Francis lay face down and anaesthetised in Theatre Three of the Birmingham General Hospital, word reached the parental home that the operation was under way. Phyllis, like Trevor's young wife Helen, was alone simply with the knowledge that it was an "exploratory" operation. In the operating theatre, the stooping figure of the surgeon beckoned two men and invited them to look down into the eight-inch incision behind the patient's right knee: "There gentlemen," he pointed out, "a complete tear of the *biceps femoris* tendon."

As the theatre guests, Birmingham City Football Club manager Freddie Goodwin and physiothera-

Roy and Phyllis Francis, the parents who left everything to rush to Birmingham when the operation was underway.

pist Jim Williams, peered into the tourniqueted leg, the surgeon commented: "When a tendon tears, it is not a *nice* tear. The ends split, so it becomes like a horse's tail. That is what I tell my students; it is like stitching together the strands in the tail of a horse." If anyone – football man or theatre technician – smiled, it was muffled behind a surgical mask.

The tail was stitched inside 45 minutes, half the time it would have taken Francis to represent his country. Rare though this particular injury is in a sportsman, the orthopaedic surgeon seemed satisfied that recovery would be complete, if tediously slow. He knew that the week's delay in getting the patient onto the operating table had placed the chances of total success near the borderline. He knew that the margin for error was fine, particularly if he was to protect the athlete's extraordinary movement and speed.

But could he, could anyone, have predicted that here in his hands was a young man destined to become the nation's first £1 million transfer? Or, moreover, that the leg would score goals for England, help win a European Cup medal with Nottingham Forest and, standing up to winters in Britain and summers in America, carry the player towards the capacity to earn a million in his own lifetime?

That Friday, November 1, 1974, had been neither

the beginning nor the end of the career of Trevor Francis; but it became, certainly, a significant turning point.

The first person to sense the severity of the injury was not even amongst the 21,639 at Bramall Lane where Sheffield United beat Birmingham City the previous Saturday. Roy Francis, a former semi-professional footballer who had nurtured his son's love of the game through most of his 20 years, was sitting in the kitchen of his Plymouth home, over 300 miles away.

"I had Radio Two on," he recalls, "and the match commentary described how Trev was through, chasing the equaliser, when Eddie Colquhoun tackled him from the back. It sounded as if he meant to bring Trevor down and there was talk of a penalty, but none was given. Anyway, as soon as I heard he was being carried off on the trainer's back, I said to myself: He won't be playing for England this time."

Mr Francis, an inveterate worrier, who cannot eat a meal on the day Trevor plays an important match, went outside to call to his wife: "He's hurt ... it sounds bad." Back in the kitchen, the radio commentary said he was back on the field, but it seemed a matter of minutes before his legs gave way and he collapsed again. He was substituted then. "I knew the lad would get hurt or something," says Roy. "I dreaded this. He'd just been selected for England for the first time ... I was near to a breakdown, on the verge I'd say. I'd been on phenobarbitone for 18 months with the worry of it all. I dreaded it every time he got selected for the Under-21s or anything, something always seemed to happen. He's got the heart of a lion, y'know; he

has, honest. So when he came off that second time I knew it was serious."

The father's anxiety had not communicated itself to Sheffield. Not initially, anyway. "All I remember," says Trevor Francis, "is going to strike the ball and somebody appearing to tackle me from behind. It was quite near goal, certainly inside the penalty area, but I didn't see who it was or where he came from. All I knew was that I had this terrible pain at the back of my leg. I was helped off for treatment, but I wanted to get back on because I didn't want to quit there. I wanted to make sure.

"I thought the hamstring had gone, although I've since learned it was nothing like the pain of a hamstring pull. I didn't think about the England squad, I just wanted to get back to play. I had a painkilling spray, and then I received the ball almost straight away and passed it about 10 yards with the side of the foot. And I just collapsed. I was helped off again by the trainer, George Dalton. It wasn't that I couldn't walk, it was just the pain behind the knee made me limp."

Drawing from Trevor the actual feelings of that pain is like asking a prisoner to explain solitary confinement. Yet as the event unfolds it will be seen to be significant to try.

What type of pain was it?

"What do you mean? Pain is pain. It hurt."

But was it violent, or an ache?

"I'd say violent."

Did you know something was torn? When

Freddie Goodwin (right), the manager who had to make a decision on conflicting medical advice; the man who then, and now, took almost a paternal interest in Trevor's career.

Olympic athlete Mary Rand ruptured a tendon, she said the pain was as if a broken bottle was being twisted inside her leg.

"Yes, I'd say it was very much like that. A sharp, biting sort of pain."

Was it the pain, loss of balance or a feeling of sickness that made you fall to the ground?

"I didn't feel sickness. It was the pain that took me down."

The staccato rhythm of that interrogation ended abruptly there. He'd had enough, poured himself a lager-shandy, and launched a new conversation.

The tackle itself is open to interpretation – or misinterpretation. The two managers, Freddie Goodwin of Birmingham and Ken Furphy of Sheffield, agree that contact was made but that it was no foul and no penalty. "It was a situation where he could have scored, it was a desperate block tackle which caught Trevor at the back of the knee, but not in my opinion a foul or a dirty tackle," says Goodwin. George Dalton is sure the blow brought Francis down from behind, but wouldn't like to say if it should have been a penalty.

A former full-back himself with Newcastle and Brighton before injury struck him down for good at 27, Dalton says: "Trevor Francis is the fastest player on the turn I've ever come across. I used to tell him he's that quick he's going to have to accept knocks and strains because, as a defender myself, I know how difficult it is to avoid catching the quick fellows."

Birmingham supporters, who stood behind that Sheffield goal, never tire of repeating that the tackle was a cynical foul. It prevented their star from adding to the 10 goals from 14 games which took Birmingham to within three points of League leaders, Leeds, and which put Francis way ahead in the First Division goalscoring chart. But their eyes are Birmingham Blue.

The eyes of Eddie Colquhoun are dark, like his beard, and unyielding, like his physique. "Naw, no way was it a foul," he declares, pulling himself to his full six foot to add emphasis. "I chased Trevor into the box and caught him here." He demonstrates, leaning back at full-stretch to put his toecap – fortunately gently – behind your knee. He winces at the memory of it. "It was nae a foul, man. Honest. *He* said that as soon as the match was over. Naw, never a foul. If it had been, it would've been a penalty. Maybe it was a desperate tackle, but nothing was given . . . and nothing intended. Trevor knows that."

What Trevor knows is, by his own description,

very little. He accepts, very readily, Colquhoun's word. Indeed, in his quiet, determined way he shows annoyance at the very suggestion that there are *any* defenders who would deliberately harm an opponent: "At times," says Francis, "the game becomes a bit too important so that some of the sport goes out of it. Everybody looks into it too deeply, questions the sport as if it were a battle or a war. It *is* only a game, after all. And a game that I love."

But aren't there defenders who would seek to prevent him exercising that love affair by putting him out of the game? "Physically, you mean?" He looks full of genuine surprise. "No, I wouldn't go so far as to say put you out of the game. They may try to stop me from playing by unfair means . . ."

By hurtful means, perhaps? "If kicking is hurtful, yes. Maybe for that game, maybe. But I'm convinced they never look as far ahead as finishing anyone's career. What you're saying is illegal. It's similar to manslaughter or murder, cutting somebody's career. I really don't believe it goes on. It's not calculated in that way. There are times when one player will deliberately set out to make another ineffective, that's part of the game really. And I'll even accept that he may resort, in the heat of the moment or otherwise, to what you call physical violence. But more often than not, it's accidental. After all, you are trying to make him mistime his tackle, trying to beat him through speed or skill."

Suddenly, aware that he has made a speech (which for him is rare), he halts the flow before saying, very deliberately: "But none of that applies to that tackle at Sheffield. It was perfectly fair. There's never been anything between Eddie and myself and we get on well even now."

In the aftermath of injury on the field, the first man to look at the damage – and the man responsible for advising the player whether to carry on – is the club trainer. Not so long ago, this was an *untrained* enthusiast who looked after the laundry and ran out to the fallen with the magic sponge and an abundance of kidology. George Dalton is not of that ilk; although the game still skimps on its medical budget, most clubs now employ qualified physiotherapists in the old trainer's role.

Dalton's qualifications came via three summers of Football Association treatment of injuries courses, plus a lot of practical work. Significantly, it was Freddie Goodwin, then manager at Brighton, who steered Dalton towards physiotherapy, partly because Goodwin himself had a fascination for the medical side after his own playing days were stunted by injury. "Do you want to stay in the game?"

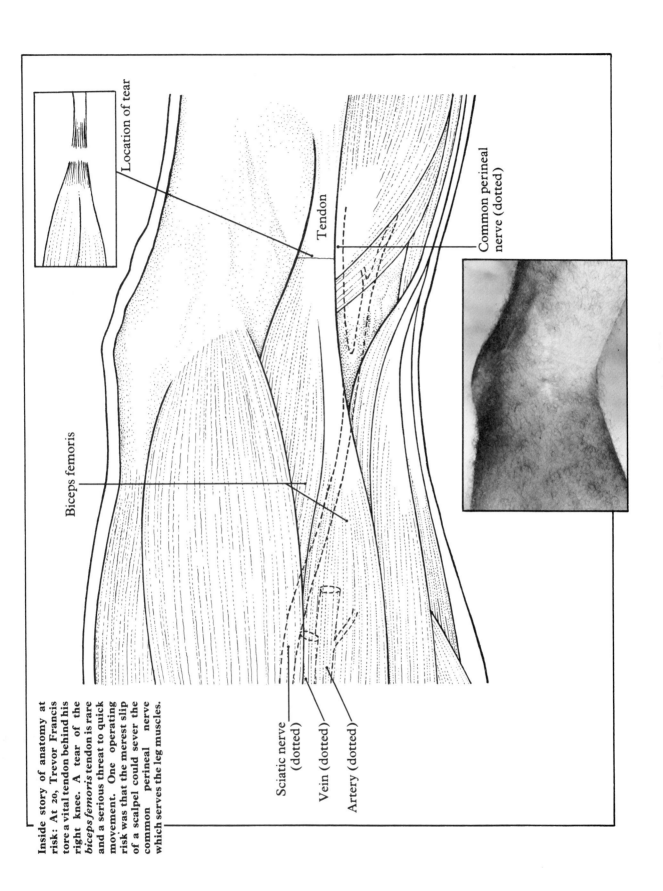

Location of tear

Tendon

Common perineal
nerve (dotted)

Biceps femoris

Sciatic nerve
(dotted)

Vein (dotted)

Artery (dotted)

Inside story of anatomy at
risk: At 20, Trevor Francis
tore a vital tendon behind his
right knee. A tear of the
biceps femoris tendon is rare
and a serious threat to quick
movement. One operating
risk was that the merest slip
of a scalpel could sever the
common perineal nerve
which serves the leg muscles.

Goodwin asked Dalton after he had broken his leg a second time. Dalton did, and we shall see how that benefited Francis.

"Only the player knows how he feels," stresses Dalton. "I can advise him on what I see. I can even advise him on the odds of his getting through a game with a certain amount of discomfort but no further damage to himself, providing there is something for me to see. When Trevor went down at Sheffield there was nothing to tell me what the damage was. I asked him to come off and, seeing nothing around the joint and that he could walk on it, I let him go back on. But it was obvious when he collapsed again that he couldn't carry on."

Dalton took Francis to the Sheffield club doctor who, similarly, had nothing to go on. They phoned the England headquarters to say he was injured but they had not given up hope because the extent of the injury was not apparent. "But I knew," says Trevor, "that I wasn't going to be ready for the England squad."

After that, his innermost feelings are now faint. Injury, after all, was not a new experience for him. He recalls watching the rest of the game, but then only that his wife Helen was with her parents in Llanelli for the weekend, that his bag was packed to join the England players in London, and that he rang his wife from Sheffield to tell her he would be going home to Knowle in Warwickshire instead.

His next recollection is travelling home on the team coach: "That journey was the biggest disappointment of my life. I was worried about the pain, but there was not a lot that could be done. I just sat there with an ice pack on the knee. I don't think I said much to anyone at the time but I remember Alan Campbell, one of our players, trying to console me, like."

One solid memory of that bus ride remains: "On the way back, I was listening to the radio and coming through was a sports programme and it just said: 'Trevor Francis was injured at Sheffield and is doubtful for the England match against Czechoslovakia.' I didn't feel too much reaction, I don't react to many things."

The team coach took the players back non-stop to Birmingham and Trevor returned straight to his house. He was resting on the settee when Helen, who had decided to travel back from Wales, arrived and switched on Match of the Day. That, too, concluded with the brief message that Trevor Francis would almost certainly miss his first opportunity of joining the England training. "Again, I didn't react much. It just sounded as if they were

Together again. Francis discusses tactics with Eddie Colquhoun (right), whose tackle appeared to cause the 1974 injury. Colquhoun later became player/coach to Trevor's American club, Detroit Express.

talking about somebody else. I'd accepted that the injury was going to put me out of the England match – and maybe much longer. The pain was enough to tell me that, although I had no idea what I'd actually done . . ."

The next morning, Francis, Dalton and Goodwin met in the Birmingham City treatment room. It was unusual for Goodwin to come in on a Sunday, but on this occasion he did and, though the full extent of the injury was still not apparent, they informed England that Francis would not be fit to join the squad. It was then that Dalton came into his own. "I was worried," he recalls, "because the tendon behind the knee, the *biceps femoris*, was not apparent. You can normally feel it, like a tight string on the outside and just underneath the knee. It didn't appear to be there. Sometimes, I knew, it can go into spasm, so the fact that I couldn't feel it didn't mean it had snapped for sure.

"Still, with Trevor being the player he was and with the England debut in sight, I wasn't happy." Dalton's Geordie voice lowers as a player at Coventry City, where he moved as physiotherapist a short while after the episode, comes in for treatment. "Anyway," Dalton picks up the theme, "I phoned a specialist, a good man attached to Birmingham and to Warwickshire County Cricket, and we took Trevor to his home in Edgbaston."

The specialist who welcomed them on Sunday morning turns out to be the man who ultimately performed the operation. His house is huge, detached and grand and when he opens the imposing panelled front doors, he peers fiercely over half-moon spectacles. He is a tall, lean man, slightly bowed from the waist as surgeons sometimes seem to be. Distinguished looking, his voice is educated and clear, with the merest trace of Brummie accent. He is around 50, younger than you might anticipate for one so eminent in the city's orthopaedic hierarchy.

Never mind. It is soon clear he cares about sport – and more important sports people – although he "never reached the heights" in school competition. He is also, when he removes first impressions at the same time as he takes off those half-moons, an engagingly patient and enthusiastic man, freer with his time than you might have thought. And he likes Trevor Francis for his polite manners as much as for his playing skill.

The examination was brief, the diagnosis categoric: there was, in his opinion, a complete rupture of the tendon; it *did* require suturing through surgery; it *meant* Francis would miss a minimum of three to four months of the season. Further, he warned that, if left longer than a week, there was a danger that the severed ends of the tendon would recoil up into the thigh and be very difficult to locate, never mind draw together afterwards.

Freddie Goodwin's head dropped. It was the last thing a manager wanted to hear. Francis was far and away the most important player in the team, a claim he did not relish but one which was borne out by Birmingham's own results. So, although Freddie Goodwin had every reason to trust the specialist, although he holds to this day a paternal feeling for Trevor, and although George Dalton was ready to agree to an operation on the spot, Goodwin dithered.

He sought a second opinion, a specialist at another Birmingham hospital who, again, saw Francis at his home. By now it was Sunday lunchtime. This time, the expert felt there was only a partial tear and that it would recover without surgery.

"So it was one for, one against," concludes Dalton. "Obviously we had to take it a step further and on the Monday Fred drove us down to Harley Street in London. The specialist there said he didn't think the tendon was completely ruptured. He also said it would recover. Fred was happy at this stage; instead of Trevor being out four months, it meant maybe only six weeks."

"It's true," Goodwin admits, "I heard what I wanted to hear in London. Four months out for Trevor would kill us. The opinions that the injury was relatively minor were what I wanted to believe. But George Dalton, my trainer, was unhappy with the diagnosis."

"That's right," says Dalton. "Over the Tuesday and the Wednesday, I kept feeling for the tendon, and it obviously wasn't there. I kept on at Fred about it and eventually he fixed up for Doc Adams at Leeds to take a look."

This perseverance by a trainer who had relatively little experience at that time (four years after his own injury) proved the critical point. Goodwin's own career had finished through injury at Leeds United, and the club doctor, Ian Adams, was a man he knew personally. "I had very little doubt that the tendon was completely torn," says Adams. "I had never come across a rupture of that major tendon before, but I felt it needed surgery, and quickly. Untreated it would have healed after a fashion, it would probably not have prevented Trevor from playing again; but it could very likely have taken the final gloss, the really quick movement away."

"So now," says Dalton, "it's two-all. We were in a bit of a quandary. Frankly even the chaps who'd said it was ruptured, qualified it by saying even so it would rectify itself in the end."

The first specialist put it this way: "If he were not an athlete by trade, if he were not a supreme athlete, I would recommend leaving the injury to heal. But in the case of an athlete who is going to make extra demands and stresses and strains on the joint, I strongly recommend that it be sutured as quickly as possible."

As they sat and talked in Leeds, the whole issue swimming around and over Trevor Francis's head, Dr Adams offered yet another expert, a specialist at a West London hospital who treated Arsenal players. It was Friday by the time an appointment could be made; Goodwin had to stay in Birmingham with

the team preparing for the following day's match, Dalton and Francis took the train to London. The hour of decision had arrived.

"This chap said he felt it was ruptured," says Dalton, "and confirmed it needed repair. Straight away I rang Fred. I stayed on the line while he phoned the first specialist, and he said to bring him back at once and not give him anything to eat or drink on the way."

Trevor Francis, in his placid West Country way, had endured the week in virtual silence. Dalton and Goodwin can scarcely remember a single moan from him. "But can you imagine how I felt?" says Francis. "I should have been playing for England, and there I was being carted up and down the country, from one specialist to another, hearing all the different views on what was wrong. Finally, by two to three, they decide on an operation to see what the trouble was."

That was it. On the final recommendation, the surgeons had decided to open up the knee as an exploratory measure; if the tendon was torn, it required urgent repair, if not nothing was lost.

What did Francis feel on that train back to Birmingham? Resentment, fear, disappointment? "Never resentment, no. I just felt disappointed at the fact that I was travelling to see people at the top of their field and they couldn't give me a definite diagnosis."

Back in Birmingham by Friday lunchtime, Trevor phoned Helen immediately to say: "Can you get my pyjamas and things ready, I'm going straight into hospital. They're going to operate." And he returned home to collect his things.

"I didn't feel frightened," he says, "more sort of relieved that something was moving. I had lost track of the days and I just wanted to get it over with.

"Helen drove me to St. Andrews (the club) and left me there. She was upset and in tears, the only time either of us really felt upset. I suppose it was all a bit quick from her point of view. One minute she's in the house wondering, the next I'm off to the operating room . . . It's worse for her really, but I couldn't do anything about it."

Strangely, as he recalled the emotion of that lunchtime, his voice reverted to the full, lilting Devon accent. Traces of his native accent are always there in his speech and Birmingham has, over a decade, not infiltrated at all. But there for once

Taking the strain. Tried and tested, and sold for £1 million, the Francis right leg now belongs to Nottingham Forest (dark shirt).

Devon came out loud and strong. Then it was gone as he continued: "Anyway, Fred took me to the General and within minutes I was going through the procedures. The quickness was incredible; when I woke up, I was heavily plastered."

The surgeon had been waiting at the hospital for Francis and Goodwin to keep the appointment. George Dalton could not be there but Jim Williams, the club physiotherapist, could and the surgeon remembers the scene with considerable humour: "I suppose you could say it was like a pantomime in there. It quite often is, with the number of people, students and so forth peering down. Fred (Goodwin), in my experience, cared about *all* his players. He very often came along when I examined injured players and he is the only manager I have had in a theatre, before or since."

Interesting, the way a surgeon will operate beneath intruding eyes while a manager in football forbids anyone to penetrate the sanctity of the dressing room. Dressing room is the operative word, for in America, where Goodwin was coach and is now president of Minnesota Kicks, the *locker* room is virtually a public thoroughfare.

However, Goodwin was in the surgeon's kingdom, even though the surgeon now admits to having felt "a bit fed up" at the time. Birmingham had, after all, "carted Trevor around" for various other opinions before, almost a week later, they came back to seek the surgery he diagnosed as necessary in the first instance. "Knowing Fred Goodwin and the club as I did," he says, "it surprised me that they dithered.

"In retrospect, I rationalised that if Fred had lost Trevor, he could see himself losing his job. He was probably fairly desperate and, looking back, I can understand his reluctance to accept a position which might deprive him of Trevor's skills for most of the season. But as far as I was concerned, by the time they eventually got him to me on the first of November, I was troubled by the delay. The body starts healing pretty smartly and if the torn ends of the tendon had contracted into the thigh, it would be difficult to get them down."

Goodwin, for his part, recalls the operation of November 1, 1974 as a child might remember its first bonfire night. "Fascinating," he says, "really enlightening. I went in there, dressed in white gown and everything, and stayed throughout the operation. I had done a bit of physiotherapy, knew a bit about anatomy, but it was really fascinating to *see* the muscles. The specialist showed me where the tendon was snapped, he said there and then that

there was absolutely no reason why Trevor shouldn't make a full recovery, said he could leave it and it would heal, but Trevor would lose a bit of quickness. The only important question was what was right for Trevor. It really wasn't a matter of getting him back quickly for the team – which leaving it to heal might have assisted. The whole thing that makes Trevor is this little bit of quickness on the turn ... there was no decision for anyone to make."

The actual operation notes read like a mechanic's list of work and replacement parts for a crash repair job – a comparison the surgeon accepts unhesitatingly. "Very little difference," he smiles. A typed sheet of plain paper, it bears the surgeon's name top left, the anaesthetist's top right, and then begins: "Repair of *biceps femoris* ... found a complete tear of the *biceps femoris* tendon approx $\frac{1}{2}$ inch from its insertion ...". It goes on to mark the spot where the tendon ruptured, to outline the method of repair and stitching, and to note that the leg was to be placed in plaster from groin to toe, including the foot and with the knee slightly bent at an angle. The plaster was kept on for two and a half months. "And in that position," observes the surgeon, "you had to be really fit to get around."

A tendon is a whitish, fibrous, non-elastic cord attaching muscle to bone – in this case the powerful muscle of *biceps femoris* to the fibula, the smaller of the two bones of the leg below the knee. The muscle travels down from the pelvis through the thigh to the knee; it helps flex the knee and straighten the hip joint. The tendon, which forms part of the lateral hamstring also divides and embraces a ligament at the side of the knee. It is extremely resilient, some half to three-quarters of an inch across, and with important bearing on the rotation of the knee is quite clearly vital to an athlete whose quickness and change of pace and direction, whose sudden turning and wriggling, is part of his £1 million value.

When the surgeon came to operate, he knew precisely where to locate the one-inch gap which had opened between the torn ends of the tendon, yet his incision was far longer than might seem necessary. This was because the tendon runs alongside a very important nerve, which supplies the front muscles of the leg, and the first major task was to mobilise this nerve without damaging it. Quite a common procedure of surgery – the ethic to do no harm – it nevertheless afforded the operator the narrowest of margins for error. Trevor Francis might miss a goal and work for an opportunity to redeem that; the merest slip by a surgeon's scalpel on a nerve could be irredeemable. Any damage to the nerve in fact represented a greater danger to the player's livelihood than the original injury but this specialist, a man used to dealing with the fine plumbing of the athletic structure – he operated on Norman Hunter's ankles and Nigel Horton's ligament – was aware of the trust placed in him.

He also possesses some facts and some beliefs that might come as a shock to those close to Trevor Francis. Eddie Colquhoun believed his tackle caused the injury, two managers, two physios, countless spectators and even two of the country's leading sports medicine specialists believed so. Francis, you'll recall, was never sure that the tackle was responsible, and the surgeon who made the repair is convinced the damage could not have been caused by the boot of Colquhoun. His reasons to doubt that are partly scientific: there was no skin blemish, no damage to the nerve or bone surrounding the tendon which would have been consistent with a blow of sufficient force to rupture the tendon. "No, it was not in my opinion caused by any tackle," says the surgeon.

What then? "First of all," says the specialist, enjoying perhaps the mysteriousness of the matter, "I should tell you that quite recently a colleague of mine, a fellow surgeon, was jogging in the street when his Achilles tendon – the one at the back of the ankle – suddenly snapped. He tells me he automatically shot round to see who had kicked him from behind. It is a very common occurrence for someone whose Achilles tendon ruptures to turn to see who or what struck them from behind; this is the first reaction to the blow back effect of the pain and even a surgeon, used to dealing with torn Achilles tendons, experienced this initial response of looking around for the villain." There was no-one, the street was quite deserted.

"Now," says the surgeon, rummaging in his notes, "when I first saw Trevor on the Sunday before the operation, neither he nor anyone else appears to have mentioned any tackle. Indeed, he had injured the knee in training six days before he came to see me. He had had previous trouble with the same knee a hydrocortisone injection was made into the knee the week before the match in which he collapsed, and he played this game the day before coming to me." It is a well-documented medical theory that cortisone injections into tendons can have the effect of weakening the tendons, but the surgeon says he saw no evidence or traces of cortisone in the tendon during the operation and would have expected to if that had been responsible;

Training in the Detroit sunshine . . . the anatomy of a trans-Atlantic player. Trevor Francis' recovery was so complete he played his winters in England and summers in America without a break for two years.

he dismisses the likelihood of the injection being the cause or contributing to the cause.

However, knowing that Francis had at that time a history of pulls and strains, which some people thought were caused by playing too many strenuous games at too young an age, the surgeon took the opportunity to test a relatively new medical belief – that the level of serum uric acid in a person's blood can affect the tendency to rupture. "I had written in my notes before the operation to check the level of serum uric acid – which is a breakdown product of proteins," says the specialist. "A number of surgeons have found that some people whose tendons do rupture have a raised level of serum uric acid. Some footballers in particular are prone to tendon injury, and we can these days bring this level down.

"Not too much has been done on this, and it is not yet written up in scientific papers, but I did find that Trevor Francis had a serum uric acid level of 7.9 against the upper limit of 6.5." The surgeon at first recommended to Birmingham's medical officer that he prescribe a course of drugs commonly used for gout; however, in his final discharge letter of January 13, 1975, he retracted that suggestion, saying that on further advice "though there is a slightly increased possibility of another tendon rupture, this is fairly remote and not worth subjecting to a prolonged course of drugs."

Francis made a good recovery, though he was treated by the same surgeon for a muscle tear in the groin in 1976. He listens, with more patience than most sportsmen, to the specialist opinion and says: "Serum uric acid – do you take it with water or straight?" He springs that slow, wary smile that often comes to him in troubled moments, stiffens and says: "I suppose this theory could apply to a lot of players, really. How would you know? We always look on the surface, don't we? In some other countries they tend to go deeper, but take myself: there are 22 teams in the First Division and if I had a medical with all of them, I suppose there'd be one or two would fail me, the same as people like Asa Hartford or Brian Little have failed; and they're still playing every Saturday. If you go deep enough these medicals would be a joke; you'd find something with everybody because not many players are fortunate to go through a career without a stitch here or an operation there."

If you watch Trevor Francis on the field, you will see him subjected to the most cynical physical abuse and rarely, if ever, react either physically or verbally and apparently not mentally either. Probe him with medical minutia, and you get the same response. His

voice is calm as he says: "I know players who would never get through even the most basic medical checks, yet are internationals. It doesn't particularly worry me to know that there is, or has been in the past, the suggestion that I might have something which someone with specialist knowledge can spot. I'm built the way I am, I can't change that. But the way it is in football, I suppose even if say Forest had found something at my medical they would still have to look on it that, if they didn't sign me someone else would."

Francis had immediately after his operation, and retains now, the attitude most of us carry through life: that the ills which befall others will not happen to us. There are something like 25 to 30 footballers invalided out of the professional game each season; that is very nearly one player for each Saturday of the season who makes a full claim on the Football League insurance scheme which pays a lump sum in the event of a permanent premature end to a playing career.

Francis, as we have seen, was surrounded by people, by George Dalton and Freddie Goodwin, who had been down that cul-de-sac; he read the papers and saw that Roy McFarland, the England centre-half, was struggling at that time to overcome a serious injury, just as players like Brian Clough, George Cohen, Tony Green, Ian Storey-Moore and so many more had fallen to the occupational hazard of their trade. "I was never in any doubt about not playing again in 1974," he says. "I don't think I'd ever give up, even if the word was bad from the doctors. I'd have to keep trying until I was too old to try any more. Playing football means so much to me – everything really."

Behind his right knee for life is a permanent reminder of a surgeon's skill. A fading scar where the stitches went in, and a small bulge, the size of a pea underneath the skin. That is where the "tail" was tied in catgut; that's where the edge to his career was put back together again.

We all know that was not the first nor the last injury Trevor Francis will get from the game of football. But there are two poignant moments which reveal that it was the closest he came to losing his gifts. Both involve Roy Francis and Freddie Goodwin.

One was the moment during the operation when Goodwin looked at Francis under the operating lights and said to himself: "We couldn't afford to replace him. There is no-one comparable in the game." And after saying that, and hearing the surgeon's confident prediction that there was no

The England caps that were denied him in 1974 began to accumulate regularly by 1980. Trevor Francis (white shirt) ... there, thanks to a surgeon's skill.

question of Trevor losing his career, he made a mental note to phone Trevor's father and tell him, ''The operation's over, his career is safe, but he will be out for up to six months.'' Roy Francis, who never told his son he worried about the termination of his footballing life, simply could not take the call: ''I heard what he said,'' says Roy, ''and I just felt faint. I dropped the phone down, let Phyl take it, and went into another room.''

The second moment, soon after the operation, was when Roy Francis met Goodwin and the late Birmingham City chairman Clifford Coombs as they came out of the hospital. ''Mr Coombs didn't know what to say to me,'' recalls Roy. ''In the end, he just said: 'You know I'd do anything for the lad – I'd build him a castle if he asked for one.''' Roy Francis choked on his reply, as he so often does if he feels he may say something his son might live to regret.

Phyllis Francis, however, knows precisely what she would like to say to a man who, for reasons of professional etiquette, prefers to remain anonymous: ''Do you know, we've never met the chappie who did our Trevor's op. Don't even know his name. But we owe a lot to that man ... whoever he is. Well, we owe him everything really.''

29

2
DISCOVERY AND PURSUIT

The first representative year – Trevor, age nine, extreme right, in Plymouth Schools Under-13 team.

"He was a name to me before I knew him. Here was a little chap who was an outstanding footballer at four-and-a-half, a nipper the older boys of 10 and 11 talked about in school. I remember the day he arrived; I used to watch them in the playground, always a good place to sum up kids. I didn't know Trevor, nor was I particularly looking for him, he just stood out. It really was a funny sight, this little lad with a big ball sort of stuck to his toes as he ran across the playground. Typical nippers, the rest all ran after the ball (there's no sense of waiting or getting into space at that age) and he suddenly put his foot on the ball, stopped and went back the other way with all the others just carrying on. I remember going into the staff room and saying to the fellow that used to take the soccer team: 'You may as well go down and see him – you can use him!' By the time he was seven, he was in the team and he stayed in it all the way through until he left. The last two years he was captain and it was nothing for him to score, oh perhaps a hundred-odd goals in a season."

Headmaster Fred Uglow must have relived that memory a hundred-odd times down the years since Trevor Francis's Pennycross Primary School days began in 1959. The look in the head's eye convinces you he is going to go on telling it long into his impending retirement. Old Cornish seadogs have their tales; Sir has his.

The way word preceded the boy into school conjures up a delightful insight into our national obsession with the game. Just imagine, some of those urchins in Trevor's very first team photograph actually knew, through their grapevine, of the rare talent in their midst. They knew about Trevor Francis before the first of the professional talent spotters, before some schoolmaster could provide the whisper that might destine a gifted boy to a Football League club. They, and Trevor Francis's mum and dad knew because, as soon as the boy could toddle, he was wheeled off down to the park with his Dad and every little "nipper" in the street who fancied a game of football.

"You've heard about my dad, then?" asks Trevor. "I think he loves football even more than I do – well, certainly as much. It is unbelievable; he would work the early shift at the gasworks – 4 am till 1 pm – then come straight home and the lads would all be waiting. He wouldn't even have a meal, he'd be off down Plymouth Hoe, or more often Victoria Park and we'd play for hours and hours ... until it got dark. I suppose it all started for me there."

In possibly any other footballing country, those park games would have alerted the soccer industry to anything approaching a child prodigy. In South America, he would have been snatched almost from the cradle into the professional net; in West Germany or Holland he would certainly have been receiving expert tuition in the youth leagues run by the big clubs. In Brazil, for example, it is not uncommon for a child of primary age to be plucked out of poverty into the hands of clubs which then nourish his body and his talent. In the Argentine, Diego Maradona, the teenage wonder boy, was

taken to specialists to beef up his physique from the age of nine and his younger brothers Raul and Hugo are receiving more of the same. And in the Netherlands, Johan Cruyff matured into the most renowned Dutchman of his time even though it was considered a bit late when he began bending soccer balls and opponents' minds at Ajax Amsterdam from the age of 12.

Trevor Francis, however, was committed to no-one until he was 15, and ready to leave school. The professional pursuit of a boy's signature is barred by law in Britain until the lad is 14, though Plymouth Argyle, naturally enough, had been watching and hoping and begging for almost two years. They then lost him to Birmingham City, who headed a pack of clubs which closed in after a much-publicised run by Plymouth in the English Schools' Trophy.

There are perhaps three major reasons why Francis was left to the schoolmasters' guidance until after the legal limit: 1. As headmaster Uglow implied, Trevor was a small child most often playing amongst older ones. 2. Plymouth is well off the beaten scouting track, and he had no international schoolboy honour. 3. His father, a cautious man, saw the wisdom of not signing his rights away in haste.

According to all witnesses the boy, also, managed to balance his priorities sufficiently to get his schoolwork and homework done in addition to satisfying his hunger for football. There came a time when he made a choice in favour of the game but by then he was 15. Even so, his father still sought the approval of his secondary school headmaster before releasing him to follow his instincts. "I was never brainy," explains Trevor, "but not the dullest, either. I like to think I have a reasonable amount of common sense. I was put in for six O Levels, but then I had to make a choice either to stay on in the hope of getting them or gain an extra year as an apprentice at Birmingham. At the time I felt that, since I had not made the England schoolboys, I couldn't afford to miss a year's apprenticeship.

"Football was everything to me. I wanted as much time as possible to become a pro. I left, but the plan was to attend night school on Tuesdays and Thursdays. English was my best subject and I was going to continue with it, thinking that if I didn't make it in football, I could work towards becoming a PE teacher. Somehow it never materialised, perhaps because things started so well at Birmingham."

The headmasterly consent was not incidentally, shared by Fred Uglow. "I remember bumping into Trevor in the street sometime before he did leave school," says Uglow, "and advising him: 'Be sensible, go to Loughborough first, then by all means get into professional football'. Of course, it was the usual, cautious headmasterly advice; my own son eventually went to Loughborough, though he was never going to be anything else but a PE teacher. The way I looked at it, Trevor was almost too nice a lad to be a professional footballer. If you sum up the average pro, he isn't likely to make money elsewhere and he's trying to make a bit out of soccer. That's not Trevor."

It is not Trevor's father, either. Roy Francis agonised and sought advice from Lionel Sim, a close friend in the teaching profession, before he accepted that the odds favoured his son's chosen path into soccer. "I must be truthful," says Dad. "There were

Pennycross Primary days. Trevor, age seven, already the apple of the headmaster's eye. The head, Fred Uglow, had heard about the boy's exceptional talent before he arrived at the school gates and, though swimming was his own forte, he was soon given to predicting that Francis was a future England player, a pupil whose good character as well as his ingrained talents would reflect credit on the school.

---

times when he studied with a textbook in one hand and a soccer book in the other. That was his love for the game. But you couldn't fault him for not caring about his schoolwork; there were times he sat up in his bedroom and worked himself up to a pitch, worrying in case he didn't come up to the mark."

Uglow agrees. "Trevor didn't have the same ability academically as on the football field," he says. "But he was still above average, well above average. And, again, it was sheer determination to do well. He would plod, he would struggle . . . and it showed in his work. He got a place at Plymouth's Public Secondary School, which was a question of passing our selection test within the city. That was sheer hard work for him because it was roughly one place in three – so he was in the top third in the city academically. And I gather that he carried on working that way when he got there. This was Trevor; only after he'd done his homework would he be back in the playground, and then even when he was only

The best Plymouth Schools forward line in memory. At 14, the boys "trained like men", at 14½ they travelled the country in pursuit of the English Schools' trophy, by 15 they hoped to be apprentices. Left to right: John Hooper, Paul Hryhoruk and Kevin Griffin who all favoured Bristol City; Trevor Francis, who joined Birmingham City; and Alan Rogers, who signed up with Plymouth Argyle. By 1979, only Francis and Rogers (then with Portsmouth) remained as full-time professionals, the others became the natural wastage of the Football League recruiting system, boys whose peak years were perhaps already being witnessed when this photograph was taken. A clue to the reasons for this can be gleaned from the relative physiques of Francis and Griffin, the two outstanding players of that 1968–69 team: Griffin at 14 was a 10.4 seconds sprinter over 100 yards, a sturdy and physically mature young man, while Francis had a lean and relatively small frame which was to fill out by a couple of stones through full-time training.

10, playing with lads of 15 and 16, it was still Trevor that was the cat's whiskers amongst them."

He was not exactly bottom of the headmaster's popularity poll, either. Everyone knew that Trevor's weakest sport, swimming, happened to be the head's own passion. Uglow, as the national schools swimming secretary would, however, only hold one former pupil up to compare with Francis, the Olympic swimmer Sharron Davies. "Trevor, you know, didn't really like swimming," says the headmaster, a tall, heavy man whose eyes give him away. They deliver the pride and the humour of a story long before he gets to the punchline. "But he was absolutely loyal – absolutely loyal and, because he knew it was the right thing to do, because he wanted to do well and because he knew I was swimming daft, he became a breaststroker of no mean ability. At a gala which was of quite a high standard, he came in third and you could see him hating every minute of it. But, because of his respect for the school – his love for the school – and because we used to win the swimming championships, he *had* to make himself a part of that team."

Pennycross Primary School, a small prefabricated building, stands above its council estate, two, maybe three soccer pitch lengths from the Francis home.

the end of it, Trevor would go out to win it, or try to.

"Well, he did get up, there was no stopping him. I felt terrible up at the school athletics with all the other Mums coming up and saying: 'He never ought to be allowed to take part. Look at him, he's so pale, he shouldn't be out of bed, the lad.' I must admit he did look awful . . . little tiny, spindly legs, nothing like an athlete. Anyway, needless to say, Trevor won the Victor Ludorum and then went straight back to bed."

Small though he was, the predictions that he would play for England had already begun to flow, not least from the head's study. Did Francis himself feel he possessed anything out of the ordinary? "No . . . well, yes, I suppose I always could strike a ball with power. I think that came home to me when I was playing in the Under-11s. A lot of teams played with little goals, where the goalkeeper could just stand and touch the crossbar. But whenever we played at home at Pennycross, we always played on a full-sized field with full-sized goals and I scored so many goals as a youngster because I could always kick the ball further. I seemed to have more power than other kids and whenever I shot, nine times out of ten I scored. I used to kick it quite high and the keeper had virtually no chance. Whenever I shot at goal I was disappointed if it didn't go in . . . I had one game when I scored eight and another when I scored six. They must have hated me, the goalkeepers."

The dangers of big-headedness must, surely, have loomed large at this stage? "No, no he was never that," insists Uglow. "The family wouldn't stand for that, for one thing. No, he was rather instead a sensitive lad. He would be emotionally upset if we lost but he wasn't a bad sportsman, never that; at any time he was justly beaten he could take it. Nonetheless, he was at nine or ten able to read the game so well it would embarrass him if we had a lazy or a biased referee favouring either side. He never let it show on the field, but he knew every move that had happened, he could tell you what every boy had done or hadn't done. He wasn't big-headed about it, he would just come and want to talk about it in a nice sort of way.

"There was one particular match upset him. He badly wanted to win a cup match but eventually we lost 4–5 or 3–5, something like that. Afterwards we discovered that our goalkeeper had had the measles and suffered double vision, but in the match every time the opposition scored, Trevor would just take over the game and equalise. Afterwards he actually

Trevor was in the playground night and day, the only time he came home was when he was hungry. He ate and went straight back again to feed his natural athletic talents – football, but also hurdling and the high jump. The year he won the junior schools high jump at 4ft he was aged 10 and would often arrive at the school jump pit at 8.15 am to practise alone. "He twinkled on his toes," says Uglow, "could turn on a sixpence. He had pace over a short distance but wasn't a good runner. His stride was too short but, there again he wanted to do well, he worked on it . . . he always wanted to *win*."

Trevor's ambition was always setting targets and struggling to meet them. It tickled his mum, and at one time embarrassed her. "He was nine, I think," she recalls. "Mr Uglow brought him home one lunchtime. 'Better put him to bed,' he said, 'it looks like flu.' Trev looked so pale and thin, but I remember saying to the head: 'You wouldn't like to bet on him not being back in two days?' It was the Victor Ludorum, and Trevor fancied his chances in that. Even in those days, if there was anything on broke down. It broke his heart, and that's how he suffered as a boy. He bottled it all up inside, and it would come out when the other boys weren't around. He'd have a good old weep in the back of the car going home.

"I watched him grow out of that. I rate him on character as one of the finest I've met. I've done 40 years of teaching, I've been a head for 27 years, and I think he's the boy I remember most about. Long before he became famous, he was a boy who stood out as an absolute cracker – not just as a sportsman but as a boy himself."

Once he had left Pennycross, Francis had to contend not only with the stony institution of Public Secondary School, with its high academic reputation, but also with bigger boys in a wider football league. Premature though it may be, the early teens are the years which begin to separate the men from the boys in terms of football prowess. With a textbook in one hand, and a soccer book in the other, Trevor Francis was out from under the admiring wing of headmaster Uglow.

Jim Liddicoat, a lifelong football fanatic, Plymothian and now retired teacher, is lodged in the Francis mind – father and son – as the man who "dropped" Trevor at 13 because he couldn't tackle. "He was right," smiles Trevor, "I still can't." Yet that incident still arouses passions around Plymouth. Before you can tackle Liddicoat on it, you have first to get past Bert Worrall, who managed the Under-15 side before becoming Plymouth Schools' FA secretary. "For pity's sake," he exclaims, "what do people want to bring that up for now? Jim Liddicoat has given his life to schoolboy football – 33 years of devoted work. I know this man ... he really rated Trevor, he worshipped the ruddy ground Trevor Francis and a lad called Kevin Griffin walked on. He was livid that Trevor and Kevin were not selected for England schoolboys. Whatever he is supposed to have said, he never dropped Trevor; all Plymouth teams – the Under-15, which I managed, and the Under-14 which Jim took – were selected by committees of five. It was never a one-man decision."

Liddicoat himself is a man who drips football. He and Fred Uglow rarely saw eye to eye, but their capacity for talking about Francis's youth runs parallel. "You can't imagine how dedicated the boy was," says Liddicoat. "He had a scrapbook on all the weaknesses and strengths of the primary school kids, you know. Yes, truly. And, my goodness, you should have seen the way he used to pad his boots. He was so meticulous ... he was a fanatic, no doubt about it.

"Now I kept my eye on Trevor, and when he came in to the senior school, I was hunting around for the Under-14s and I had him and Kevin Griffin in my side at 13, you know. I based the whole team around he and Griffin; Trevor for me was the Bobby Charlton of the side and the boy Griffin more of a Jimmy Greaves, the finest goalscorer I have ever seen at schoolboy level. In their different ways, I looked on them as equals, you know?" Liddicoat's photographic memory can outline the shape of hundreds of goals the pair scored, not only in the green and white of Plymouth but also in Ernesettle Athletic, a youth team managed by Griffin's father.

He can and does give a convincing appraisal of the development of the two boys, their speed, timing and personalities that in many ways accords with their own. But on the point at issue, Liddicoat says: "I don't agree that I ever dropped him, you know? Not from the Under-14s, he was always automatic choice in that. But he didn't get a place in the Under-15s quite as quickly as the other boy, Griffin. Now I think Trevor and his Dad got the impression this was my doing, but don't you believe it. The selection committee, probably on my recommendation as Under-14 manager, chose Griffin at 13 to go into the senior side, but that was purely a matter of physique. Griffin, you know, was a much bigger boy. We only needed one of the two at the time, and Griffin had that slight edge. That didn't alter the fact that Trevor did get in at the back end of that season, and that he scored one of those goals only he could score. I was on the line, and I remember saying this is a goal long before it happened. You could see him shaping up, you know?"

But did Liddicoat tell Francis he was not being selected because he couldn't tackle? "Not in so many words, no. But I don't deny I chivvied him a bit – he ain't done badly since, has he? Now I sometimes wonder how he manages to cope with Old Cloughie and those announcements in the paper – not very professional are they? No, Trevor was always a sensitive lad, and I realise that I was probably the first to bawl him out.

"It was during a match against Torbay Schools and I can see in retrospect that I probably put him off his game. I wasn't trying to say he was a fairy, you know; size for size he would win the ball. No, I was trying to let him know in no uncertain terms that in my team he had to pull his weight. By that I meant it was no use him standing around waiting for the ball to come to him, as he had been able to do as such a small boy playing with bigger lads up to that time. If I said he wasn't winning the ball

The slender physique, the emerging style. Trevor, in 1969, challenging for Plymouth Schools at Home Park, the "golden year". Mother's note: "See the way he holds his hands – piano fingers."
Left: Age 14½, about to join an FA course at Bisham Abbey that was to assess him as "fairly skilful, but needs speeding up."

enough, it was in the sense of going looking for it, wasn't mobile enough for a midfield player. I may have upset a few people at the time, but I reckon I probably also put him on the right lines, showed him what he had to do from being absolutely supreme amongst his contemporaries to go into sterner company and fight for it a bit you know?''

Thirteen years on, there remains a complete difference of opinion and approach by two school-masters, and a player and his father who still regard the period as a significant and perplexing stage of his development: "My recollection is not that good now," admits Francis, "but I felt it was a setback, my one real setback, really. I thought, looking back, that I was dropped from the Under-14 side because I couldn't tackle and was too small, but I wouldn't argue. I certainly don't feel bad about it now, although it did disappoint me at the time."

That leaves Fred Uglow and Jim Liddicoat still

mentally squaring up like two children in the playground. "This fellow Liddicoat had no love for me," says Uglow, "and personally I think he was inclined to take it out on Trevor. I'm quite sure he didn't let Trevor play his own natural game and that this would not have helped Trevor's development."

"Oh, don't you listen to Old Uglow," retorts Liddicoat. "He's a great man for sport, Fred, but he's not a great expert on football, take it from me. I was aware of Trevor's natural talent, and I think he knew that. He's never held any grudge, Trevor; he and I have been very friendly since."

Any differences were laid aside for the 1968–69 season – "The golden period of my life and many other people's besides", says Bert Worrall, then manager of one of the best sides ever to represent Plymouth Schools. "We had an absolutely outstanding group of lads, and an outstanding group of parents, too. As we progressed through the rounds of the English Schools Trophy, whenever and wherever we had a match the parents would be there without interfering ... the Francises, the Griffins and a good many others."

Here was the epitome of schoolboy soccer; teamwork and harmony, leadership and success. There were times when the schools association funds foundered as a result of the expense of unexpected travel, but only once, in the quarter-finals against Liverpool, did the goals run out. Inevitably, League scouts came like moths to a flame and no less than eight of that team attracted major clubs.

Inevitable, too, was the degree of the limelight focussing on Francis and Griffin, the Little and Large of Plymouth Schools. In south London, as Blackheath Schools were conquered 3–1 and Griffin scored twice, the local paper reported: "Griffin now has eight goals in four matches, but Francis was the boy behind this win, taking complete control of midfield." Plymouth had to travel in the following round and this time Francis, the skipper, hit a memorable hat-trick in a 5–0 victory – a volley from 25 yards, a calmly placed cross shot, a lob over the goalkeeper from the edge of the penalty area. The venue and the opposition? Birmingham. And, significantly, Birmingham, Arsenal and Wolves had scouts there.

In between that, and a disappointing 0–1 defeat by Liverpool schoolboys in front of a crowd of 6,764 at the Plymouth Argyle ground, Home Park, Francis and Griffin scored nine of the 12 goals by which Plymouth Youth Committee League thrashed South Dorset, and an average six goals a game for Ernesettle

Athletic Club. The success of the team accelerated the stripping down of its components. One by one, like little green bottles, the Plymouth lads fell into the professional nets.

Goalkeeper Hugh Scott was sought by Wolves; full-back Alan Holloway, and forwards John Hooper and Paul Hryhoruk interested Bristol City, who also gave trials to centre-half Andy Knowles and reserve David Pook; Plymouth Argyle captured winger Alan Rogers and half-back Ian Towlson. The fickle returns of youth meant that only Rogers, a clever and cheeky but never quite sturdy player, who had come the whole way with Francis from Pennycross, was to make a permanent League career with Argyle and later Portsmouth.

But the last two bottles, where would they eventually fall?

Griffin made a snap decision and joined Bristol City; Francis waited and watched and listened before leaving his chum and rival and going north to Birmingham. Up to that point, Jim Liddicoat's assessment that Griffin had the edge would not even draw argument in the Francis household. "He was faster than I was," recalls Trevor. "That's true, that is," says Roy. "Faster and a better goal-getter than you as a boy, Trev. He was Plymouth 100 yards champion and so good in front of goal you'd never want to give him a chance."

Yet when Bristol did give Kevin Griffin a chance, it did not work out. Why? "I think perhaps Roy influenced Trevor a little bit there," says Griffin. "I was very impatient to become a footballer. It was my lifelong ambition, probably the same as Trevor, but I went in for the first club that came whereas Trevor sat back and took his pick. Really if I'd waited, I could have done better myself. After I signed for Bristol City, five or six other clubs came in. I think it over and over, you know, and I believe the only mistake I made was to pick the wrong club."

So the only boy who could rival Francis at school had, he says, chosen in haste. We shall meet him again later, but what is significant here is that in 1979, while Francis was scoring goals for England, Griffin was a part-time player, scoring goals for £25 a match with Southern League Gloucester City.

The chances of Francis joining Griffin at Bristol City or joining Alan Rogers at Argyle were never as high as some people imagined. "I think I always knew that I wanted to get away, to start in a fresh environment," says Trevor. "Certainly I knew that the club and the people inside the club – and most important the opportunity they could offer – were,

ST. ALBANS CITY F.C.

Clarence Park, St. Albans

The English Schools' Football Association

INTERNATIONAL TRIAL

SOUTH EAST v SOUTH WEST

SATURDAY, JANUARY 25th   K.O. 2.30 p.m.

This afternoon we have very much pleasure in staging this English Schools' trial and welcome officials and players to Clarence Park.

SOUTH EAST (White Shirts)

1 C. JAYES (Leicester)
2 T. SAMPSON (Blackheath)
3 J. FLAHERTY (South London)
4 N. HOWELL
   (St Augustine-Canterbury)
5 A. MARCHANT (Barking)
6 R. FULTON (Barnet)
7 S. PHILLIPS (Harringay)
8 K. DOVE (Northampton)
9 A. WAREING (South London)

10 A. TAYLOR (Barking)
11 E. McCOOLE (Watford)

SOUTH WEST (Red Shirts)

1 L. BOND (Yeovil)
2 S. FLOWERS (Mid-Warwickshire)
3 S. OLROG (Swindon)
4 P. ELEMENT (S.E. Staffs)
5 J. IMPEY (Exeter & E. Devon)
6 L. JENKINS (West Bromwich)
7 K. STROUD (Swindon)
8 K. MORRIS (Wrekin)
9 T. SPINNER
   (Aldershot & Farnborough)
10 T. FRANCIS (Plymouth)
11 P. CHRISTOPHER (Poole)

Reserves to play :
A. ACTON (West Suffolk)
A. MAYES (Mid Herts)
P. WHITWOOD (Thurrock)

Reserves to play :
M. TRIGGS (East Cornwall)
D. DAY (King's Norton)
R. ROBBINS (Torbay)

Referee : Mr. T. BARKER (Welwyn Garden City)
Linesmen: Mr. J. WHITE (St. Albans)—Red Flag.
Mr. D. WILLACY (St. Albans)—Orange Flag.

Duration of game : 40 minutes each way.

Selections will be made after this game for a team to represent the SOUTH of England against the NORTH at Swindon on Saturday, 15th February, 1969.

INTERNATIONAL PROGRAME

England v Scotland	Burnley	22nd March
Wales v England	Cardiff	29th March
England v Holland	Coventry	5th April
England v Wales	Wembley	19th April
Germany v England	Berlin	26th April
	Hamburg	29th April
Ireland v England	Belfast	17th May

OFFICIAL PROGRAMME - Price 3d.

In 1969, the first and last chance for schoolboy honours. Trevor was hung-over from flu, the England selectors and big club scouts were not impressed even then, the main things I was looking for.''

Roy Francis can remember eight clubs – Arsenal, Bristol City, Birmingham, Chelsea, Plymouth, Spurs, West Ham and Wolves – showing varying degrees of interest. He told everyone the same thing: Trevor would decide and he would sign no pieces of paper until he was absolutely sure of that decision.

John Sillett, a former Argyle player and a friend of Roy Francis, was at that time recruiting for Bristol City, but he already knew he would not get first prize. ''I remember standing on the touchline with John when Trevor was 14,'' says Roy, ''and after he'd seen Trev kick a ball for 10 minutes he said to me: 'I'd sign him tomorrow, Roy'. Even then, I told him I wouldn't influence Trevor in any way.''

Later Roy Francis and John Sillett stood together at a match in which nine Bristol juniors were on offer as free transfers: ''That's the end of the line, that is,'' says Roy. ''I said to John, our Trevor will have to do a lot better than that.''

One man in Plymouth, meanwhile, was regretting every minute of the schools team's success. ''It was that cup run did me in,'' says Ellis Stuttard, Argyle's chief scout. ''Bloody hell, I'd had the schoolboy forms in my pocket until they were fraying. I'd been out in all weathers, I'd seen it all in Trevor when he was 13. I'd never wanted a player more in my life ... he had the lot, skill on the ball, passing, shooting, speed. Complete he was. People said to me he'd never be strong enough but I'd seen it happen before at Swindon; lads thicken out amazingly fast once they get full training. Anyhow, it wasn't as if he was a wafer, there was plenty to build on.''

A small man, nearing his sixties, Stuttard has large, intent grey eyes and the brisk manner of a scout: ''You talk little, d'y'see? Otherwise you let on, don't you?'' His accent is pure Burnley but he transferred to Plymouth as a young player and, apart from a highly successful period when he spotted the embryonic talents of Ernie Hunt, Mike Summerbee, Don Rogers and Bobby Woodruff for Swindon, he has been at the Argyle for 40 years as manager or scout. ''I thought he was coming here, y'know?'' he admits, ''I thought I'd done enough, but you take nothing for granted in this game.

''I used to see the mother on the touchline most weeks. She'd give me tea from a flask, and I'd tell her I'd still got the form in me pocket. I've spent hours, days in that house, trying to get them to sign, but Roy would say to me: 'Ellis, we're leaving the boy to decide ... leave it yet, Ellis ... it'll be all right when he's ready.' You've to get the school, the father and the boy all to sign and all I could do was keep watching him.''

And watch in silence, for the one privilege a good scout never affords himself is the line, told you so. ''Oh, I seen it all right,'' says Stuttard, ''but the least you say about the good 'uns the better. You don't broadcast it, do you? You hope that, being a bit isolated down here nobody else will get to notice it from the big clubs.''

Stuttard began to feel it slipping away the night Plymouth drew in Devon with Blackheath which took them to a London replay. ''On the Monday, certain scouts from the London area were on to me, asking if Francis was signed to anybody. And of course I was telling 'em lies – white lies, like – telling 'em, 'Oh yes, he's our player'. At first, that put 'em off, but then the team played the next round up in Birmingham, and it all started again. I saw it coming, tried to get him to sign, but he was free at the time and both Birmingham and Wolves invited him up to show him around and that was it. Shortly afterwards he signed for Birmingham.''

Somehow Ellis had felt he would keep Francis away from the big clubs. ''I did. I felt that because we look after lads here, because he used to come up to the club for treatment, we had a start. But, y'know even at the death, I called at the house on the Sunday – 24 hours before he went to Birmingham. Even then I was trying everything I could, but Roy again said: 'Ellis, we're leaving the decision to him.' When I could see Plymouth hadn't a hope, I even tried to sign him for Arsenal – I still had connections there – but the boy's mind was made up. I walked out of that house that night. I thought back over the months, the years. I thought of the whoppers I'd told to put the London boys off the scent. Hell, I'd have given anything to sign him up. He's without question the best to come out of this area.''

Anything? Did he consider a bribe, a present, shall we say?

Stuttard shook his head, he looked pained.

It is well known that parents of talented boys sometimes finish up with new carpets or cars or colour television sets in exchange for a signature, isn't it?

''Yeah, yeah ... you hear it happens sometimes. But we didn't do it. What I tried to say to the parents was we'd not interfere with the lad's studying, we'd send him to night school ...''

Did he wonder what Birmingham, a Second Division club, could offer that Plymouth could not?

''You wonder, aye ... but I didn't know.''

People in Plymouth do talk of a backhander, in fact Roy Francis gets accused even now by Argyle fans of selling his son, what do you think?

"What did the family tell you?"

They say Birmingham did not pay a halfpenny.

"Okay. If that's what they say, that's it . . . I just don't know."

Meanwhile, up in Birmingham, Don Dorman, the chief scout, sits behind his desk. An outspoken Brummie, he was a war-time paratrooper taken prisoner at Arnhem. He looks like a centre-half but was a wing-half for Birmingham before joining the same Coventry City team for which Nottingham Forest assistant manager Peter Taylor kept goal. "Harry Storer's team," says Dorman. "He taught us the basics."

Dorman's voice booms through the thinly-partitioned offices of Birmingham City. In 23 years as Birmingham chief scout, he's operated on a shoestring of 10 part-time scouts. "I'm very friendly with a lot of schoolmasters, y'see. You get to know the judgment of schoolmasters; mind you, when you get there sometimes you could cry; sometimes you go to see one lad and you come back sold on another. That's what happened with Trevor Francis.

"Y'see, the situation was, I used to go down and watch Devon schoolboys and Cornish ones, too, before Christmas. You had to get your homework done by then because they reverted to rugger, a lot of them, in the New Year. Well, I'll be honest with you: I'd got a tip-off to watch this lad Griffin – and he was good, the lad was, I'd have taken him make no mistake – but at the time I was more interested in the lad Francis. I remember my contact asking me: 'Well, what do you think?' 'He's good,' I said, 'but what about this No. 10?' 'He hasn't done badly,' said my contact, 'but Griffin . . .'

"Hasn't done *badly*, the man says! My God, you only wanted to see him once. The thing that really hit me was he was so quick. Really quick – quick and natural. But there was something else, something you don't see in 99 per cent of schoolboys today: He struck a ball beautifully. A lot of lads scoop the ball up or what have you, but Trevor's touch was lovely and clean. Beautiful it was. After that, I saw he had two good feet, a bit slim but a nice enough build for the equipment he'd got."

Your mind flips back to Ellis Stuttard. Good scouts don't talk? Try and stop Dorman. "Like I said," he goes on. " You only need to go once to see it. The reason you go again is to keep contact with the parents, put yourself about. Having seen the talent that's there, you follow it around because

Don Dorman, the scout who did his homework and signed a £1m player for peanuts. "I believed in Trevor, I told him so."

you've got to win it. Once I'd made up my mind he's good enough for a pro future, it's solely me that gets him here. So I'd been following him around, getting to know the family when he gets selected for an England schoolboy trial at St. Albans (Hertfordshire) in the January (1969).

"I'd been talking to the father on the phone a few days before and he said the laddie's down with flu, what was best, play him or not? I suggested if he wasn't fit he shouldn't play, but in the end the lad didn't want to miss this chance, felt he might never get another . . . anyway, he played. I'll always remember that day; I took three scouts from this club with me. It was a practice of mine not to mention names, let them form their own opinions. Well, he had a stinker, and my three and a lot of others didn't rate Trevor Francis too much on what they saw.

"It's amazing, really. When you look back, that

day probably threw some of the bigger clubs off his trail. Anyhow, it finished up between the Wolves and ourselves, and we won him, put it that way. All your top scouts as they call 'em – I class myself one of them – came to me when he broke into the team and asked: 'Where the hell did you get him?' I told some of 'em they'd seen him ... there was Charlie Ferguson of Sunderland, Charlie Faulkner of Spurs, Gordon Clark of Arsenal, they'd all been there at St. Albans. I told 'em to go and look in their programmes. 'But he did nothing that afternoon,' they said and I told 'em: 'You're right, and it's to my advantage.'"

Dorman is amused by reports published over the years telling how Stan Cullis had watched Francis during a trial game and turned to tell his chief scout after 20 minutes: 'Don, that's the one we must sign.' Cullis was Birmingham manager at the time, but what the press called a trial was in fact a game laid on by the club "to impress *them*, the lads we had already decided we wanted to sign". Dorman's system was that he signed apprentices and told the manager afterwards and, as it happens, 20 minutes was correct – that was all Cullis saw of the match after returning from a Football League meeting in London.

Don Dorman was aware that Ellis Stuttard had tried, at the eleventh hour to divert Francis to Arsenal. That, he feels, played right into his hands: "I'm a great believer in telling young lads to forget the glamour clubs. They may be interested and all the rest of it, but think what you've got to compete with. Come to us, we've got all the facilities, and we'll get you in the first team as soon as possible. It's no good being a reserve player – playing in the youth and reserves in the Central League for two or three years will kill you."

He pauses, looks you in the eye, and continues: "I'll give you an example. It's a classic. Right on our doorstep. A lad called Colin Booth, played for Manchester schoolboys, England schoolboys ... every representative honour. He was chased up and down the country by 14 clubs. I wanted him here, I'll admit it, but the lad chose Wolves. Now the Wolves at that time had two of the best inside-forwards in the League – Broadbent and Mason. It was a fine tradition to follow, but it meant that all Colin got was the odd game.

"His class had got him in the reserves, and in no time – that's because he was a very good player. But this is my point; he got used to the lack of atmosphere and pace of the game and by the time he got a transfer to Forest it was too late. He got no higher

and is out of the game now." Dorman looks and waits for the reaction. If necessary, if a youngster like Francis looks suitably impressed, he will conclude briefly that Colin would have made it here at Birmingham; if there is still doubt, then – Dorman might tell him how Terry Hennessey, the Welsh international chose Birmingham instead of Manchester United (though not, presumably, how Hennessey finished up an early casualty to the game).

Not only Trevor, but Trevor's Mum and Dad were given this verbal persuasion. "A good chief scout," says Dorman, "will sell himself before the club, if you see what I mean. If I can convince the parents that once the lad comes to the club he will be under my supervision and my charge, if I can make the parents believe in *me*, that is more important than selling the club. The coaches and the manager at the time may not have won Trevor over, but I believed in Trevor, I told him this. It was important he believed in me, important because if he was coming to Birmingham, 200 miles away from his home, in a strange city with a strange manager and coaches and players, he had to have someone there who believed in him."

He visited the family home in Plymouth, then entertained them at his home and over drinks at his club outside Birmingham. He even invited Trevor's Aunt Doris, who kept The Cherry Tree pub on the Pennycross estate and whose phone was a vital link. He realised they were a home-loving family and he talked at length about the digs he would put Trevor into.

We reach the same stage in the conversation, as with Stuttard, where the answers shorten appreciably. Once again we asked whether there was any question of a pay-off? It's well known that fathers of promising boys finish up sometimes with a new car, carpets or TV, especially where there's competition.

"Never came up. They were more concerned that he went to the right club, which it proved he did."

In Plymouth, there's people who say he should have stayed at Argyle, would have done if Birmingham had not lined the family pockets?

"Typical of the narrow-minded attitude. A boy has gone away from them and done good, so all they can do is point the finger, say he must have been bought. Load of bloody nonsense."

It does happen though – unless you are insisting it never occurs?

"I've heard it happens, but not with Trevor Francis, not with Kenny Burns, not with Terry

Hennessey, Bob Latchford or any others I've brought to this club. We don't do it. Look – you're talking illegal payments, right?''

Right.

"Do you think if I had made any I'd tell you about them?''

Why, is there a possibility?

"None whatsoever. Look, supposing I had paid Trevor Francis's Dad X amount of money to, let's say scout for me, put it that way. Supposing Trevor had gone out of the game at 17, I've got the father on my back then. Those clubs that do it make rods for their own back, put themselves in jeopardy because that can put them out of business. It's not worth considering. The money talk is jealousy, it's maybe a good excuse for those who fail to sign him.''

Was Trevor hard to win?

"A little, yeah, yeah. They are when they're intelligent.''

By the time Trevor Francis was asked to make up his mind the two principal scouts who got closest to him had each, in a different style, tried everything they knew that was legal to tempt him. Ellis Stuttard had lost to Don Dorman, it was perhaps as simple as that.

Ironically, both were to get a visit from the player last autumn, Stuttard by way of a testimonial match between Plymouth Argyle and Nottingham Forest, which gave him £15,000 less expenses for his 40 years in the game. Dorman, in Worcester hospital where he was recovering from a heart attack suffered on the M1 motorway whilst returning from a scouting mission to Bedford. He was then 57.

Roy Francis, whose memory is something the family all lean on, has far greater recall than Trevor of the weekend which altered the course of his life: "Trevor had gone up to Birmingham for a weekend as guest of the club to look around,'' says Roy. "My sister at The Cherry Tree sent a message on the Saturday to say Trevor had rung, could we go and phone him back. Trevor said Don Dorman wanted to know if he could stay an extra day because he didn't want to send him home at night, and when Trevor came home that Sunday I knew as soon as I saw him, he'd sign. He liked it up there, enjoyed his weekend. He felt the people were right and he would get a chance of a better start . . . a quicker start.

"He had offers to go to other clubs, spend weekends at other clubs, but he came straight out and said he wanted to sign for Birmingham. I asked him 'Are you sure – you can have another weekend up there if you like, to help you decide.' He was sure. That was when we went up; we were invited to

spend a weekend in Birmingham. Well, we were already pretty sure Trevor was going to sign for them because I'm not the type to go and spend a weekend just to get a free weekend. We left here quarter past four on the Friday, got there about quarter past ten that night and Dorman took us to his working men's club – Acocks Green it was. He never asked me there and then, but if he would 'ave I'd have told him Trevor was making up his mind.

"I think it was finally on the Sunday lunchtime that Don Dorman asked me: 'What's it to be Roy, what's Trevor going to do?' I said he'd make up his own decision but that if he said yes to Birmingham, I'd ensure he kept his word. That was it, gentleman's agreement . . . Trevor went to Birmingham.''

There remained one final question to put to the Francis family – the same one that has been whispered around Plymouth for a decade. Before you put the question, you believe it an imposition and what is more an unnecessary one. You could no more envisage Roy Francis taking an inducement to give up his son than see Trevor Francis as England goalkeeper. He is too principled a man. So the question is defensive:

I believe that if you were offered money for Trevor to sign you would have said no?

"I would 'ave accepted it. Yes I would 'ave . . . that's telling you the truth. Because we had nothing. Nothing at all. I'll tell you, my wage at the time was £97 a month, that was to feed, clothe and keep a family of five. No, there were eight clubs in, and not one offered a thing – no, I tell a lie, there was some talk of one paying me £4 a week to be what they call a scout. You read in the papers of five thousand quid being offered for this boy and that, but it was never suggested to me. Being honest with you, I look back and don't know if I could have turned it down. I had the rest of the family to think of . . . but I never had any decision to make.''

He pauses, looks you straight in the eye as always, and says: "You can put this down. You should do. I'd never been in debt in my life. What we didn't have we saved for, but when Trevor went to Birmingham it cost us money for a new suit, new shoes – £21 if I'm not mistaken. And we had to have a car which we couldn't afford; I bought an old Morris 1000 off my sister, she was going to Singapore for a time and I used to do jobs, painting and decorating, in her guest house to work the £200 off. Phyllis was taking in sewing because the one thing we could never do was just leave Trevor up there in Birmingham without us going up to be there when he needed it.''

3 QUESTIONS OF ORIGIN

Family portrait, 1960. Roy and Phyllis Francis with Trevor (left, age six), Ian (age three-and-a-half), and Carolyn (age one).

"Coaches don't make footballers," rasps Bill Shankly. "Mothers and fathers make footballers."

The old Scottish sage of Anfield seldom needs to summon many words to get to the centre – in this case, the womb – of a footballing matter. If, as he implies, you have to be *born* with talent, then Trevor John Francis was invested with his gifts on April 19, 1954, at 41 Morley Place, Plymouth.

The house no longer exists, the place is converted into a shrine to another form of ball control, ten-pin bowling. But some say it was there, in a small two-floor flat, that the skill was brought into this world along with the hernia which Trevor Francis had at birth. They, and Shankly and philosophers and men of the arts down the years, support the belief that talent can be developed, but not taught.

Trevor does himself. He was teaching young boys on the lush carpet of an American Astrodome in the summer of 1979 when he turned to reflect privately: "They haven't got the eye for it. I always knew what I wanted to do with a ball, or a cricket bat. It's either there or it's not, it's something born into you.

"All the enthusiasm in the world won't make up for it. I often see youngsters – at home as well as here – try to pass a ball. And they don't know how to pass it. Really, they've no chance ... though you don't tell them that."

That judgment and the role as teacher may later mature into something else: Francis is, after all, a gifted athlete young enough to suggest he has yet to reach his own prime. Yet to see him with children, to see his eye search for and encourage precocious skills, is to recognise a tutor in the making. A coach of youth, perhaps, rather than of men.

But how does Francis, the player, reconcile a belief in natural ability with the extreme dedication to self-improvement which began long before he turned professional at 15? "I find it difficult to talk about," he admits before, as so often, doing just that with a succinct and articulate summary: "Heading, volleying and general fitness were made by coaches working specifically on those aspects. But I never had to practise dribbling, chipping and seeing things. People have always said I've got vision; it's more, I'd say, alertness. I'm a quick driver and my wife Helen often remarks on things I've done or avoided before she's even seen them.

"You can improve *every* aspect, but you've got to have a foundation to build on."

Foundations, however, are useless without builders. Even genius, without discipline, amounts to waste – as we have seen with George Best and Stanley Bowles. Without genius, without apparent natural brilliance, we have also seen players like Alan Ball and Kevin Keegan drive themselves, as a result of overwhelming enthusiasm and determination, towards magnificent achievements. So, is the brilliant player to be born not merely with touch and timing and awareness, but also the perfect temperament?

And is that combination an act of God? Is it genetic? To what degree is it conditioned by environment, by parents and teachers who help draw the talent out?

"Aye, ye can help a man be a better player," concedes Bill Shankly. "Ye can get him fit to play – fit for football, not for running miles. Derek Ibbotson came to Huddersfield to train while I was manager; he could run a mile in 3 minutes 57 seconds, the players couldnae do that. But he was finished in half-an-hour at five-a-sides. See what I mean, son? You've to get fit for football.

"Now Trevor Francis is a natural runner to start with. A loose runner, quick, sharp. He's a nice, easy kicker of a ball. I watched him score a goal at Everton – aye, it was his left foot, too. It was a gifted shot. It was not an ordinary football shot at all, more like something Jack Nicklaus would play with a golf club. There's no coach helped him do that."

Another legendary figure who believes football, particularly Trevor Francis's brand, is a natural endowment is Jackie Milburn – Newcastle's "Wor Jackie" whose own pace was said to be like a whippet out of a trap, whose two-footed finishing carried the Geordies to three FA Cup Final victories in the early Fifties: "It's to be born in you, all right," says Jackie. "There has to be something there, but after that it depends what you did as a kid. Who you played against at school, how often you played and such-like.

"I was born in a footballing street, but the next street's game was shields and chucking stones. I could have been born in the next street and been a stone-thrower. But I was never out of our street; I firmly believe that what made me so accurate was I was always kicking a small rubber ball, the size of a tennis ball, up against the coalhouse door – hitting corners from angles and that. It's just habit ... and it becomes habit and habit and habit until it's natural."

Milburn in his Ashington street of terraced miners' cottages and coalhouse doors; Francis in the Pennycross playground and parks ... the image is mirrored. Constant repetition – practise, practise, practise, until the light dies. And then take the ball home and practise knocking it against the living-room door. Quick movement, according to recent scientific discovery, is implanted by nature in muscles, but even scientists could devise no more persistent stimulation for reflexes than have Jackie Milburn, Trevor Francis and their like. It is, moreover, to be found in the boyhood of so many "natural" players. Watch Trevor Brooking, and you see an elegant player of insight, touch, instinct; talk with him, and you learn that all this blossomed after years of constant practice with elder brothers in an Essex backyard.

Who is to say that the quick "eye", which is assumed inborn is not, in fact, the product of incessant demand? Are not fathers, brothers, playmates the first coaches? "Eh, well it is possible to manufacture one or two players by coaching and by help," Bill Shankly admits. "But the likes of Trevor Francis are born. A pianist is born. Ye can teach somebody to play the piano, but you find these people who play naturally and play better. We are born with a voice to sing. Nobody made that voice, God made it. Ye can train a voice, the same way it's possible if a player is right-footed to improve his left out of all recognition. But even then it's balance, it's something that's given you to work on."

Shankly's religion may be football, yet he in common with sportsmen in general, constantly refers to God as if the Maker apportions athletic prowess to the chosen few. Even in the age of science, we have no way of disputing it. They may have been matching thoroughbred racehorses at stud for years, yet John Hislop, whose lifetime's study culminated in the pairing that produced Brigadier Gerard, contends that mating best with best often backfires in offspring too highly strung to race.

In human sports we have not yet (to our knowledge) tampered with deliberate selective breeding. Hitler did order a purpose-bred athletic master race, but although his plan probably gave some pleasure to a number of Bavarian champions, he lost the war and the experiment perished, leaving intact the mystique of the genesis of athletic excellence.

And yet we do not have to look far to find genuine family trees sprouting sporting success. "If you get a good boy and ye cannae trace his football to his parents," suggests Shankly, "ye often come across it further back." Bill Shankly himself, a rousing Scottish international wing-half, reputed to have

Passing it on. Trevor's first coaches were his father and schoolteachers. Now he, in England or America, likes to pass on tips to youngsters.

been the finest No. 4 in Preston North End's proud history, adds: "My football background came from my mother's side. Two brothers were players on her side. My father was a professional quarter-mile runner, so maybe I got the fitness from him. Anyway, he was involved with football, and my four brothers were all professional players before me. It's a throwback, you might say."

Milburn's pedigree is as firmly rooted. He was born into football, married into football. Great grandfather Milburn was Northumberland county goalkeeper in 1888, four of Jackie's cousins were League defenders (as he was in the beginning, before being converted to centre-forward) and another cousin, Cissie, is the mother of Jack and Bobby Charlton. Even the women in the Milburn family played football.

Further afield, the Jones family of Penyard in South Wales, again of mining stock, produced eight professionals over two decades, including internationals Ivor, Bryn and Cliff. And when England schoolboy striker Wayne Clarke – the image of his famous brother Allan – joined Wolves, he became the fifth son of a Staffordshire family to wear League colours.

A newer fashion is the father overseeing his son's first professional steps: Both Ken Barnes and Johnny Aston, once players with Manchester City and Manchester United respectively, stayed on as chief scout with their former clubs and ushered in their lads Peter and John. While managers at Norwich, Queen's Park Rangers and Stoke City, John Bond, Les Allen and Tony Waddington all hired their own sons Kevin, Clive and Steve.

But why be so insular when we can just as easily look beyond the country and one sport for similar evidence of family leanings? In 1975, Oleg Blokhin, a Russian winger was carried by sheer turn of speed to the European Footballer of the Year title; unsurprisingly, his father was once Soviet 100 metres sprint champion and his mother the best 80 metres hurdler of her day.

Parental influence, or genetic inheritance? Perhaps it is no more than in any other walk of life, where a craftsman's trade, an artistic bent or even a factory bench is handed down. Clearly it is universal: In Sweden, the world tennis champion Bjorn Borg merely chose a bigger bat and ball than his father, who was once table tennis champion. His compatriot, Kjell Isaksson was world pole vault record holder, and Isaksson's father was a champion cyclist, his mother a top-class rower and gymnast. South Africa has one obsessionally brilliant golfer

and another on the way up – Gary and Wayne Player.

Back in Britain, Richard Hutton and Chris Cowdrey wield cricket bats something like their famous fathers, Sir Len and Colin. Alan Knott defied his father Eric to pad up behind the stumps and maintain family tradition. Buster Mottram's temperament is different, but his tennis is in father Tony's image; Denise Burton is pushing pedals now on mother's bikes; and Peter Duke may well have been designed to fit in Geoff's motorcycle slipstream.

Finally, in an area where privilege and certainly familiarity offers a leg up, the equine world echoes with recurring names: Lester Piggott derived his pedigree from a father, grandfather and two uncles who lived in the saddle, while Pat Eddery's Irish background shows the same form, with an extra uncle, a third, thrown in. Wally Swinburn has groomed son Walter, and there's also Joe and James Guest, Dick and Merrick Francis, and Michael and Peter Scudamore. Show jumping, too, has its paternal influences, where Robert Smith threatens to upstage dad Harvey.

And Trevor Francis? There is no sporting fame in the Francis family tree, no seething soccer hotbed in Devon to compare to the mining communities of the north-east of England, of Scotland or South Wales. There is, however, an inescapable affinity with the game in the family home.

Roy Francis had played semi-professional football for Plymouth Argyle, as well as Launceston and Newton Abbot. He was, as we know, something of a footballing Pied Piper of Plymouth Hoe (or Victoria Park), endlessly passing on his affection and his knowledge to any youngster who would follow him down to the park. Even today, he cannot pass a youth team game or a kick-around without stopping to cast his eye on skills there to be encouraged. And, yes, he feels the urge to get amongst them; one stray ball in his direction might just entice him in.

He watches the boys, but he watches the fathers, too. He understands their aspirations and their pride. "I watch the youths when I can," he says. "I think it's a shame sometimes the way certain things are drummed into them. I sometimes think, I must admit, 'Surely our Trevor wasn't as bad as some of these?' But the parents who come to watch their kiddies must get a thrill out of it at representative level. It's not for me to criticise; I keep my thoughts to myself."

Quite often, Trevor's dad receives letters from people asking if he can give them hints on coaching

Father and son, tutor and pupil . . . Roy and Trevor Francis. "You can't teach skill – you encourage it."

their lads. "Some ask if I would give the boy a coaching lesson," says Roy. "The truth is, you can't coach a very young lad. All you can do is help them. Encourage them."

Roy Francis played even his serious football for love rather than money, "like most people in those days." The most he was paid for a match was £3, although that took care of the rent and insurance and club money. He turned down an offer to become a full-time pro with Southampton because he and Phyllis, Plymouth born and bred, were reluctant to leave. Besides, football then was low paid and precarious, so they clung to the security of his job at the South West Gas Board, where he began as teaboy in 1942 and worked up to shift foreman.

"We're not a family that daydreams," says Roy Francis. "We didn't leave then, and I don't think we ever would. We're set in our ways, happy as we are. We have our health – money can't buy that –

and it's not often I can be tempted out of the house. If anyone wants to discuss football with me, I'll discuss it. Otherwise, I'm perfectly satisfied in the house."

The house, the same one for over 20 years, is a three-bedroomed council semi at Pennycross. The gas board van stands outside the gate, and at the front door R. E. FRANCIS is printed onto a narrow metal plate beneath the letter box. Phyllis Francis is waiting, motherly and full of bonhomie. It takes five seconds with Roy and Phyllis Francis – and brother Ian, who shakes hands shyly, switches off his TV programme, and sidles out of the room – to understand why Trevor's feet never got lost in clouds of adulation.

Ian, at 23 almost three years the junior brother, never wanted to nor was ever made to kick a ball. "Carolyn probably had more kicks than Ian ever did," smiles Roy Francis. Carolyn, slim, dark-haired and vivacious is coming up to 21, the baby of the household. She has been trying to persuade Ian to take her out for a driving lesson; a visitor's entrance clinches it.

The living room is neat and unpretentious. In a corner stands a polished wood cabinet colour television, bought by the 17-year-old eldest son out of his first inflated wage packets after he shot into Birmingham's team. Two England caps nestle behind glass in a wall unit, blue velvet caps bearing the inscriptions: "Netherlands 1976–77" and "Switzerland 1977–78". Did Phyllis Francis realise the Netherlands was the *first* cap? She did not, though Roy would know.

She lifts it out, looks curiously over it as if this is the first time she has handled it, and says: "Can you see any honour in getting one of these velvet things? I ask you. It'd be better if they gave him a medal. It seems to rule our Trevor's life at times. When there's an England game, we always like to go if Roy can fix his holiday days. So Trev rings us as soon as he hears the team; when he's left out, he's down in the dumps, terrible. When he's in, he bubbles down the phone. Can you understand it, for that?"

Her alert eyes study you for a moment, amused, knowing that her questions are rhetorical. She sees your gaze settle on a small silver salver which shares the inexpensive wall unit. "The only thing he won with Birmingham," she observes. "It was for promotion from the Second Division."

The one other symbol of her son's achievements on display is a framed photograph on the dining room table. Trevor, long-haired, 17, and with boyish grin, poses with Pele. "My favourite picture," says

Mum. "Pele's club from Brazil came over to play Aston Villa and Fred Goodwin (then Birmingham City's manager) phoned Trevor at his digs to tell him to put his best suit on and go down to the Albany to meet Pele. The papers made a lot of that."

Phyllis Francis cannot for the life of her understand how anyone can be surprised that Trevor remained outwardly unaffected by being promoted in his early teens alongside the world's greatest footballer. "I don't know how anyone can be anything but normal," she insists. "We're all normal, aren't we? You know, we have a Birmingham family that regularly writes to us about Trevor. We've swopped visits and they're daft on Trevor. We can't see why it's so marvellous just to know Trevor's family. We're the same as they are ... it's just that somehow, because our son happens to be able to play football, there's an image that he or we are different."

Upstairs, Mrs Francis has a bulging and lovingly kept scrapbook, measuring 20 inches by 12. It covers the Pennycross Primary days through to the Birmingham "superboy" image, and it encases the pride the family might otherwise ostentatiously display around the home. Admittedly, once the headlines became a daily affair, and once the Francis' family realised "half the time the stories are made up", scrapbook fever waned. Now the hundreds of cuttings and photographs which arrive in the post usually find their way into a huge carton of uncertain destiny.

The scrapbook, however, would make a useful exhibit for anyone wishing to make a case for skills that owe nothing to professional coaching. The *Western Morning News* and *Western Evening Herald* are consistent witnesses, with reports like:

"Francis (Public) rewarded Plymouth with a gem of a goal. Three players were beaten in a close dribble and a left-foot shot left Torbay goalkeeper Robbins helpless."

"Captain Trevor Francis's creativeness and distribution was of such a high calibre that it suggests he may have a career ahead of him in League Football."

"Skipper Trevor Francis (Public) showed why he is interesting several League clubs with a match-winning hat-trick. He opened the account with a cracking 25-yards shot that gave Keith Clarke no chance in the Birmingham goal. Fourteen minutes after the restart, Francis struck again with a well-placed shot from a pass by Kevin Griffin (Devonport High). Goal number three from Francis came four minutes later when he calmly lobbed the ball under the crossbar from the edge of the Birmingham penalty area."

Photographs in the scrapbook clearly chart the developing boy. Not until the Birmingham days did the physique begin to fill out from the greyhound figure inherited from his father. And some of those

photographs capture the parental support; there is Roy sponging down his son at half-time during an Ernesettle Athletic club game, Phyllis standing on a deserted touchline on a cold and misty morning.

Roy Francis, shy or at least reserved on first meeting, tells you: "No-one pushed or prodded Trevor into football, or anything like that. Anyway, he was a weak baby, born with a hernia as you know." Almost before his sentence is complete, Phyllis says: "Did Trevor ever tell you he was on the touchline two weeks before he was born?"

She waits, eyes again full of humour or mischief. "He was, you know. I wasn't interested in football until I met Roy when we were 15, but after that I used to go on the touchline. Never missed a match Roy played. I was going to matches till a fortnight before Trevor was born, and took him to the touchline a fortnight after."

Bill Shankly was right. Trevor Francis was, in a manner of speaking, born to football.

It was also no accident that his Christian name and his initials coincide with those of Trevor Ford. A few months before Trevor's birth, Ford had been transferred from Sunderland to Cardiff City, the second time he had fetched the British record fee of £30,000. But it wasn't money which caught Mr Francis' eye: "Oh, what a footballer he was," says Mr. Francis. "Best to come out of these parts."

Ford happens to be a Welshman, but that is fair

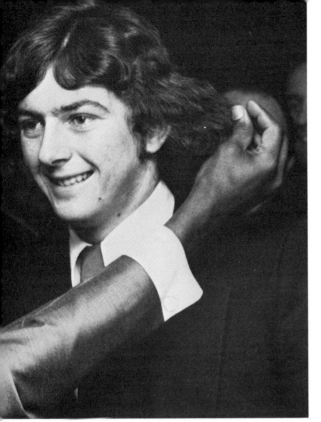

Trevor, at 17, the "superboy", with Pele in Birmingham.

League matches, and 23 in 38 internationals for Wales.

"A different type," says Roy. You almost daren't ask which type he prefers, the touch player he reared or the crash bang hero of his own day. "I've always been careful not to praise our Trevor," admits Roy Francis. "I didn't want to see him bigheaded. If he can keep his head, it's a great life and, to be honest with you, he's a credit to the game and to us. That's true that is."

Roy Francis, still lean, though hair grey now, looks almost sheepish at letting this fatherly pride slip from under his belt. There is a lot of him in Trevor; the blue-grey eyes, the polite manner, so mild and yet quietly determined.

"I'll say this to you now," he begins again. "I never gave Trevor any credit. I reckoned once he reached England standard, that was the time to start. I knew he was waiting for something from me. Well, when he got there, I think what I said was: 'That's the start of the job, now go and get some more.'"

Roy and Trevor Francis even search for the same word, though not in each other's hearing. "I've never once heard my Dad say I did anything ... well, brilliant," says Trevor. Perhaps he hasn't, to his face. But try asking Roy Francis what he thought of his son's European Cup Final performance in 1979. The pupils dilate at the memory ... "Brilliant," he says. He doesn't elaborate.

Probe him, and Roy Francis will dig deep to put his pride into terms that are, well, brilliantly clear: "It's not just what he achieved. It's that he's done it right. His job now is to stay there, but the greatest thing we've had from our three has been respect. We always could take them anywhere and they would know how to behave."

Again, try to get Trevor to explain how he managed to keep his feet on the ground. "I don't even feel I want to answer that," he says. "It's not even a problem. I'm more concerned with what people say about me off the field. If they criticise me on the field, I don't like it, but they are entitled to do that. But if they start criticising what I do off the field, I'm upset because I go out of my way to make sure I conduct myself right.

"To be honest with you, I want everybody to like me. Obviously not everybody can do, but I try to look for respect. I want people to think that I'm honest, that's my priority. And, I wouldn't say intelligent, but I'd like to think that people thought I'd got enough common sense. The other thing I hope I am is mannerly ... I owe that to my parents, I feel."

West Country licence considering how impoverished those parts are in footballing terms. Plymouth, anyway, was a place for sailors, explorers and navigators, as the view from Trevor's boyhood bedroom demonstrates: it is dominated by the solid, square building of H.M.S. Thunderer, the Royal Naval Engineering College. Phyllis Francis's family conformed to Plymouth tradition, her father serving 27 years in the navy; Roy Francis's family has served the South West Gas Board for generations.

If, through the name, Roy Francis had hoped his boy would follow in Trevor Ford's boot prints, he was right in many ways, wrong in others. The boy did become a professional footballer, he did break the record transfer fee, and he did play for his country. The style, however, bears little comparison, except that goalscoring is the end result of it.

Trevor Ford was a rip-roaring centre-forward. He stands 5ft 10in, the same as Trevor Francis, but he carried at his peak an extra stone, which was predominantly around the shoulders and used to barge past centre-halves and knock goalkeepers into the net, preferably with the ball. He went where the money was, transferring from Swansea to Aston Villa, to Sunderland, Cardiff, PSV Eindhoven and Newport County. He banged in 177 goals in 349

Like father, like ... well, not totally. "Trevor is softer than Roy ever was as a player," says Phyllis Francis.

"Not softer, Phyl..." contends Roy.

"Nobody ever hit his father and got away with it," explains Phyllis. "Trevor never hits back, but his father did. If somebody kicks our Trevor, he just says that proves he's got their measure, and goes out to beat them again. But his father? He'd kick right back, especially if there was anything sly."

"That's true, that is," agrees Roy. "Trev reckons if he's fouled, it's proof he's got 'em going, but I used to dish it out too. I reckon I had to; apart from one season as a semi-pro with Argyle – they were short – I played in Cornish soccer. A hard school, that was."

"But just the other day," Phyllis reminds him, "That Webb was marking Trevor for Derby, and Trev was taking all the punishment at the back. Roy was saying: 'I'd have him. I'd tread on his toes, he wouldn't want any more.' But Trevor just took it all ... that's the difference."

There were other differences. Roy was a defender who came forward to join attacks, a fierce competitor whose forte was to head the ball from the halfway line deep into the opponent's area. "I reckon that's why I get these migraines now," he confesses, "but I was a really good header at the time."

The father's pleasurable memories of his playing days are only slightly blurred by these headaches. The mother, on the other hand, has a clear and also painful recollection of her son's early obsession with a ball. "He was two-and-a-half," she says. "I remember that so exactly because I was pregnant with Ian at the time. We were living in the three-room flat at Morley Place, and I was at the top of the stairs carrying a bucket from the kitchen to the bedroom.

"I hadn't realised Trevor had thrown his ball out of the room ahead of me. I stepped on it, and down I bounced, all the way down the stairs with the bucket clattering after me. At the hospital, they said it was a miracle I didn't lose the baby."

The baby survived, but in it not the merest inclination towards ball games. Maybe, if footballers are born, non-footballers are born also; and maybe that quick descent down the stairs pre-conditioned Ian's lack of interest? "He never partook," says Roy Francis. "Even on the beach, you never saw Ian kick a ball. Carolyn would have a go at anything, but Ian didn't even want to go to the school sports day. People just don't believe it; they think it should be obvious that if one played so much the other would too."

Yet the brothers are close. Whenever Trevor is at home, he and Ian chat for hours between themselves. "We never learn what about," says Phyllis, "though I shouldn't think it would be football. It's funny you know, Ian is so serious it's not true. Trevor, when he's home, is always skylarking. When they were little, Ian never touched a ball and you could never interest Trev in anything else. He wouldn't bother to play cowboys and Indians, that was kids' stuff. He was off pestering the bigger boys to play football. Quite often he'd come home crying because he got a knock, but his Dad says he could always cope with the older boys for skill and he learned to take the knocks."

Does Ian ever pause to consider what might have been? What if he had inherited similar skills, does it haunt him that he never at least tried to find them? "No, not at all," he says. The voice is quiet, even by Francis standards, and the accent more pronounced. Even his physical appearance is different; Ian is more solidly built and studious behind his glasses. "I was never interested in sports," he adds, "probably because Trev was so good at it and I could never match what he was doing."

Teachers at Pennycross and Public Secondary naturally tried to thrust his brother's mantle upon him: "Oh, yes, always on at me to try," Ian concedes. "I did once – no twice – go in for galas at Pennycross, but it didn't work out. I came second, and I think third, but I didn't like competing. When I went to Secondary, they put me in for a trial at football, but I hated that. Couldn't wait for the finish. I just didn't want to partake."

Academically, Ian did well, finishing with five O levels. He had no hobbies to compensate for Trevor's pre-occupation with football, though the brothers share the same feel for music and have built up collections of similar records. Otherwise, says Ian, "I keep my views to myself. I never think about sport, although I'm very interested in Trev's career. Possibly I missed out; I look at what he's achieved and what he's got, which is probably more than I ever could get."

Jealousy? In others it could sound that way, in Ian it is straightforward, reserved realism. He and Carolyn, a data processor, are learning that a brother's celebrity can often rebound on their own achievements. In 1979, Ian traded in his Mini and, with cash he had saved hard to accumulate, bought a new car. "Nice car, Ian," the neighbours said, "I expect Trevor's bought that?" In fact, Trevor had given Ian a contact in Birmingham where he could negotiate a discount for himself.

Previous page : Reaching out to get to grips with the £1 million presence the privileged boys at Nottingham Forest greet Trevor Francis as he emerges from the players' tunnel. They get as close as most opponents. Witness, *(above and left)* Ipswich Town defenders struggling with footholds and ways of keeping him down while *(right)* a Southampton defender has accepted an invitation to go the wrong way as Francis, eyes on the ball, balance suddenly diverted from left to right, seeks a way out. The pictures capture the essence of Francis's style under pressure, as much as the unforgiving determination of defenders not to give him a yard.

Signs of our times in the home of European champions. While the masses must view from behind wire fencing *(above)*, the camera's eye provides in a single frame *(left)* the style of England past and present. Beneath a skyline dominated by rustic red brick chimneys and typically British terracing behind the goal, Trevor Francis obeys the modern dictate that forwards must also defend. He waits on goalkeeper Peter Shilton's left as the last line of defence against a Bolton attack.

"You've got to bear it, Ian," his Dad told him. "We all have. Every time we buy anything new, it's 'Oh, Trevor's paid for that'. Well he did buy us that colour TV set in the front room, but this one here in the back we paid for ourselves. It's disappointing for Ian to make good on his own and have things thrown in his face, but we have to bear it."

Perhaps the real test of family unity is to be able to absorb the fame of one member without isolating him, feeding off him, using him. The Francis family remains powerfully-knit, the Plymouth council house still "home" to which Trevor, his wife Helen and baby son Matthew return at every given opportunity. A postponed match at Nottingham provides the trigger for a motorway dash of 300 miles for a relaxing two-day break.

"It's a funny thing," says Phyllis Francis, "but when we are with Trevor in company up in Birmingham or Nottingham, he's not *ours*. He's good mannered and that, all the things we brought him up to be, but I don't know him, I can't believe it's our son. Trev's a bit of a loner, you know. Outsiders never get close enough to him to know him. In his sort of surroundings, he can't confide in any one person.

"But when he's here, he can relax completely. He's ours again, skylarking with the rest of us and letting himself go. And he's always bringing people home with no warning; we've had most of the ELO (Electric Light Orchestra) sleeping here. And would you believe our Trevor throwing a cup of water from the bedroom window?"

Over who? "Family and friends, usually when they're sunbathing in the garden. He and Helen love a good laugh. They used to go down to Looe in Cornwall and one day Trev came back wearing a hairy face mask. Grotesque, it was, like an old, crinkly face. He wore it coming over the toll bridge, gave the chap his money and drove off. Then he drove past a chap on a ladder, beeped his horn and the chap almost fell off. And when he came home, he went out pretending to sweep the street in the mask; frightened the lady next door to death. Helen was so embarrassed she was hiding her face."

The pride and satisfaction the family shares in Trevor's career is a personal thing, contained where possible within the walls of the home and carried around quietly. Roy Francis has been known to partake for hours in football debate without ever pulling rank or even letting on that his son actually plays for England. He and Phyllis have also turned down invitations from local television studios to talk about Trevor. "It's not us, is it Roy?" says Phyllis. "We agreed they could come to the house to film a

Roy Francis, the father who handed down his love for football. He suffered when Trevor was injured, but now looks on with pride because "we've seen a bigger difference in Trevor's physique than his ego."

bit of background for one programme but that was okay because we didn't have to speak. I just sat there looking through the scrapbook."

When they do see Trevor put on a pedestal, do Ian or Carolyn – or the parents – ever hanker after his success? "They never hanker after anything," says Mrs Francis. "Our kids always had the belief we were well off, maybe because we've always been in a position to give them most of what they wanted. The three of them never really wanted for anything, and I've been in the same position."

A visitor to the Francis home will want for very little, either. You share a hugely proportioned dinner, and wonder how Roy remains so lean and how his footballing son could ever have been considered too skinny to grow into a professional. Halfway through the meal, the father politely excuses himself from the table and from the next room you overhear the familiar voices of BBC Radio 2 sports broadcasters. The others look towards the door, smile, say nothing . . . and at that moment you appreciate exactly from where Trevor Francis derives his consuming passion for sport.

4 MAKING OF A LEGEND

TREVOR FRANCIS — At 16 he is one of the youngest and most exciting players in football. He caused a sensation in his debut last week against Oxford United by scoring a goal which gave City a valuable point.

FRANCIS WINS BLUES LEAGUE CUP PLACE

by NEVILLE FOULGER

TREVOR Francis, Birmingham City's 16-year-old "discovery," will be in the side against Colchester in the League Cup replay at St. Andrew's tomorrow night . . . on merit.

Francis was given his chance in the first team . . .

KID FRANCIS SUPER SHOT

Birmingham 4, Bolton 0

TREVOR FRANCIS, Birmingham's 16-year-old striker, became the Pride of St. Andrews by punishing . . .

throw a curtain around the youngster to try to destroy his talents.

But four minutes later Francis struck again.

It was not until the seventy-eighth minute Francis . . .

It's four-goal Franci

TEENAGE ACE KEEPS BLUES BUBBLING

By FRED BATES
Birmingham 4, Bolton 0

IT WAS the Trevor Francis super show in this smashing Birmingham victory!

This brilliant 16-year-old striker was given a standing ovation by the 25,000 St Andrew's crowd as he staged a four-goal spectacular to demolish the Bolton defence virtually on his own.

And what a superb, goalscoring machine this Plymouth-born lad is turning out to be. His four goals—all so coolly taken—took his tally to 10 goals from . . . Seven

veteran Warwick Rimmer to shadow the much-publicised youngster, but it made no difference.

After 16 minutes Gordon Taylor, who had a great game against his old club, headed on a free-kick and Francis ghosted clear in the penalty area. His shot was blocked, but he coolly moved through and headed in.

Four minutes later, Phil Summerill headed down to Francis and he nonchalantly picked his spot from 10 yards.

It was nearly all Birmingham. Poor Bolton . . .

Summerill's header which hit the bar.

Much of the game after the interval was pretty aimless until Francis struck near the end.

Bolton substituted big John Manning for the injured Phillips but it made little difference and Manning missed their only real chance of the second half.

Francis completed his hat-trick after 78 minutes —an easy one after Bosswell could only parry a fierce drive by Summerill.

And four minutes later Francis again brought the house down, heading in from close range from Dave Robinson's centre.

Brilliant

. . . gave by Bos-

Francis hits his first for Blues

EAM debuts for two West Midland teenagers. Sixteen-year-old Trevor Francis
d for Blues in his first senior game at St.
rew's, and 19-year-old Ken Hibbitt was on
t for Wolves at Chelsea.

goal from Francis came after an hour and

Two quick goals set alight St. Andrew's

Francis is the hero

Great goal, then Blues pegged back

by BOB BLACKBURN

Birmingham City 1, Oxford Utd. 1

BLUES fans will remember 16-year-old Trevor
Francis's first full League game for a long
time. He gave a fine display against Oxford at
St. Andrew's and scored a great goal.

He blasted Blues into the penalty area and was brought down
lead and brought the crowd by Martin.
Sloan, moving across fast to se

ues babe cheered off after League debut goal

SIXTEEN-YEAR-OLD Trevor Francis, Birmingham City's apprentice from
Plymouth, limped off the field at St. Andrew's—he was the last to leave
—with the cheers of Blues' supporters ringing in his ears.

The youngster had shown tremendous potential in his
first full league game and
capped his display with

THE INDEPENDENT

ANG! Now everyone is talking about super boy Francis

by HARLEY LAWER

OR FRANCIS doesn't give a decimal
r publicity. Which is just as well
ering the amount of newspaper
that has been generously doted on
5-year-old Plymouth whizz kid since
rmed on to the soccer scene this

RANCIS IS SUPERB" and "BLUES' NEW
STAR" screamed just two of the headlines
latest two-goal adventure for Birmingham
inst Sheffield Wednesday at Hillsborough
urday.

goals brought his
tally to six in
Second Division
for the Blues—
an enough to send
riters in raptures
undoubted star
l.

's father—Mr. Roy
former Argyle
er and now a plant
with the South
Gas Board in Ply-
reads every adu-
because he still
y grasp what is

HUFFED'

thumbed through
rave nobles cut
a place in the
ance scrapbook,
said he was
nuffled to read
ere saying about
l.

ather wouldn't
d. "But Trevor
r a bit what
akes no notice.
Just a job to
glad he has

of Melrose
erone, is still
revor's antence

'I suppose

would improve my son's
game so much in short
time.

"He always had a gift
for football, but the coaching has improved his skills.
He is so much quicker off
the mark, and some of his
goals have been as good as
the newspapers have de-
scribed them !

"In fact, his manager
Freddie Goodwin has told
him that it's about time he
scored a few bad ones !

But Goodwin is careful
not to put any pressure on
the lad. "He seems deter-
mined not to over-expose
him too early in his career."

"He advised him not to
talk to some reporters that
wanted to interview him
recently and refused to play
him every week.

"He tells him to go out
and enjoy himself. If he is
not enjoying his game he
takes him off. He gets no
special treatment and as he
is still an apprentice, he
has to sweep the dressing
rooms and do all the jobs
that apprentices do at their
age."

"My wife and other son
Ian and daughter Carolyn
travel up to see as many of
his games as we can. We
went up early the other day
and, although he was play-

ing next day, we had to wait
on the Friday lunch time
until he had scrubbed the
dressing room balls before
he could join us.

"But that's how it should
be and we wouldn't want it
to be any other way. He
comes home about once a
month, but won't stay too
long in case he misses any
training at St. Andrew's."

CHOICE

Few youngsters in the
West Country in recent
years could have had a bigger choice of clubs queueing
up for his signature after
his performances for Ply-
mouth Schoolboys had stood

head and shoulders above
the rest.

Arsenal, Wolves, West
Ham, and Birmingham City
were among the leading
contenders. It was because
of the fierce competition
that Argyle, as Manager
Ellis Stuttard has explained
before, didn't stand a
chance. But with every
Francis goal, there is crit-
cism that Argyle missed the
boat.

"It wasn't like that at
all," insists Mr. Francis.
"Ellis Stuttard is a personal
friend of mine and he
chased and chased Trevor
and did everything he could
to persuade the lad to go to
Home Park.

"Even three days before
he was due to go to Birm-

ingham, Ellis was still trying to change the boy's
mind. I felt sorry for him
and, in the end, left the
choice completely to Trevor.

"He visited several clubs
and eventually chose Birmingham because of the way
he was treated by Stan
Cullis when he went there
for a schoolboy trial.

stories that he must have
had a book-binder from
Birmingham. But that is
ridiculous. We never received
a penny and didn't expect
it either.

Now Francis fans in Ply-
mouth are likely to have a
chance to see Trevor in
action when Birmingham
City parade their team

ncis's permanent
at Home Park is
ext.
Francis's move
April made for me
youth to con
sh of the F.A. Y
Machinery on P
arce ground
give me mu
a chance to
a certain to w

● Trevor
Francis—
heading for
soccer
stardom.

TREVOR IS SHAPING UP WELL AT BRUM

THE FUTURE for Trevor
Francis, the former Ply-
mouth schoolboy star who
joined Birmingham City last

By any standards, the induction of Trevor Francis into the Football League was phenomenal – even in an age which spawns athletic child stars just as previous eras produced infant pianists and actors. At 16, Francis was not exactly a child but he was years off physical maturity, a boy scoring goals of breath-taking quality in a man's world where muscle and might often obliterate skill.

It is hard today to rationalise what happened in that 1970–71 season. But it was also hard at the time. Fifteen goals in his first 15 games including four in an afternoon, launched a Francis cult in and around industrial Birmingham; a following that gained impetus even when he was deployed as creator rather than pure goalscorer. But did the lad create the following, or was it there waiting? Was it the arrival of youthful innocence that excited the community, or the people willing youth to score goals from angles and distances experienced players deemed impossible?

Maybe it was a natural occurrence – natural in a city for so long bereft of a sporting hero that it should over-react to a gifted boy. Everything else in society seemed to be going instant so why not the heroes too? The career of Trevor Francis was not allowed to evolve; it exploded at such a pace that the well-meaning manager trying to hold him back, to put a normal perspective into the development, was simply yanked along in his wake.

The truly impressive aspect, however, was that Francis came through the idolatry with a reputation for level-headedness, good manners and club loyalty which are anything but automatic in the successful sportsman today. Somehow, although he outgrew the "St. Francis of St. Andrews" and "superboy" tags, and although he did try to leave to further his career on several occasions, he never lost his rapport with the Birmingham crowd. There was little harsh judgment even when he did get away. Deep down they felt he was entitled to pursue greater ambitions and they respected the fact he never used the modern ploy of forcing the club to sell him by not giving his best.

The nine, almost 10 years at St. Andrews were the longest of his professional life, the most intently monitored, in some ways the most enjoyable and in other ways the most frustrating. "People ask if I would have preferred a quieter, more normal start than the pressure at 16," he reflects. "If I had the choice, I'd have it exactly the same way. At 16, it was ridiculous having people tip me for England, but I enjoyed it. It put me on the map straight away, but *I* wasn't green enough to believe it."

Roy Francis, his father, would have been a steadying influence whatever temptations came his way. "He left home at 15," says Roy, "a boy come a man. But he knew one thing from the start: he had to dedicate himself to it. For some of them it's one big joyride but Trevor would see it the way I do... you either want to do the job or you don't."

Phyllis Francis, naturally, watched him go with maternal misgivings: "Straight from school, he went," she says. "Do you know what he missed first of all? The sound of the sea. He'd never known what it was like, going away, and I remember we spent hours looking round for a stuffed seagull to give him as a joke. Never came across one, though. But at first he was so homesick, I don't know how he stuck it except he wanted to be a footballer so badly. Mind you, I was no better. He came home every third weekend, but it almost did more harm than good ... I'd be crying while I was changing the sheets as his dad was taking him back."

In the early years, Roy was committed to driving to Birmingham for every home match. "I believed he neeeded us there," the father explains. "He appreciated it. He could talk to us where he couldn't to anyone else." However that journey, combined with the uncertainty of the demands on Trevor, put Roy Francis on phenobarbitone. "There was no M5 motorway in those days," says Roy, "and it used to take me seven hours to go up. I'd arrive at one o'clock, have a snack and flask of tea in the car park, have an hour with Trevor in the tearooms after the match, and drive off back to Plymouth, picking up a bag of chips on the way."

Mrs Francis usually took in sewing and tailoring at six shillings an hour to pay for petrol. The family at one time seriously considered a move to Birmingham, but Roy could not escape the pace of city life quickly enough. He, too, was accustomed to waking to the sound of seagulls, to wandering down to the beach when the mood took him.

Trevor, meanwhile, was learning how totally the football experience consumes adolescence. He had three lots of digs from the ages of 15 to 17, finally settling in a home from home, with a large family. Even there he had a 10.30 pm curfew and a demand for written permission before he was allowed to see in the New Year at 17.

And although he keeps in touch with all three "homes" with the occasional visit, Phyllis Francis will never forget the remark of Iris Wright, the third landlady and still a family friend: "You missed out on a lot in life with Trevor ... the teenage years. I had them."

Not that they were swinging. "*I* missed out on my teenage years," observes Trevor. "They say those are the best years of your life. I could have been downing pints or going to discos, but I'd have ended up on the scrapheap. I was playing with men of 30 and I socialised with them instead. I chose to miss out. Don't get me wrong, I wasn't an angel. I like to enjoy myself like anyone else. But though it would have been easy to go out every night, it just wasn't me to do it. I had to decide what was best for football, and football was everything to me."

Most people were kind. He was stopped in the street to shake hands, asked for his autograph on buses, chatted up by girls. But recognition had its drawbacks. "There was one time I was sitting in a pub, drinking a lemon and lime because I was 17, and some City supporters were chatting to me, friendly like, when somebody in the background spat all over my face. I just had to sit there and take it. I mean, what would it have looked like if I'd got involved in a pub fight? But why would anyone want to do that?

"I had to watch my step all the time. It was too easy for people to jump to wrong conclusions. Sometimes they rang the manager and said I was roaring drunk around town, other times they came up and said: 'You were putting them away last night, weren't you? Never seen a whisky disappear so fast.' The manager knew the strongest I drank was a shandy. He told me to laugh at it, but I made a point of letting him know if I was going into licensed premises, even for a meal."

Before he broke into the first team, Francis believes the first two months' professional training sharpened him almost beyond recognition. Don Dorman, however, reckons they can be the most vulnerable months. "When Trevor came as a boy," the scout recalls, "he wasn't known except by me. Now clubs always used to keep the contact between the apprentices and the scout; the scout used to run the youth team, pick it, train it, look after their welfare and everything. I used to sit on the platform hours with Trevor while he waited to catch the train home; it's times like that you can listen to the lad, reassure him.

"But y'see, now, with all that modern thinking, they bring in coaches, all that bull from Lilleshall. And straight the way, lads are out of the scout's hands. Now if a feller has a badge that says he's a coach, okay, I'll accept that. But I don't know if he's a *judge* – that's my responsibility. And if it's not my responsibility to bring lads I choose through, then who gets the sack if they fail? The coach or the scout? What's more important if you break the contact with the scout, the lad could fail because the coach doesn't rate him a player."

As it turned out, no-one had cause or time to question the judgment of bringing Trevor Francis to Birmingham. Stan Cullis, the manager at the time he actually signed, was sacked shortly afterwards. Freddie Goodwin said, however, almost at the start: "You looked at Trevor and saw everything you want in a footballer. If a manager is lucky, he comes across a youngster like that once in his career. Looking for comparisons, I'd say Jimmy Greaves, Denis Law and that's it. Francis is in this exclusive scorer's bracket."

The only question, the responsibility, was when and how to wean him. "He was always an appreciative lad," says Goodwin. "From the start he would work hard and play hard and listen to you. So many players once they get into the first team start to believe their own press and stop listening to the coaching. There was an excitement for the coaching staff because we could all feel – know – Trevor was going to the very, very top. He was so level-headed. Even when he was reading about himself as the ultimate star, he was concerned that his sudden promotion in the headlines wouldn't take away his willingness to learn or his ambition."

It was ironic that Goodwin should bracket the boy Francis with Greaves. Even then Francis felt comparisons were ridiculous, but Greaves, who was nearing his own premature retirement, saw the link: "I wouldn't like to be Trevor Francis, just breaking into the game," Greaves said at that time. "The game has gone sick and the demands on players are increasing every season. I don't think he'll get the chance to enjoy it in the same way I did."

Greaves, 13 years previously, had scored 22 goals in his first season as a 17-year-old with Chelsea. "I remember I felt older than boys my age," he said. "But Trevor Francis and Charlie George and Alan Hudson will grow up even quicker with the extra pressure they face."

Down in Cardiff on September 5, 1970, Trevor Francis came on at half-time, as a sub, in his first League game. But the introduction was not to the disillusioned fate Greaves had described; instead he found a pocket of good old-fashioned sportsmanship. "My marker talked me through the game," recalls Trevor. "He was saying things like 'Are you all right, son? Not too tired? I know what an ordeal it is, but there's only half-hour to go, lad, then you can go upstairs for a drink. Tell you what, I'll buy you one myself.'"

The first of many ... Francis is helped to his feet by Phil Summerill and greeted by Ray Martin (No 2) after scoring in his League debut.

Even when Trevor lost the defender to hit a post, the opponent's attitude remained unchanged. "And y'know, Trevor was one you could think to bully," remembers his dad. "Such a skinny little lad, skin and bones. They pushed him in so quick." And even today, Roy Francis can recall the name of that opponent: "Gary Bell," he says without hesitation. "He went to Newport from Cardiff."

The more cynical side, however, was to come. Once the flow of goals made Francis a household name, his nerve was put to the sword. "Defenders read the papers too," Francis says, "and some were really looking for me. 'Broken leg for you today, son', 'This is a man's game, sonny'. Some others tried to be patronising 'Never mind, you'll learn, son' and then there was the time at Huddersfield that I got pushed onto the cinder track." Roy Francis was there, too, with his memory: "Geoff Hutt, that was," he says. "Trevor's teammate Alan Campbell said to Hutt: 'If that had happened at St. Andrews, you'd have been lynched.'" Hutt had earlier warned that he was going to "kill" Francis.

Trevor was at the time an £8-a-week apprentice, scraping mud off the boots of players like John Vincent, Trevor Hockey and Malcolm Page, playing alongside them on Saturdays, and then mopping out the dressing rooms and baths. In between, the television cameras were lining up for him, but as early as the fourth match, against Bristol City, the dangers of a growing adolescent pushed too quickly were apparent when he was taken off exhausted in the 85th minute.

"I found myself caught by the speed with which he made the grade," admits Goodwin. "I was learning about him, I didn't know how much he could absorb. It's not natural to have those pressures at 16, that's why we have apprentices. The idea is for them to learn as they make mistakes, to be allowed to make mistakes as part of their development.

"I didn't want to deprive Trevor of that learning process. I also felt we had a responsibility to continue his education in soccer. We still had a responsibility to coach him, even if at the time it knocked back his own stardom. He had so much ability, he was taking control of games in the last five minutes, taking on responsibility in a way you expect from more mature players. And all this besides scoring goals that were just zooming in. I looked at this boy, just 16, and thought it can't last."

Goodwin found himself in a classic juxtaposition: a dilemma of conscience and temptation. Francis was scoring wonder goals week in week out, yet the manager was trying to persuade him to look for easier ones, start the habit of picking up goals in the six yards box. "I didn't want to hold him back, but I just felt he couldn't go on scoring these fantastic goals," Goodwin says. He was also aware that a youngster could be hampered rather than helped by exposure at this level. He expected that, "for all that the crowd and press expected it of Trevor", he would have to play him in spurts, three or four games, a break, then six or seven games.

Goodwin explains: "It was an unreal situation. The fans in Birmingham were looking for something extra special, something to cling to after bad times. They'd never really had someone so young and so gifted, although good players like Bob Latchford and Kenny Burns were coming through the same youth process. But I had to consider that Trevor is fairly high strung, so keen to do well and do right, keen to try to live up to this image of the superstar. He wanted to be as good as everybody was saying he was, and I was telling him nobody could be that good."

Usually at the manager's side as he tried to detect signs of strain on the young player was trainer George Dalton. His eye as a former defender told him that Francis was quick, quicker than any player he'd had to mark. He saw the lad score "goals you never expect to see the likes of ... he went into positions experienced players would never go into, and he scored from them." But Dalton's role was to deal with the cramps, the muscle fatigue.

"You're bound to have a stamina problem at 16, 17 or 18," reasons Dalton. "It's asking a kid to do a man's job. He's bound to get knackered. There comes a time when teenagers physically drop, and they become prone to strains then. Trevor got his full strength at about 19, but before that, even when he used to get physically drained in games and you'd think he should be given a rest, all of a sudden he'd turn on the ball, beat a couple of men and score a goal nobody else would. The manager couldn't leave him out. Usually when the fitness drops, the performance goes as well, but Trevor has so much skill he overcame that." Added to his skill, Dalton says, Francis had a capacity and a determination to train well. His ability to take the training load, the trainer believed, was evidence that "the strain was not leaving a permanent mark."

Goodwin tried to shield his young star from all the clamour of press and public. He rested him just before Christmas 1970, explaining that while he was the "best prospect since George Best" he should not be spoilt or burned out. A week later Francis was back, scoring irresistibly with the left foot, a goal which rewarded him with a cancelled Christmas leave. The Birmingham tradition was to allow apprentices to go home for the holiday but the manager announced: "For Trevor it has got to be different."

Even before the legend of the young Francis became national property, rumour was flying. It may or may not have been true that Arsenal was prepared to pay a then incredible £150,000 for a 16-year-old, but on February 20, 1970, he astonished everyone by scoring four goals in the 4–0 defeat of Bolton Wanderers at St. Andrews. The faithful amongst that 25,600 crowd can recite the goals chapter and verse like a bible reading: 16 minutes, Francis beats the goalkeeper in the six yards box to head the first; 19 minutes, a Francis half-volley from 15 yards; 78 minutes, Francis following up after the keeper drops a Phil Summerill free-kick; 83 minutes, Francis collides with the goalkeeper but scores with a near post header.

The most personal memories of that afternoon are not what you might expect. Trevor Francis regretted that he had to leave the field with a leg injury, after scoring the fourth, because the sub missed a chance to make it five. "And the day afterwards, the boss had me cleaning the terraces, baths and boots ... there was no way I could possibly believe the wonderboy tag." Freddie Goodwin remembers: "What thrilled me was that three of the goals came in the six yards box ... that proved he was listening to what I'd been saying." And Roy Francis? "Trevor doesn't bother about the rave notices. He knows he has a way to go yet, although some of his goals have been as good as the newspapers describe them."

Apart from the physical and mental acceleration into Second Division football, Trevor had to cope with the pedestal he was thrust upon. A small but significant incident followed the match against Orient in London on March 13, 1971 when Francis's novelty put 4,000 on the gate and his 14th goal in 13 games was described by Orient manager Jimmy Bloomfield as "a goal out of nothing." But Francis had slipped the press. He was caught on his way to the station, an overcoat hiding the club blazer: "I know the dangers of getting big-headed," he said. "And I really hope it won't happen to me. I don't think it will because you can never tell how long success will last – anyway the lads make sure I keep cool."

While Francis was determined to keep cool, while he was going to football matches in his spare time with goalkeeper Mike Kelly – "a good friend to me, and besides he has an FA coaching badge and can give me tips" – the Brummie fans were working up the Francis cult, with its own jargon: "The Francis Special ... Francis Flick ... Francis Magic."

The chemistry that evolved between this gifted youth and the folk of Birmingham was at the heart of a phenomenal peak in the club's crowd appeal. During Trevor's first two seasons, while the club was in the Second Division, it attracted crowds of 49,025 against Cardiff City and 45,181 against Blackpool; then, in 1972, the first year of promotion, Manchester United swelled the St. Andrews attendance to 52,104 and Liverpool to 48,114 ... crowds literally four times the hard-core gates of just over 12,000 which watched Birmingham's decline after Francis left in 1979.

"I don't expect to get ever again such a lift from the crowds as I got at the start," says Francis. "It was staggering, really. People have talked about some of the things I did as a teenager, saying how I just used to go out there and do things naturally.

Well, I felt inspired to do so by the crowds. Can you imagine what it felt like as a 16-year-old to come out at 2 pm to inspect the pitch before a match against Cardiff and find 20,000 people already there cheering you?

"I used to feel it wasn't just me, or just 11 Birmingham players against the opposition; Cardiff that day found themselves playing 49,000 as well. I remember Mel Sutton fouling me early on and the crowd – which used to get so incensed if anybody so much as touched me – was unbelievable. Somebody ran on to the pitch from the Kop and chased after Sutton, wanting to fight him.

"Those supporters literally shouted us to promotion. We had left ourselves needing three points from our last two away games. It was a tall order because although we won most games at St. Andrews we didn't have a good away record. But the first game, against Sheffield Wednesday at Hillsborough, saw thousands and thousands of Birmingham supporters cheering us, and it was an incredible feeling for me to score the winning goal there. In fact, we heard later that Millwall, the other team hoping to go up, had won its last game and the Millwall crowd at the Den had danced all over the pitch because the loudspeaker had announced our result wrongly. They thought they were up.

"For our final match, against Orient, 33,000 packed into Brisbane Road; there were well over 25,000 from Birmingham, hardly anybody from Orient, and the rest from Millwall. We won again, 1–0, with Bob Latchford getting the all-important goal, and I shall never forget that day. The atmosphere was electric; somebody threw a knife in the area where I was running, the Millwall fans massed around the pitch trying to get the game called off, and the stands were evacuated because of a bomb scare. In fact, in the dressing room we heard a loud blast as we were beginning to celebrate. It was a firework, I think.

"There was another reason I'll never forget the night. It was two weeks after my 18th birthday, and of course the team went out to celebrate in London. I got very drunk, something I deeply regret now because it was the first time I had tried vodka. I never even finished my meal. I suppose I thought I could put vodka back like some of the older professionals.

"Anyway, I missed the celebrations. Mick Kelly helped me back to the hotel, and he says I kept falling against shop windows in Regent Street while he was struggling to make me walk straight. I suppose if anyone doubted it, that proved I was

human! But it taught me a lesson; instead of enjoying the night, I was back in my bedroom, feeling ill and I've never been like that again. All I'd achieved was getting drunk; when Forest won the European Cup I enjoyed the night far more with just a few glasses of lager shandy."

Francis's one wayward night of mispent youth did not, however, blur his memory of the fun those apprentice years were. Roger Hynd, a beefy fitness fanatic in Birmingham's defence, was at the centre of three vivid instances which embedded themselves into the Francis memoirs:

"Roger was such a big man, we called him Garth," Francis recalls. "And I remember when we were training in the Malvern Hills, before our FA Cup semi-final against Leeds United, the sight we must have been in our special training routine. Leeds at that time used to come out to the centre circle, wave to the crowd and then perform a limbering-up routine. I'll never forget the faces on some of the Malvern locals as we spent our week working on our own 'dance' routine in answer; we were practising it for half an hour every day, making a fine art of it with stopwatches to perfect it. Can you imagine Garth, at 14 stones, doing a Nureyev?

"We all thought Freddie Goodwin was joking at first but he was dead serious. It was all part of his plan to unsettle Leeds in the Cup game at Hillsborough. The trouble was we were absolutely brilliant in our dance routine . . . but we lost the match 3–0."

Trevor almost 18. A year earlier, preparing for a match at Swindon, he experienced another unforgettable scene when Roger Hynd, warming up as usual by heading the ball in the dressing room, put his head through the ceiling. Literally. "Someone unkindly said he never even noticed," smiles Francis.

The third Hynd special, recalled with as much humour by the big defender himself, came in Tahiti. Knowing Garth's obsession never to duck a challenge or be beaten by anything, the Birmingham players asked him to try to reach the bottom of the clear waters near to the hotel. He tried, and declared it impossible. However, goalkeeper Mick Kelly dived in (concealing a handful of sand) and came up after a very few seconds sprinkling the grains through his fingers.

Inevitably, Hynd tried and tried again to match the feat. The players believed the joke was over that day, but the following morning, Hynd's room mate, Paul Cooper, another goalkeeper, reported the big man rising at 6 am, going down to the water, and practising enormous deep-breathing exercises before attempting the dive. The fun had a slightly wry sequel when Roger Hynd's eardrum was affected, fortunately only temporarily, by the water pressure.

"But there always was plenty of laughs around Birmingham," says Francis. "Jasper Carrott was a supporter of the club before I arrived and we became friends soon afterwards. He takes his own football unbelievably seriously – he's a defender with Hockley Heath Rangers – but at the club the joking never seemed to stop. When he was invited to become a director at Birmingham after I left, he came to discuss with me what he saw as a potential problem, the fact that he is so close to the players. It seems to have worked out okay."

Despite Trevor's "desertion", they remain good friends, even though Jasper Carrott's source of humour on stage or record can very often be Francis himself. "Birmingham City's flying winger had a *magnificent* game for Birmingham yesterday," goes the Carrott line, "scoring all 16 goals in their eight-all draw with Doncaster. He had to leave the field every 15 minutes to wipe the dead flies from his glasses."

Jasper Carrott, and the mass of Birmingham supporters, live on memories such as the day Trevor Francis hit a hat-trick for the Blues . . . and Malcolm Macdonald replied with three goals for Arsenal. "We were both writing columns in Tiger magazine at the time," recalls Francis, "and there were one or two comments about us believing too many stories out of comics."

Less amused, possibly, were the defenders who had to keep the "Francis Magic" under control. Here was a teenager already being urged to begin an investment by buying his first house, and here for a time at least a player earning a reputation for "diving" to con referees into awarding him protection. Liverpool and England captain Emlyn Hughes was once sent off after hitting Francis with his elbow or fist, and claims still that the teenager had got him sent off by falling as if pole-axed. "If it happened today," Francis admits, "I wouldn't go down. It was a controversial incident, and I remember at the time Emlyn waiting for me outside the dressing room door after the match. He muttered a few words, but since then we've got on well together.

"Looking back on it, I must admit that there was a time it seemed fashionable to over-emphasise things. There were times I could have got up a bit quicker, and I am not proud to have to admit it. I was booked once, by Norman Burtenshaw, for supposedly feigning an injury, although on that occasion I really was hurt. That's justice, I suppose.

"I think a player has failed if he gets booked. It happened to me twice, once when I was chasing a through ball and caught Bob Wilson with my boot. I was immediately surrounded by jostling players and the referee said he was booking me because there was a big hole in the goalkeeper's jersey.

"The other occasion was with the England youth team in Spain. I lost control of myself. I was rooming with Gary Locke from Chelsea and he was fouled and suffered the nastiest gash I've ever seen. I was incensed and the next thing I did was barge into the goalkeeper . . . it was a total lack of self-control. My own fault, and I learned from it."

The maturing player maintained his special rapport with the Birmingham crowd, for whom he could do no wrong. "But looking back," he says, "I think the supporters were too fanatical, too brilliant at times for Birmingham's good. I know this is difficult for supporters to accept, coming from me, but I believe they were so loyal to the club that the directors had it too easy. While the cash kept flowing in, they were never forced to go out and buy the real quality players any club needs to succeed.

"We had an incredible nucleus of young players – Kenny Burns, Bob Latchford and myself in one year, then Joe Gallagher coming through as well. But whereas Nottingham Forest for example would go out and spend £300,000 on Peter Shilton, Birmingham would tend to try to buy half a team for the money. But look how many points Peter's been worth at Forest. Anyway, I believe that the massive following Birmingham had began to get disillusioned when they saw the club gradually selling off the best players. Bob Latchford and Kenny Burns went before I did, and I'm really sad to see that now Birmingham has probably its best side ever, the support has dwindled."

And if one supporter could take it upon himself to represent the commitment of the terrace fan, it was Michael Overs, a 21-year-old car worker. Throughout the 1970s Overs worked on his great labour of love, a personally compiled and typed tome of 259,700 words, 72 pictures, 350 match reports, and comments, tables, statistics. Whether from his personal view, or culled from papers around the world, there is not a match Francis played anywhere that goes unreported . . . even in the American seasons, for Overs wrote to Detroit Express and found himself invited over on the next plane at the club's expense.

He presented bound copies of the book to Trevor and his parents in 1979, and says now: "No-one blames Trevor for leaving. He was bound to do so because the club never achieved the promises it made to help him win things here. But when he left it seemed to knock some heart out of the club. We will never replace him, it's as simple as that.'' Yet Overs had not transferred his allegiance to Nottingham: ''I thought I might go across from time to time, see how he's getting on ... but somehow family allegiances to the Blues are too strong to break, even without Trevor.''

Out of all his words in the bound volumes, perhaps the most significant came in a sentence of personal observation: ''It was indicative of Trevor's international fame that BBC's Sports Report announced this afternoon 'Francis did not score today'.'' The date? February 1970. Francis was two months short of his 17th birthday.

While this worship was building up, while extra weight-training was beginning to shape the eventual stronger physique, so Freddie Goodwin found himself in a curious position. ''You know what I was doing at this time?'' he asks. ''Trying to deprive the lad of praise! I didn't want it to appear we were a one-man side. We had good young players and I was always conscious of the resentment that could spread around Trevor. So I was trying to get the praise shared around.

''There was a danger of Trevor getting isolated and lonely, apart from the group, not so much from the behaviour of the players but from outside influences. I recall a shoe company coming in to do a deal with Trevor, golf shoes actually, and while I didn't want to deny him the sponsorship, I persuaded him to get all the lads a free pair of shoes.''

If Goodwin sounds a somewhat more rounded and perceptive man than the caricature generally presented of the British football manager, then it is not unfounded. He is a tall, stooping figure, a serious, deep-thinking man whose pronounced Lancashire accent and paternal manner at times disguises a personality forever seeking new ideas and putting innovations to the players. He learned his managerial trade under Sir Matt Busby and then Don Revie (who actually recommended him to Birmingham) but had been to America as a pioneer in the infancy of North American soccer and returned with a determination to attend night classes in psychology.

He hung slogans on the dressing room walls – ''Hard Work Brings Its Own Rewards'' – and introduced yoga to training schedules. ''It didn't do a lot for me,'' smiles Trevor. ''But then I'm so stiff, I can just about touch my toes doing a hamstring stretch.''

The coup de grâce of Goodwin's managerial surprises at Birmingham, however, involved an American professor of psychology, Bruce C. Ogilvie, who has travelled the world examining the motivation and, the mental and emotional factors of sportsmen from the Olympic arena to the professional boxing ring.

''The psychological aspects of soccer have always been very much an unknown quantity,'' stresses Goodwin, ''so I invited Bruce Ogilvie to Birmingham where we put all our players through tests of 190 questions and then talked to the players about them.''

Trevor Francis was barely 17 when the tests were carried out. ''A very young player,'' agrees Goodwin, ''but the tests suggested it was very doubtful if he would ever reach full potential. One thing that was said about Trevor was that he was a person who at that time was living as if poised on an egg shell. He was a superstar, right up there, but the whole thing could collapse unless he was made to appreciate, in future, the real world as against the world of adulation in which he was involved.''

Francis, the maturer man of 26, has since read the entire Ogilvie verdict on his likelihood to realise his potential. He has re-read the 190 questions and feels ''I would probably answer them the same way today.'' He isn't shocked by the professor's assertions that he ''lacked mental toughness'', was ''extremely non-aggressive'', scored low on determination, and, surprisingly low on coachability, emotional control and conscientiousness.

In fact, as the player says: ''He doesn't seem to have had a good word for me, does he?'' Francis smiles, slightly. How many of us could withstand having our souls bared at the tender age of 17? And tender is the conclusive remark of the report. Does it perturb Francis to read it? ''No. I don't attach that much importance to this kind of thing ... in fact I think it's rubbish.'' The verdict sounded somewhat more assertive than his Motivational Profile indicates, but Francis adds: ''I don't mean to be rude. Maybe there's some merit in things like this, but for myself I've always believed that sport is a personal thing. You motivate yourself in your own way.'' In other words, questions are answered on the field of play.

Psychologically, Francis has always been something of a realist, a traditionalist who trusts his instincts and his willingness to work and learn to pull the ability out of him. He says his natural resistance would rule out hypnosis, which helped golfer Tony Jacklin and Test cricketer Bob Willis.

And drugs are right out; they have never been tried or considered.

Throughout the Birmingham days, however, he clung to a pre-match ritual: "I liked to come out behind the goalkeeper, always carried a ball, and didn't allow photographs prior to a game," he says. "Then there was this drink, Dynamo. We all drink that. Maybe its psychological . . . but there are just certain things you like to do. It's like having oil rubbed into your legs. I don't think for one minute it's going to do any good, but if players *think* it's doing them good, why not do it? We have a young black player in the reserves at Forest who gets a big tube of cream – hot stuff – and plasters it all over his legs and thighs. Like ice cream it is."

There is one more Francis ritual: Sleep. "I always look at what time I go to bed. I take a long time to get to sleep, but I always try to gauge exactly how many hours I've had. I don't like anything less than eight hours and, though it's ridiculous, if I only get 7½ hours, I do feel a bit tired."

The real test of character for a fledgling player, however, is to prove that his initial impact has not depended on just the element of surprise. Freddie Goodwin always maintained that Francis's second season – when defenders marked him in pairs, when the tackling was hurtful and when Francis was asked to play varying roles – proved more than the phenomenal goals that heralded his beginning. "As word got around to make life tougher," says Goodwin, "Trevor came through a more dedicated, more responsible player."

Second Division managers voted Francis the 1971–72 divisional player of the year in the season Birmingham won promotion. Yet some fans, failing to detect the workings of transition, barracked the 17-year-old so harshly Goodwin rebuked them: "He did miss a chance. But he also produced three or four touches beyond the scope of every other player on the field."

Goodwin had already attempted to put the club's money where he placed his praise, offering Francis a 10-year contract for his 17th birthday. Francis preferred a four-year bond which increased his £8-a-week apprentice wage to £50 a week though then, as now, he attempted to keep his income private. And, though visibly overburdened by the strain of promotion, he flew off to join the England Youth team for his second International Youth Tournament, at £5 a match.

The boy come a man was still growing. He coped with the First Division, where physical emphasis is slightly less obsessive, though the know-how and

Sixteen . . . and Birmingham hails St. Francis of St. Andrews, the boy who exploded into a man's game.

Impact. There was often a degree of niggle between Trevor Francis and Kenny Burns in the Birmingham camp. Here, on opposite sides of the England–Scotland divide, they compete on aggressive but equal terms.

sharpness infinitely superior. He learned to live with close-marking and to free himself at vital moments, or to tow men out of position to assist colleagues. He mastered the art of pace control and, though Birmingham was struggling, he was growing as a player and a man. In three seasons he put on three inches and a stone and a half.

Then came that fateful autumn of 1974: Francis, remember, was top scorer in Division One and Birmingham were five points off the leaders, Leeds United, but by the time he returned from the five-month absence, forced by his torn tendon, Birmingham were relegation candidates once again. "We couldn't replace him," says Goodwin. "There was no-one comparable, even if we had had that kind of money to buy."

Yet, as haunted teams sometimes do, Birmingham grittily fought through to the FA Cup semi-finals without its leading scorer. It was a measure of Francis's importance, however, that the manager was trying desperately to accelerate his return, sensing that his touch might mean the difference between a Wembly final or nothing at all.

The gamble was extreme. Francis played his first practice match on March 8, less than a month before the semi-final. He managed 60 minutes. On March 12, he played a private practice match at Coventry. "Frightened to death, I was," he remembers. "I hadn't seen a ball for over four months. But a defender came up behind me and I felt a boot in the back of the right knee. As I was falling, he shouted: 'Just testing your leg for you'. I felt more annoyed than hurt . . ."

He was through the first test. Now he was training seven days a week to try to recapture that special sharpness in tight situations. His first public match drew a postwar reserve record of 6,030 to St. Andrews, and the attraction was not Bournemouth reserves. The pitch was heavy. Francis created two goals in the first half then, after 49 minutes, he chested the ball down on the right wing, ran to the edge of the penalty box, and curled a shot around the goalkeeper . . . with his *right foot*. He stayed 80 minutes and went off to a standing ovation.

Both Goodwin and trainer Dalton agree that the gamble of playing Francis in the semi-final did not come off. The player was not mentally or physically fit, as Dalton knew when he spent the week before the game kicking balls up to Trevor to encourage him to turn sharply. "I knew he just didn't have that zip," admits Dalton, "and you could say we could have lost that semi through playing him, yet we had to try." In fact, the first game at Sheffield ended o–o but the replay, at Maine Road, Manchester, was won by Fulham with the only goal in the last seconds of extra time. "I was so sick, I cried," admits Francis.

Although Francis and Birmingham survived relegation, and although Freddie Goodwin persuaded him to sign a new three-year contract, the manager's days at Birmingham were numbered. His sacking in September, 1975 was, in the words of a High Court judge, "done in a particularly nasty way . . . Mr Goodwin was summoned before his employers like a schoolboy sent for by his headmaster" and told to bring along his junior – coach, Willie Bell – to be told his junior was replacing him as manager. Goodwin, the judge considered, had served Birmingham excellently and done nothing to deserve summary dismissal which caused loss of status, humiliation and distress.

Trevor Francis felt a personal distress at the sacking of the man who, less than a year earlier, was driving him to reserve matches "just to get me out of the house with my tendon injury." He went first to Goodwin's house, to offer an inscribed silver cigarette case saying "Thanks for everything", and later to see the chairman Keith Coombs because "I was concerned about the future and how it might affect my game." The chairman reassured him about "certain things" and Francis announced after that he was not asking for a transfer: "I am happy to stay and will do all I can to help get the results we need."

Willie Bell was put on trial for five matches before Birmingham judged him a success. Three wins satisfied the board "we have appointed tomorrow's man rather than yesterday's man". But, tomorrow's man never really got to grips with at least one situation at Birmingham.

On November 3, three weeks after Bell had been confirmed as manager with former Leeds United coach Syd Owen as assistant, there was a highly publicised incident between Kenny Burns and Trevor Francis at the Damson Lane training field.

Francis had walked off the field, changed and gone home without finishing training after a tackle on him by Burns. Rumours have festered from that day to this about the intent of the tackle, but Bell said: "I was told he (Francis) walked off because he had a knock. I've told players to do this. Later he phoned me to say he was all right and asked if I wanted him for further training."

Even now, Francis is reluctant to talk about the incident. "Things that happen in the past don't seem so important today," he says. "It was a bad tackle, but some of the things that have been said about it are ridiculous, as are other things people used to say about Kenny and myself. What disgusted me at the time was not so much the tackle as the fact that nothing happened because of it. I was incensed with the manager, who was taking the training session, because he appeared to turn a blind eye.

"The biggest problem that we had was that Kenny was a player who needed discipline and he was given a free rein at Birmingham. I blame management more than anything else. It got to the stage where Kenny trained when he felt like it. There'd be mornings I'd come in at 10.30, and Kenny would be showering ready to go home. They couldn't cope with him. We laugh about it now, Kenny and myself, because if he was even minutes late at Forest it would cost him. But he never is – mind you, he wasn't late at Birmingham, he was early in fact!"

Francis admits there were occasions he and Burns did not speak to each other, even while playing as twin strikers feeding off each other for goals. They are quite different players, Francis quick and sharp, Burns strong and aggressive. "But," insists Francis, "I've always rated Kenny as a player. He was born with talent and proved on many occasions he could score goals."

Consider for a moment the Birmingham or any other dressing room. It is a marriage of personalities, players drawn from totally differing environments and upbringings, cloistered together to live and work in extremely tense and emotive circumstances. It is like the trenches must have been: you may not like the fellow next to you but you have to fight on his side.

And few relationships could epitomise this more than the Francis–Burns one at Birmingham. There is scarcely a greater geographical or environmental divide in Britain than the 488 miles between the placid nature of Plymouth and the harsh elements of the old Glasgow streets. Yet that is Francis and Burns; the one raised and still welcomed in a demonstrably caring home, the other an orphan who learned to live on his wits, take advantage of situations around him. Francis who has always believed that to be cautioned by a referee is a disgrace, Burns who might have been a Glasgow Rangers player had his "uncontrollable" temper not got him sent off in three of four youth matches.

How on earth could you reconcile the two? "There was a clash of personalities," admits Freddie Goodwin. "I always had a lot of time for Kenny but he had great difficulty in controlling his tempera-

ment, his emotions. I don't think it was jealousy between him and Trevor, although they were together in the youth team and Trevor got into the first a lot sooner. No, there was a different type of friction. Kenny, mind you, could clash with anybody – he respected only force and discipline and if he felt he could get away with it he tried. I had to fine Kenny Burns so often I can't recall every incident, some at the training ground, some in matches."

Yet ask Freddie Goodwin, ask any member of the Francis family, and particularly ask scout Don Dorman who actually signed Kenny Burns at the home of his brother in Glasgow, and they all see a lovable side in Burns. He never bears a grudge, he can take the dressing room ribbing; he came from nothing and had to fight himself to achieve (under Brian Clough and Peter Taylor) the ultimate accolade as Player of the Year.

Dorman has a special affection for Burns and feels the frictions should have been seen, discussed and finalised by the managers – particularly Bell and his assistant Owen. Eventually Dorman felt let down when Bell, having fined Burns and even ordered him off the field during a League match, "gave Burnsie away at £150,000."

A sequel to the overlapping Francis–Burns careers came in Munich immediately after the two played for Nottingham Forest in the European Cup Final in 1979. "I was standing outside," says Roy Francis, "when the lad Kenny Burns came out. We hadn't seen each other since that day he tackled Trevor in training, but Burns came straight up to us, said 'Hello Mr. Francis' and started chatting about what was going on in the dressing room."

But back in November, 1975, Francis handed in a written transfer request, three days after the training upset, though he said it had been on his mind for some time. The request was rejected and Bell openly admired the fact that Francis stuck to his word to give 100 per cent, to carry on another relegation fight and play through a succession of injuries. "The constant relegation factor was the real reason I want to get away," said Francis. "I would like to enjoy my football more, to play without fear for once. My game is about expressing myself but in a backs-to-the-wall situation all the time I can't do that."

Arsenal, Everton, Derby County and Leeds all made no attempt to hide their admiration for Francis but he had said: "It's well known there are methods you can employ to get away, but I can't go out there and not try, even in training."

It was known, even then, that Francis might fetch

a transfer fee of £½ million if Birmingham put him up for sale. "It would," writer Cyril Chapman memorably wrote, "be like a Rembrandt coming onto the open market."

But Birmingham's need was greater still. In April 1976, Willie Bell admitted that Francis was playing game after game despite being unable to train and having injections into a strained groin. "If it weren't for our fight against relegation," said the manager, "I would have given him a rest a long time ago. But it is typical of him that he insisted on playing."

The club's status was saved again. Francis finished the season with 17 goals from 35 games ... and two months later was fined £100 by Bell for saying: "We must buy players if we are going to make an impact. If some effort is made during the close season I shall be happy to stay at St. Andrews and help the club to the success the fans deserve." Bell retorted: "He'll be telling us how to cut the grass next."

By December 1976, there was yet another example of Francis's almost obsessive determination to play under any circumstances, and the club's willingness to allow it. After he had scored the winner against Sunderland, Bell told reporters: "Trevor spent all day yesterday in bed with a heavy cold, but when he arrived at the ground, he said he wanted to play. It is all credit to his courage that he was able to do so well. I wanted to bring him off towards the end, but he would not hear of it. He looked really poorly in the dressing room and I sent him home. Maybe the fact that he had played three hard games in the last week drained him."

By coincidence, the day after that statement, Christopher Brasher wrote a major article in *The Observer* entitled "A risk athletes run shrugging off a cold". He reported the deaths of two orienteers who had trained or competed suffering from a heavy cold and flu, and that medical science now suggested that the stress of activity combined with the weakening effects of flu could kill.

When this article was shown to Francis, he scanned it, looked faintly surprised, and said: "The truth was, I had been in bed three or four days. It's got to be something really wrong for me not to play. I got out of bed at one o'clock on the Saturday, came down in my pyjamas and my dad who was staying with us said: 'What are you intending to do?' 'I shall go in,' I said. The manager didn't ask how I was. He started talking about how he wanted me to play. During the match, I spent long spells bent over and coughing."

Francis in fact came through that season without missing a game, and with 21 League goals as Birmingham achieved a mid-table position. Willie Bell, however, was never given time to build on that. Four defeats at the start of the next season and he went the way of Goodwin, to be replaced by a Birmingham City director, Sir Alf Ramsey. Bell, after a further short spell managing Lincoln, gave up football to join a religious order in America.

Willie Bell departed but, via the air waves of Radio Birmingham, delivered a subsequent sour reflection on Francis. Referring to a transfer request at a time the club was out of the FA Cup and floundering as usual in relegation waters, Bell said: "I think it's a disgrace the player, in particular Trevor, one of the highest paid in the country, should throw in the towel. This is where character comes in. There's another 30 players at that club and they're not picking up the money he's getting. He's picking up two or three times their wages."

Francis, who replied that there was never a good time to ask to go, that he could wait for ever, felt the remarks created more dissension amongst the players than anything he might do. His quarrel with Birmingham had never been a financial one; it was simply that the years were passing and his chances of ever winning anything seemed as far away as ever at Birmingham.

Enter Ramsey. "The first problem we had about Sir Alf Ramsey was what to call him," says Trevor. "He made it clear, very clear, that he wanted to be called Sir Alf. He took the team meetings and we knew exactly what was wanted. The thing he stressed more than anything was work-rate. He set out to play a certain way, 4-4-2, based tactically on the success he had with England winning the 1966 World Cup. And it proved fairly successful. Keith Bertschin and myself were given similar roles to Geoff Hurst and Roger Hunt in the World Cup and we got some good results, although I always felt it wasn't going to last for ever."

Ramsey began by saying: "There is no better player in the country than Trevor Francis." Then, by demanding the effort and loyalty around him which he inspired in 1966, he achieved an overall record, in his short term of 26 matches at Birmingham, of 10 wins, 4 draws, 12 defeats, 38 goals for, 41 against, and 24 points. By Birmingham standards it deserved an almost ecstatic reaction. Significantly, Francis scored 14 goals, of which nine won points.

"What Sir Alf had was certainly the utmost respect of all the players because of his achievements," says Francis. "I think, at the start, everyone tended to think that he had some influence over the team before he was made manager because, as a

Helen, the wife who has to share the controversy as well as the good things in a footballer's life.

director, he used to come into the dressing room. But that wasn't so. I never did see him talk to anyone about the game.

"There was always so much speculation about clubs coming in for me at Birmingham that people think all I had to do was put in a request and I could leave. But it was never as easy as that. For a start, I was never told at the club if anyone was showing interest, although I knew I had admirers. But if anyone could have told me how to get away without cheating or not trying, I'd love to have heard it. I asked Freddie Goodwin two or three times, though not in writing; but the fact was I felt so much for the club and the supporters, I kept being convinced that there was some glimmer of hope things would change. I was hoping I would be part of success *at* Birmingham. In any case, the times when I became unhappy were never that many. Obviously, it made headlines when Kenny Burns and myself were at odds, when I was being fined or asking for a move, but it boils down to six or seven days in nine years.

"But the years had kept going by and I began to feel, in the end, that there was no hope. As you get older you can get harder, but although I'd ask for transfers I was never prepared myself to play badly in order to force them to sell me. I think they used that to keep me there – someone said, as a prisoner – and I think that's right. In the end I had to resort to something I never wanted to do, which was going to the press, trying to antagonise them by writing a

couple of articles which I knew would bring me heavy fines. When I look back on the nine years at Birmingham I think that's the only black mark I really had against me."

Francis was fined a week's wages for each of the articles, one in *The People* and one in *The Guardian*, in 1978, because they liberally quoted his dissatisfaction with life at Birmingham City. When Sir Alf resigned as manager – or consultant manager as he termed it – in the March, he claimed Francis was encouraged to deliberately flaunt the club rules in the articles "because he received more money than he was fined."

Francis refutes the implication that he negotiated the fees on a profit motive. "I don't think I did receive more than I lost," he says, "but if I did get a bit extra it wasn't important. It wasn't something I negotiated. Before I put anything in the press, I obviously wanted to make sure that I wasn't losing on it. We are not talking about a fiver or £10, we are talking a lot of money. I'd be as naive as some people say I am if I threw that away."

Ramsey further remarked: "He's had his say. His wife's had hers. Now I'm waiting for the dog's turn." A reference obviously to an interview given by Helen to a national newspaper emphasising that her "softhearted" husband was more interested in the move than the money, was answering dozens of letters of support every day, and in her opinion should be allowed to move on to seek some success in his final eight years or so.

"There had been no problem between Sir Alf and myself until I asked for a transfer," says Francis. "But the biggest surprise I had from him was when he announced after he left that he had advised the board to sell me. He had told *me* all the way through that he wasn't letting me go. He told me he was advising the board *not* to let me go. That's why, in the end, I went to the press."

According to Sir Alf's public resignation statement, and subsequently reiterated in a newspaper column headlined "Francis—the £1 million headache! Why I had to quit over him", the board, having accepted his recommendation to list Francis at £750,000 on a 4–1 vote, changed their minds three days later. It was Sir Alf who left and not Trevor Francis. If the player was unhappy at that, it again wasn't reflected in the scoresheets as he struck goals in each of the next seven games for Birmingham to finish the season with 27 goals.

Jim Smith, former manager of Blackburn Rovers was the new boss. "Jim Smith was a man I took to," says Francis. "He came to me the night before his

Why I quit

BY JEFF FARMER

BIRMINGHAM'S refusal to consider the sale of England striker Trevor Francis was yesterday revealed as the reason why Sir Alf Ramsey has left the club.
The future of Britain's most valuable

Sir Alf blames the Francis decision

first game and said: 'I understand you're unhappy, tell me about it.' The first thing that occurred to me was how honest he was. The next was that for the first time somebody at the club could understand my feelings, how I felt after so many promises over so many years had gone unfulfilled. Even Freddie Goodwin didn't agree on that, although naturally he was there at the start and there'd been a lot more promises since.

"Jim Smith said he wasn't going to promise anything but what he would like me to do is to forget all about asking for a transfer. He told me his plans and said that if things weren't any better in six months he would do everything possible to help me get away. I like Jim Smith; it might seem rather weird to some people because he was the man who eventually sold me, but we still see each other socially. He impressed me."

That April, Jim Smith announced his controversial plan to allow Francis to share his talents between Birmingham and Detroit. "Trevor has received fabulous offers to play in America," Smith said, "and this may be the only way we are going to be able to compete with the slumbering giant of American soccer. Renting out our best players for the summer is better than losing them forever."

Freddie Goodwin, by then coaching at Minnesota, had made the first contact, but Trevor admits he was astonished when Birmingham said he could play there during the summer. "I felt that fed up at not winning anything, not being involved in Europe, that I felt America was the one way I could do something different as well as earn the money which I don't deny attracted me. Would anyone else, all those people who criticised me for going, turn down such an opportunity?"

Thus for a time, it looked as if Francis might actually still be at Birmingham to receive his testimonial, which was already being organised in the city. However, after the turn of another New Year, Birmingham's season virtually ended with no cup involvement and almost no hope left in preventing relegation. Jim Smith, remembering his

A former England manager makes his exit at Birmingham City.

word, suggested to the board that it might release Francis; there was a £750,000 bid outstanding from Arsenal. The board said no.

"I didn't ask for a transfer," says Francis, "but I admitted to the chairman and his brother that I couldn't face another season dragging on towards relegation. This time anyway we were so badly entrenched it didn't look possible to do our Houdini act once again, and I felt it was in everyone's interests if they let me go. I told them I would do my stuff, there was still no way I would not try my hardest; I couldn't do anything less than that. But my heart was no longer in it. I didn't care about the testimonial money, which was going to be more than I would get from a transfer and it wasn't a question of anything they could offer. Money wasn't the thing; my heart was no longer in the club."

A few days after that meeting, Jim Smith told him the board had decided he could go ... at a million pounds. Ironically, the word came to Francis at precisely the same time as a close friend of his, Alan Cooper, was being told: "One thing about Jim (Smith), he'd sell his wife before he'd sell Trevor."

Birmingham City, after its allegiance to a single star image, suddenly became a buying club. Jim Smith required 10 months to reinvest the Francis million, buying a goalkeeper, two defenders, two midfield players, a winger and two strikers. Four of them, Archie Gemmill, Colin Todd, Frank Worthington and Willie Johnston were experienced internationals ... and now Francis was gone, Birmingham suddenly had a team that might have suited his talents.

That irony tells you the truth about Birmingham City. That it just never had the money, or perhaps the will, to invest in a successful side. As the new side began to challenge for promotion the Blues fans started calling it "The team Trevor Francis bought".

69

5
SKILL
AND STYLE

The eyes of Peter Taylor are constantly wary, as if he mistrusts everybody and everthing. Yet they are a gambler's eyes, too. They are the organs which led Brian Clough and Nottingham Forest to pay the first £1 million transfer fee in the history of British soccer. The million bought flesh and blood – one player. In fact, it was more than a million; Birmingham City's ransom for Trevor Francis was £1,150,500 inclusive of taxes, and it was Taylor, whose judgment Clough trusts implicitly, who made the commitment to pay it. "After that," he says, "I phoned Brian to tell him what I'd done."

What many of us would have given for a crossed telephone line that evening! What Taylor had done was double the transfer record overnight. Why? What does Francis have that Forest wanted so badly? "All round ability," says Taylor, leaning his hefty ex-goalkeeper's frame back against the chair. "Everything . . . he's got it all.

"He's quicker than most, his control is better than most, his composure's better than most . . . all qualities that make a top class player. If you want me to elaborate . . . pace, craft, control, composure . . . he appears to me to have an abundance of all these, more so than the average player. In my bracket, a player of possible greatness – hence the fee."

Pele once described his own art as "the ability to create something out of nothing". The attributes Peter Taylor saw in Francis, a heightened sense of scoring opportunity and an ability to deliver with either foot, come close to that art. More so, certainly, than the average player.

Ability is all, but we have yet to scratch the surface of Trevor Francis's endowment. Before we try, bear in mind that the real magnitude of Nottingham's gamble lies in the use it makes of the talent, and in imponderables concerning team blend, heart and commitment, fortune and management. How, for example, do the first medals, increasing wealth, the birth of a son, affect ambition? In a succeeding chapter we shall share thoughts from Clough, Taylor and Francis on the best ways to prevent any squandering of talent.

First, we thought we should define the skills built into the anatomy of a million pound player. They are so complex that five club managers, and as many at international level, have juggled in varied ways with Francis's gifts. They peer at him apparently through their own particular prisms and cast him in the images they perceive, most likely where their teams are weakest. Right wing, second striker, left or right of midfield . . . no-one has tried centre-half or goalkeeper yet.

When Trevor Francis flies to America, he goes Concorde. When Francis takes wing on the field Tampa Bay hunt him in threes. Around the V.I.P. in this picture are Mike Connell (6), Sandje Ivanchukov (18) and Farrukh Quraishi (16). They've travelled far and

Before he had finished being a teenager, Francis made a plea for understanding in Birmingham City's programme: "When you consider that to date I have played in four different roles for the Blues, you must also consider that opportunities of scoring arise with a different frequency in each position." It read like a political manifesto but it was a young professional's cry from the heart. "On the right wing or in midfield, I am more a provider than a taker of chances, but that hasn't released me from criticism that I am not getting sufficient goals. I like to see my name in the goal charts, like any player, but it has become not the most vital thing in my game. I do not know where I shall eventually finish with regard to the tactical plan."

Freddie Goodwin, Birmingham's manager at that time, now admits: "I don't know his true role for sure. He has fulfilled himself in more than one role. I felt eventually his best position would be outside-right, but he hates it. From a club point of view, we had Bob Latchford, Bob Hatton and Trevor, all good goalscorers, down the middle. Partly because

wide but is any of them fleet enough of foot to catch him? Just in case, Niels Guldbjerg (also numbered 18), Detroit's Danish forward, waits unmarked for the pass. "I don't mind three marking me," points out Francis, "because it means somewhere there are men free."

stand on the halfway line, knowing he's the best deliverer in the business ... *I* want him to be the best, the best tackler forwardwise, the best header forwardwise, and the best sticker-in forwardwise. That's the way we work."

At the time he said that, Brian Clough was using Francis as a midfield player, again because it suited the team's need. Ultimately, when Tony Woodcock was sold to F.C. Cologne, Francis was released to chase goals alongside the centre-forward "shield" of Garry Birtles.

Francis was 26 last April, and there remain more options about where to play him than clubs which could buy him. Willie Bell, Sir Alf Ramsey (who described him a year ago as the outstanding attacking Englishman in the game) and Jim Smith allowed him the role of his choice, alongside the centre-forward, at Birmingham. Don Revie observed that the less space Francis is given, the more dangerous he appears to be; he saw him as a player with his back to goal, spinning to take on defenders. Ken Furphy used Francis that way for Detroit in the summers of 1978 and 1979.

Crystal Palace manager Terry Venables, who may in time succeed to the England managership, says Francis's killer instinct is too valuable to fritter away any distance from goal; like Ron Greenwood he foresees the future forward as a sharp, fast-paced, infiltrating player with good control, breaking down international defences. Manager Ron Atkinson, having watched Francis at close quarters from West Bromwich Albion, reasons that his speed over 30 yards is the best in the game and should be used to run at defenders.

A voice from Francis's past, schoolmaster Jim Liddicoat, differs from all the professionals: "I suppose I shouldn't argue with Clough, with his record," says Jim, "but if I had anything to do with it, Trevor would be the Bobby Charlton in Greenwood's side. Although he scores goals he's absolutely brilliant in the centre of the field, moving about, making his own game, making the others respond to passes of real class. And y'know, I reckon he would score more goals from midfield than Charlton did. I think his all-round ability is limited as a striker."

Jim Liddicoat and Roy Francis, differed before, and they do still. Last winter, when Francis had a quiet moan to his father about the changing demands on him, Roy told his son: "You don't have to worry. You have all the skills you need to do a job anywhere on the field." But does Francis senior have a favourite role for Trevor? "There's only one, really. He's best in front of goal off a main striker."

of that, partly to protect him from the real robustness, I played him at outside-right for a spell. He has all the equipment to be a winger – the dribble, the pace, the accuracy – but he was unhappy; he prefers to be inside and involved. Wingers are a special breed. They hear all the comments of the crowd; a lot of players don't like playing next to the crowd and that's why there is a shortage of wingers in the game. I don't think Trevor ever accepted how good he is in that position."

Now contrast that assessment from the man who nurtured Francis' growing skills, to that of Brian Clough, who bought the maturing player: "Trevor Francis's *only* position, not his best position, is playing off an extremely brave centre-forward, God didn't give us everything – none of us y'know. God gave Trevor Francis extraordinary pace, God gave him the ability to put the ball in the back of the net. He made him the best *deliverer* of a ball we've seen; I worry sometimes that he'll settle for being such a great deliverer. I'm not bloody well having him

Clearly, if Francis listened to everyone, he would never come up for air. He is pliable enough to do his best wherever he is asked to play, but do not confuse that with a lack of will or preference. Before giving voice to that, let's allow one more opinion, from John Hollins who has defended for England as well as for three London clubs in over 600 games. "Having to play in various positions can't do any harm," Hollins says. "I've played right-back, centre-half, midfield and even had a go up front. It puts a new edge on your game, helps you understand how the other fellows want the ball played, and what difficulties they have in getting it where you want it. Trevor will be a better player for it, believe me."

What about the player himself, would *he* like to say a few words on the true position of Trevor Francis? "No." You wait for the boyish smile. It appears, settles, and drifts away. "Okay. First of all," he begins, serious by now, "I never understand why so many people say they'd give up football if they could make money at something else. I love playing, I love having the ball, doing things with it.

"I like to attack players, go at players from the centre of the field. I don't mind being made to go either way. I'm obviously stronger on my right foot and defenders know that, but if I've got to, I'll go the other way. Birmingham people will tell you better than me, but I've scored some good goals from outside the box with my left foot. I suppose I always could strike a ball with both feet and with *power*." He uses that word with an emphasis designed to re-create the impact verbally. "It first came home to me when I was in the Under-11s."

Talking about himself places Francis out of position again. At other times his conversation can flow as fluently as he does over the field, but self-effacement is his natural disposition and he wriggles uncomfortably through cross-examination on his attributes. He looks for support, for the easy way out.

Finding none, he attacks: "I prefer to play as a forward. I know what I'm doing up front. Even if I'm not seeing a lot of the ball, at least I can move off the ball and be some use by keeping people occupied. In midfield, I have to think before I act. I can rush about, but I don't always know if it's right or wrong. It doesn't come naturally to me." Yet, he acknowledged in 1979: "If I was manager of Forest, I'd have done the same thing... I think I would, anyway, because it's the best blend. They've had success with that formation, so why change it because they've bought a player?" In the event, Francis justified the demands, scoring 11 times in 25

games from midfield, including the goal that won the European Cup in 1979.

That goal, like some of the others, came at the end of a 50 yards sprint into the goalmouth, and the sharpness with which the ball was despatched removed lingering doubts about his stamina. The other doubt which clings on is about his aggression, or lack of it. That isn't to imply cowardice, but a tendency to think too little of his own ability. "He doesn't take a game by the scruff of the neck," says his father.

"Trevor's not a physically aggressive player," agrees Fred Goodwin, "yet at the same time he goes into areas which demand bravery. Teams very quickly find out a player, particularly a goalscorer. In that position, you cannot hide any weaknesses such as lack of bravery or frailty."

John Wile, the West Bromwich Albion captain, is a defender who gives no quarter. Anyone who witnessed Wile driving his team on in the 1978 FA Cup semi-final, blood seeping out of a head wound, will appreciate the Desperate Dan code by which he judges bravery.

"There are not many very, very brave forwards," Wile says. "I wouldn't place Trevor Francis in the same category as Andy Gray, who is so absolutely fearless he picks up more injuries than he need simply through flinging himself in. But I won't have players criticise Francis for lacking determination – or whatever word they use. At The Hawthorns a couple of years back, he went off early in the second half with concussion after colliding with Alistair Robertson. Birmingham wasn't having a very good time, and the first thought that crossed my mind was: 'I don't suppose we'll see *him* back on.'

"He'd been the only one posing us any threats and I thought that knock was his perfect excuse to stay off. But he came back, almost scored with his first touch and later with an overhead kick. He didn't pull out of a thing and was still posing the major problems. That told me a lot about the lad's character.

"There was, mind you, a stage when Trevor Francis tended to make a lot of a tackle, you know fall as if pole-axed. It was a stage he went through; I've played him at least a dozen times and I've learned that if there's anything worth going for –

"Legs of pork," Trevor's friends call them, but look at the power that can be generated from thighs built up on weight training and running. Look, too, at the left arm, and ask yourself if this is a player who isn't prepared to fight for the ball.

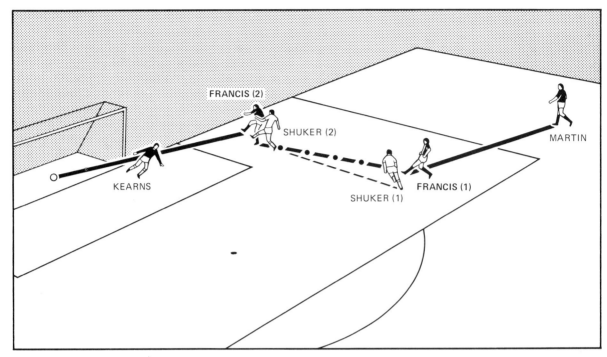

FRANCIS (2)

SHUKER (2)

MARTIN

KEARNS

FRANCIS (1)

SHUKER (1)

September 12, 1970 – Birmingham City v. Oxford United: In his first full League match, Francis scored a goal that looked simple. In fact it was a small masterpiece from a 16-year-old apprentice, a goal of anticipation, acceleration, timing, balance and nerve. He sprinted onto a pass from Ray Martin a yard inside the penalty box, controlling the ball at full stretch with his left instep 12 inches above the ground. He accelerated, ran seven strides, and hit a right foot shot behind Irish international keeper Mick Kearns who had rushed towards him. A waif of a lad, he withstood a tackle in the back from John Shuker, an experienced pro. That tackle forced Francis onto his back, his feet pawing at the air like an overturned turtle. He suffered cramp; he was a boy delivering the first of over 100 Birmingham City goals. The match was drawn 1–1 and Birmingham's 22,346 spectators had a dissatisfied hero: "I wish," said Trevor, "it could have been the winner."

the possibility of a goal or a chance to set one up – then he'll go for it, never mind the consequences."

A major change in Francis's attitude towards defensive duties might be attributable in part to Don Revie. In 1977, on the eve of his debut for England, Francis reflected quietly: "During the past year, I've looked at the names in the international squads. My name was not among them, and I thought, as I was getting my best form, I *ought* to be there. So I began to analyse myself, and decided I'd do almost anything because I wanted it so much. But you can't make yourself ruthless if it's not in you, and I'd never been brought up to do anything sort of dirty. I couldn't do that, but I decided that if I lacked anything it was what Mr Revie had said himself when he picked me for his first squad before my injury in 1974: he talked about aggression and tackling back."

Revie had preached his gospel of work-rate and commitment. He had turned Francis's head, telling him what his best friends never dared. "I'd never been much of a tackler," Francis said at that time, "it wasn't born into me. But I decided I could make myself more nuisance value by putting pressure on defenders when I hadn't got the ball. I took Kevin Keegan as my example. He was England captain and he wasn't the greatest tackler. Maybe I shouldn't say that? What I mean is, he puts defenders under pressure by getting under their feet. To be honest, I never thought I needed to do it. Perhaps I was wrong. I don't enjoy chasing defenders. But if it gets me into the England side I'm delighted I've done it."

Three years on, a more sustained approach was built into Francis's game – though he rarely appears

Right: The style is the man – on artificial turf or on grass, only the speed of things has to be quickened up. On artificial turf, the ball rolls freer and techniques have to be sharper to control it.

Tampa Bay's 6 ft. defender Mike Connell dwarfs Francis in height and poundage, but by controlling the ball on the outside of his right foot and placing his body between, Trevor is using his body as a shield between opponent and ball. It is impossible for Connell to tackle without committing a foul and this is a technique used to perfection by even the slenderest of players, such as Johan Cruyff.

to "chase" defenders. "He does put the fright into defenders," conceded John Hollins, "but by skill. You can't put the Andy Gray aggression – meeting fire with fire – into a player; in any case it would take away from Francis's game. The thing is, if you rap someone on the shins, they're going to be looking for you and you'll spend half the game looking over your shoulder.

"People know Trevor's a nice lad. They'll kick him, he knows that, but they won't do anything more than they've been told to do at the start, they'll mostly be trying to win the ball. But if he started anything rough, he'd find himself out of the game, as others have in the past. He doesn't need that."

From defender to attacker, sweet music. The trouble is, John Hollins is also an exceptionally nice fellow. Brian Clough, who has seen harder times, insists Francis "*does* lack aggression, though I'm not sure what aggression is. People who look just for the physical thing all the time are barmy, they couldn't build a sandcastle let alone a team. But

there's never ever been a great player without the ability to look after himself – some do it physically, some by an awareness, some by extra vision. Franz Beckenbauer strolled through things with this extraordinary vision, but he was quick to look after himself; Wilf Mannion looked after himself and he had to. A very small bloke, a frail man with a touch as delicate as anybody today but Wilf had an awareness of a defender which enabled him to avoid injury. Trevor's got to find something, the young man has."

Among the things the young man relies on to ward off injury is a physique more resilient by far than in his youth. His thigh muscles have built up so that, in his mid-twenties they seem positively gross in proportion to his torso. This, he assumes, develops out of extensive weight-training following injuries, though he says they are really not his at all. They are on lease, to be returned to Roger Hynd after use. Mr Hynd is otherwise known as "Garth", the fitness fanatic who dwarfs most players by inches

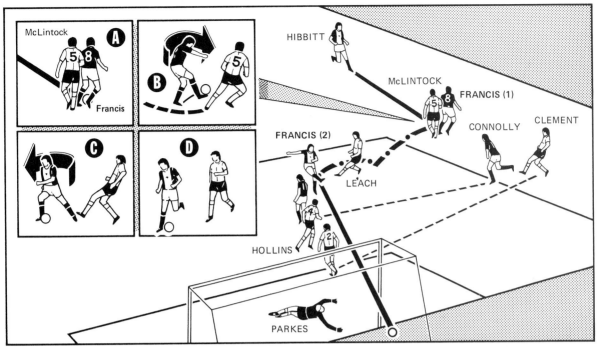

October 30, 1976 – Birmingham City v. Queen's Park Rangers: The ability to create out of nothing. Thank heavens Trevor Francis is less modest with the ball than with his description: "I started on the edge of the box, did a little bit there, came across and shot low and hard to Phil Parkes's right." True, but it misses one or two points. Like the fact he had his back to Scottish international

Frank McLintock when the ball was played up to him. He hit it gently into the air, caught it on his right foot and turned to go right. McLintock followed the turn but suddenly Francis turned full circle and slipped past McLintock's left. "He has the movement of a snake," says McLintock, "he flows from one direction to the other without braking. He glides." He accelerates, too, as first McLintock

and then Mick Leach discovered. And then he shoots on sight, using his right foot to score just inside the post. The flowing movement followed by the deadly finish of McLintock's snake. "What made it even better," says the Scot, "is that it was soft and slippery underfoot that day. I dug in, and he seemed to move on top of the surface, flowing this way and that without stopping."

and who once blockaded the Birmingham defence.

An equally significant development had been in the mind. Francis never fitted West German international Paul Breitner's identikit picture of "those players whose brain begins at the feet and terminates in the knees" but nowadays he has more knowledge of and control over his skills. At close quarters, and at full throttle, you can actually *see* the mind at work.

From the stands, he has style. It looks sculptural and almost serene as he moves on his toes at genuinely quick pace, achieved apparently without the kind of effort that interferes with composure. Down at ground level you get to feel the power that is laced into that burst of acceleration. It seems to yank you forward in its wake; it scares you coming at you for a moment because you wonder how he can possibly avoid a collision.

Then you look at the face. Concentration is absolute. At that instant he seems to sense that the defender at his side has lost the pace and you can visibly detect the moment his mind switches, even before he is free, from the effort of rounding the defender, to glance up into the goalmouth, perhaps to pick out another red shirt or to strike at goal. If it is a centre, he begins the movement with a long sweep which guides the ball to its target with precise accuracy, and invariably the momentum lifts his other leg off the ground and deposits him on the seat of his pants, quite often with the full-back on top of him.

All done in fractions of seconds, on a good day, when Francis has the beating of a full-back time and again, you can study the change of speed, separate exact moments of thought and movement as he beats his man, looks for the next move, and delivers. From the stand again it appears one continuous movement of rhythm and flow; down below beauty is blurred by the sheer suddenness, the sweep fragmented into separate actions. Aggressive actions, too.

The essence of it is not merely that he has pace, but that somehow he has absolute power of control over that pace, the concentration to ignore tackles that would grind his bones. You see a face more alert and determined than at any other time in his company, you sense that his faculties are working at greater pitch than at any other time in his life.

Immediately after the match, you want to question him, to ask if he really is aware of all that you thought you saw, to determine whether he operates with calculating powers or whether, like the pigeon, he possesses homing instinct. But he can't tell you, not then. Not for hours before or after the play. He isn't on drugs, but he is locked into a concentration so deep it is an effort for him to observe his own social courtesies.

And this concentration can last for hours. All night even. "My mind is going over and over all the moves, especially things you might say I've done well – but also the bad moves. I'm telling myself I should have passed to set up a goal for Tony, or should have shot or attempted a tackle. Sometimes it's so bad, I'm useless. I can't socialise. Other times I go for a meal with Helen and maybe close friends, but I'm just going through the motions." Relief comes, as it has since boyhood, with a couple of Mogadon sleeping tablets, "only after a game – I've never taken anything before. I don't know anyone who has taken stimulants. I've certainly never needed anything to put me in the mood to play. It's just after the game."

On the field, verbal communication is cut to the bone. He converses with his body, so opponents get closest to his thoughts. "You daren't get too close, mind," warns John Wile. "If he draws you in, he's deadly. I suppose the most predictable thing about him is the number of times he spins away from a close-marker. You know he's going to do it, but you can't do anything about it. *He's* gone.

"If you back off too far, he'll run you and again you've no chance. The only thing to do is to try to push him into a situation where you've got other defenders to back you up or, if you have to make a tackle in the middle third of the field where his pace is exceptional, you'd better make sure it counts. There'll be no second bite."

Frank McLintock made two, almost three second bite tackles when Francis turned him almost a figure of eight to score against Queen's Park Rangers. "He has this movement George Best used to have," says McLintock. "It's like a snake, it flows one way and then the other without braking. You are tight up against him, reading every twist and turn, but as your boot digs into the surface to get some purchase, his seems to glide over it."

McLintock's team-mate that day, John Hollins again, tries to develop a rapport of movement with Francis. "Often, I try to let him *have* the ball. I'm fairly quick, but not as quick as him so, like John Wile, I'd try to slow him down so that I can get some support. Sometimes I come in ever so quick, as if I'm going to slide tackle, but then I stop quick and back away. Hopefully, he's thought I was going to tackle and he's stopped the ball or dropped his shoulder to feint to go one way. That way I've prevented him getting into his stride."

After that, still with Hollins, it gets more complicated, a unique *pas des deux*: "If you're up tight, at his back, he'll turn halfway, use you as a shield, and when the ball comes to him he'll chest it or go towards your goal with such speed you can't counter it. Keegan does the same. A lot of people can't understand that you're watching the ball, but you're also watching for the time to tackle. And yet you're trying to watch *him* as well.

"Watch only the ball and you fall for every trick, every shuffle he does over the ball. With experience, you learn to watch Trevor's body as well as the ball. The trick is to try to rock your body movement to the same momentum as his; you do exactly as he does, so that if he only half commits himself one way and springs off the other, you can respond with him. You can't just stand there and watch; he's that quick of movement you wouldn't even see him go . . . Are you still with me?"

Almost, John, almost. "The trouble with Trevor is that after a time he spots what you're doing and he throws in a few more tricks. With most players, you know they always drop a shoulder and go because that's their only trick. But Trevor's a class player, and a class player has the advantage because he *knows* where he's going to go with the ball."

"That's right," says Francis. "I know when I'm going to do it, usually I do anyway. I try to work out when the player is going to deliver the ball to me and I try to feel how tightly the fellow behind is marking me. He's probably not exactly touching me but I know where a defender is in relation to myself even if he's a couple of yards off. There are certain things I do without having to plan them, I don't even have to think about them.

"If I get to the byline, for example, I seem to be able to catch the ball and cross it when people think it's running out. I don't have to practise it, I just do

1

2

3

4

5

In America, the opponents may be cosmopolitan, but the technique has to be the same. Englishman Alan West (10) and South African Ace Ntsoelengoe (11) converge like cymbals but Francis's balance, as much as his sheer pace, takes him through them. West, the blond Minnesota Kicks midfield man, is the more dogged in pursuit but is shrugged off with a little help from Francis's right elbow before Francis sidefoots a pass to a teammate. The end result, typical in the States, sees the Francis ankles kicked from under him.

it. I can show you how it's done; it's just the general body movement that enables me to do it. I can't really explain it any more than that.''

The common advice from managers to their players is ''Be wary of Francis's pace in tight situations''. They might as well tell a goalkeeper to be on guard for a sudden shot from nowhere or the reptilian reflex action which Francis has been aware of since his childhood. ''I've always had quick reflexes,'' he reassures you. ''I've always kept wicket when I play cricket and I'm pretty quick around the tennis court. It's born into you, I think.''

The ability to move quicker than his contemporaries does indeed have to be born into a player. Scientific analysis of athleticism is now measured in the laboratory, where the technique of muscle biopsy can clinically define whether a man is born a sprinter or a stayer. It depends on the ''twitch'' in muscle fibre; the twitch being the speed of the fibre's response to a nerve impulse – fast indicates suitability to short bursts of activity, and slow provides endurance. Thus the sprinter, like the hare, has a preponderance of fast twitch fibres throughout his muscular structure, while a marathoner is a slow twitch man. This relatively new science has superseded the criteria that the ultimate factors of athletic prowess are heart rate and lung power. They remain vital, but the reason for speed lies in the muscles, according to modern research.

Trevor Francis would no more give up a sliver of muscle to science than abandon football for a motor assembly line. He knows he is fast, and that in retrospect the only men who ever doubted it were some Football Association coaches at Bisham Abbey who sent him home after a week's course at age 14½ with the words: ''A fairly skilful ball player, but needs speeding up in his actions.'' The echo now merely provokes that slow, placid smile. Francis has since had such consolation as the word of Syd Owen, former coach to Leeds United, Birmingham City, and now the Manchester United youth team: ''Trevor's acceleration from a standing start is equal to any I have seen in 34 years working with top class players.''

No amount of training can alter the balance of muscle fibre, though speed training works wonders with sluggish footballers. It may only be developing responses that lie dormant, but Ron Jones, the former Olympic sprinter who works on Queen's Park Rangers' players, says: ''I believe if you take the average footballer, you can improve him by about 10 per cent through continuous quality work. I don't say you can take a bloke at 10·4 and push him

down to nine point something, but you can improve an 11-second sprinter down to 10·5 simply by good quality training.

''The traditional attitude of an easy football session is one run around the park; a hard session is three times around. It's as fallacious as saying you've got to train in a mud bath to be able to slog it out on heavy pitches. To improve the quality of speed you have got to improve the condition of muscles, and this can only be done on good surfaces, such as Tartan or at least a good cinder track, using spikes.''

Footballers complain that their muscles ache like hell after a Jones session. ''I say bloody good thing,'' he smiles. ''You can't be that fit if a bit of quality running hurts that much. It's horses for courses, really; I remember I once tried to improve my stamina by running miles in the winter. I got extremely fit, but when I competed I came a steady fifth or sixth. I looked a fast half-miler. You don't see the great American sprinters running cross-country in winter. They sprint all year round.''

Francis, though he says he improved beyond recognition after a few months at Birmingham, impresses Midland athletics coach Charles Taylor more by his smooth change of pace than his flat-out sprint. A few years ago, Taylor coached Steve Kindon, the former Wolves winger, to compete at the Powderhall professional sprint championships in Scotland. ''In a straight line,'' says Taylor, ''Kindon would be faster than Francis. But he hasn't got Trevor Francis's grace. It's more the attribute of a ballet dancer – the ability to turn, to change direction quickly. Francis has what Stanley Matthews had, this brilliant ability to move through a gear without obviously changing pace, even when running a straight line. It's so smooth you can't detect it in the action.''

Francis attributes any grace or style to nature's endowment, though curiously for one of the few whose fluency so gracefully disguises the effort, he can't bear to watch himself on TV or film. ''I don't like looking at myself,'' he says. ''I don't know why. I like to study other players, the way they move, but I don't like the way *I* move. I'm embarrassed.''

Professional footballers still do shy away from discussion on style, and particularly grace, as if it has effeminate connotations. Yet there are experienced managers, men like Don Revie, Malcolm Allison and Terry Venables whose teams are not noted for lack of toughness, who have hired a Geordie dancing master, Lennie Heppell, to teach body movement to players. ''Malcolm Allison has

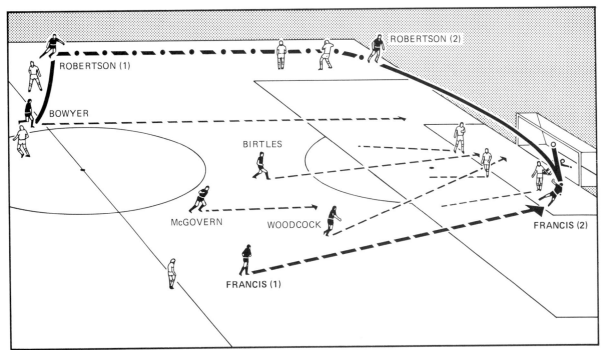

ROBERTSON (2)

ROBERTSON (1)

BOWYER

BIRTLES

McGOVERN

WOODCOCK

FRANCIS (2)

FRANCIS (1)

May 30, 1979 – Nottingham Forest v. Malmo: "Not as good a goal as people made it out to be," says Francis of the European Cup winner. No? "No. I remember that John Robertson had the ball and was going down the left flank, so I thought I ought to get in at the back post in the hope he would put it across. As soon as I saw it coming, I thought I've *got* to score here. I'd have been disappointed if I had missed." Francis devalues his art again; his reading, though accurate, ignores the anticipation of the preceding 11 seconds. Ian Bowyer began it with a pass out of the Forest half and, as the pass found Robertson, so Francis began a loping run towards the Malmo goalmouth. Robertson swept past Roland Andersson and then Jan-Olof Kinvall and, while Garry Birtles and Tony Woodcock moved to the near post, Francis timed his 50-yards run almost to perfection. "As the cross arrived, I saw that the goalkeeper had come further across than I anticipated, so I headed it back across him. I was pleased with it, but it was a goal I ought to have scored."

me in three times a week," says Heppell. "I'm working with super athletes, so obviously I'm scraping the barrel looking for tiny flaws that upset a player's balance.

"Now to me, Trevor Francis is near perfect. In full flight he's like a deer. He twists and turns so beautifully . . . he's probably the best balanced player in the country in full flight. To move gracefully and well, you've got to use the ground. Trevor Francis is balanced for ice, he's got muscle control in his whole body right through to his fingers. You can see it.

"But he could be even better. I've seen a flaw," Heppell confides. "You see, in certain situations he'll fall over – when he makes a reverse pass, he falls over; when he does a turn from a standing position, he falls over; when he makes a cross or a shot, he falls over. It starts from the basic way he walks, the way he stands. Now 'Pop' Robson (Heppell's son-in-law) hasn't got Trevor Francis's skill to beat a player, but he can turn on a sixpence because he's crouched like an animal. He didn't used to be, mind, . . . he worked on it. Trevor Francis is a great player, it's just that with this little thing I keep mentioning he could probably be the world's *best* player."

You leave Heppell, the dancing master who teaches balance to pro footballers, and you look again at Francis in action. Maybe he does stand erect, maybe he does finish off a great deal of movement on the floor, but isn't he just about the fastest player on the turn in the game? Isn't it perhaps just a question of style, even of habit? Couldn't it be that if you tampered with the mechanics of a player whose amalgam of balance, control and swiftness drew the first £1 million bid in British soccer history, you might dismantle the whole package? Francis himself listens with unfailing politeness. He offers no opinion, and he looks

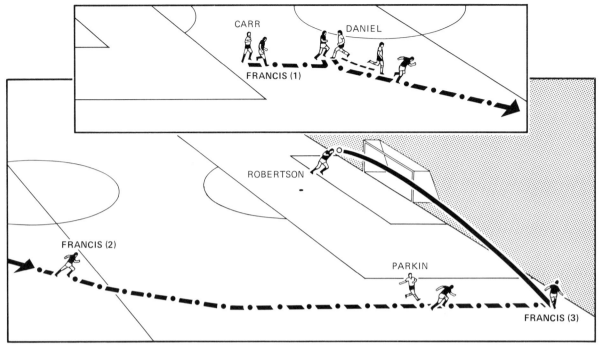

FRANCIS (1)
CARR
DANIEL
ROBERTSON
FRANCIS (2)
PARKIN
FRANCIS (3)

October 6, 1979 – Nottingham Forest v. Wolverhampton Wanderers: Francis, the creator, beat three opponents in a run three-quarters of the length of the pitch and delivered an accurate cross to the head of John Robertson. "Actually," he admits, "I didn't set out to do that – a lot of it just happened." He "happened" first to snatch the ball from Wolverhampton's Willie Carr near the Nottingham penalty box, then to surge towards midfield where he skipped past Peter Daniel's tackle. "I think I was forced into the situation after that by Daniel," he says. "He chased me out wide, and I felt he was going to foul me. Probably if I'd had close support, I'd have knocked the ball off, but I had to try to shrug Daniel off. After that, I saw only one player, Derek Parkin, ahead so I felt I had to try to get past. When I got to the line, I saw Robbo making a run for the back post so the cross was the obvious ball to attempt." Robertson's header came to nothing, but that does not detract from the pace, vision and fluency of Francis's creation. Since he happened to be barely half-fit at the time, it says much for his athleticism, too.

bemused. Change the subject; men of art are seldom given to examining their navels.

Neither does Francis welcome comparisons. From the earliest days, when he began scoring in a men's League for a boy's wage, he sidestepped attempts to liken him to those great predators of the goalmouth – Denis Law and Jimmy Greaves. They, themselves, should not be compared, he points out; Law was a spectacular, athletic finisher and Greaves achieved the same ends through subtlety. "Myself, I loved to watch George Best manipulate the ball," says Francis, "and Johan Cruyff is obviously one of the best players I've seen. He affects the whole team. To compare any of them serves no purpose."

Football is a changing game and so are the people in it. What has never changed, however, is the special thrill of goalscoring. "I don't think that'll ever change," says Francis, "I'll certainly always feel it. I like to think I'm not an out-and-out goalscorer; that there's more to my game. I enjoy creating things almost as much, but I sometimes think that because of that, other people aren't aware that I can do that job. If I've got a disappointment in football, it's that so many goals I've scored for Birmingham were witnessed only by Blues supporters and a few people in the opposition. Unfortunately in football, people are only recognised when they are playing for successful teams. Struggling sides don't attract television."

When pressed, he has a video-like recall of his

Right: Timing is of the essence, for camera as for striker. It took you longer to scan these pictures than it took Francis to score against Bolton. At three frames per second, judge the speed of thought and movement as he moves where others hesitate and then squeezes the ball in from an angle so acute Brian Clough described it as "genius". Francis prefers to attribute the goalscoring knack to a good eye and constant practice – and wonders what the manager would have said if he had missed!

Blues goals. "Well, there were a couple of mazy runs, I suppose; I sort of started on the halfway line and passed three players and scored. And I remember a left-foot volley from outside the area at Leicester, and two goals against Blackpool. One was a free-kick from about 35 yards; direct it was and . . . well, I spoke to people afterwards about it and they thought I was crazy actually thinking about shooting. I took a long run at it – and it just flew in the net.

"I remember that one. Then there was another at Blackpool. My dad was there behind the goal. I was about 25 yards out and Bob Latchford won the ball in the air and as he went to nod it down I met it on

Some have grace and favour, where others must have sweat and toil. A contrast in styles, as Bolton defender David Burke attempts to keep at bay the Francis speed. Men of exactly the same height (5 ft. 10 in.) and similar weights (11½ st.), and each endowed with more than average acceleration, the comparison ends there. You can see how Burke's cheeks are blown out and sense the aching in his lungs as the effort makes its demands. Next look at Francis, up on his toes, eyes on the ball . . . getting there with time and energy to spare and with thoughts already striding ahead to what he might invent out of the situation once Burke's challenge is thrown. Burke, that afternoon, was run time and again so mercilessly he will be the last player on earth to subscribe to the theory that Francis lacks aggression or perseverance.

Balance is the springboard to invention. Francis is poised over the ball, his weight firmly anchored down through the hips, ready to spring him this way or that once his eyes have told him which colleagues are in a position to exploit the situation. "I can sense, as well as see people around me," he explains, "and although I have my eye on the ball, I can still quite often see people moving into position some distance away." The coaches call it peripheral vision; Francis's word is awareness.

THE GOALSCORERS

Men who score goals will always fascinate. Figures alone cannot capture the degree of difficulty or spectacle involved, but in this random selection it is clear that Francis's finish puts him up there with the greats. In bygone days, when goals were easier to come by, Dixie Dean hit 60 League goals in the season 1927–28; today's hero is a 25–goals a season man, a player who unlocks systematic defences. And even in the seventies, it has to be taken into account that, whereas Jimmy Greaves was a goalscorer pure and simple, Francis, like George Best or Martin Peters, doubles as provider. In Greaves's favour, he scored every one of his goals in the First Division, while Arthur Rowley, the League record goalscorer, was a "banger" who finished off what others created largely in lower standards: only three of his 19 seasons immediately after the last war were spent in Division One.

GOLDEN OLDIES

	goals	games		goals	games
Arthur Rowley	434	619	Tommy Lawton	231	390
Jimmy McGrory	410	408 (Scottish League)	Stan Mortenson	225	395
			Peter Doherty	197	403
Hughie Gallacher	387	541	Tom Finney	187	431
Dixie Dean	379	437	Cliff Jones	182	511
Steve Bloomer	352	600	Jackie Millburn	178	354
John Atyeo	315	597	Johnny Haynes	148	594
Nat Lofthouse	255	452	Len Shackleton	126	384
Brian Clough	251	274 (Div. II)	Stanley Matthews	71	698

MODERN PLAYERS

	goals	games	average per game		goals	games	average per game
Jimmy Greaves	357	517	0.69	Peter Osgood	133	408	0.32
Ron Davies	276	537	0.51	Phil Boyer*	131	449	0.29
Roger Hunt	269	478	0.56	Brian Kidd*	128	388	0.33
Kevin Hector	258	606	0.42	John Richards*	124	277	0.45
Ted MacDougall	248	499	0.50	Trevor Francis*	124	300	0.41
Martin Chivers	220	466	0.47	Alan Gowling*	121	335	0.36
Allan Clarke*	220	501	0.44	David Cross*	117	333	0.35
Derek Dougan	219	546	0.40	Ian Moore	116	273	0.42
Denis Law	217	458	0.47	Duncan McKenzie*	111	289	0.38
Francis Lee	216	471	0.46	Don Givens*	103	373	0.28
Tony Brown*	214	558	0.38	Stan Bowles*	100	345	0.29
Geoff Hurst	210	518	0.41	Stuart Pearson*	99	268	0.37
Pop Robson*	209	523	0.40	Derek Hales*	96	203	0.47
Bobby Charlton	206	644	0.32	Paul Mariner*	90	233	0.39
Malcolm Macdonald	191	372	0.51	Mike Flanagan*	85	254	0.33
Don Rogers	182	500	0.36	Kevin Keegan*	86	354	0.24
Mick Channon*	178	462	0.38	Ray Kennedy*	85	337	0.25
Rodney Marsh	169	408	0.41	David Johnson*	70	255	0.27
John Toshack*	167	374	0.45	Charlie George*	65	239	0.27
Bob Latchford*	162	351	0.46	Peter Withe*	54	170	0.32
Martin Peters*	161	658	0.24	Andy Gray*	54	112	0.48
Alan Ball*	160	607	0.26	Kevin Reeves*	48	159	0.30
Bob Hatton*	156	450	0.35	Frank Stapleton*	44	146	0.32
Frank Worthington*	149	458	0.33	Joe Jordon*	44	214	0.20
George Best*	147	406	0.36	Kenny Dalglish*	41	84	0.49
Colin Bell	142	476	0.30	Steve Coppell*	36	211	0.17
Joe Royle*	140	398	0.35	Alan Sunderland*	34	218	0.16
Jimmy Greenhoff*	134	483	0.28				

* Denotes current player, total does not include 1979–80.

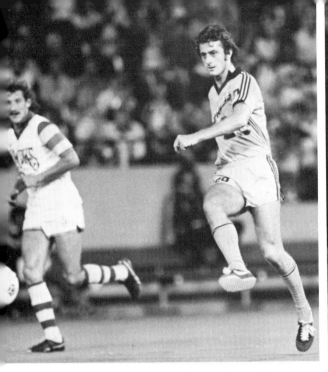

The art of shooting. At the age of seven, Francis's ability to strike a ball so cleanly with either foot was noted by schoolteachers. At 15, it was the main reason Birmingham City signed him. Francis himself was always aware of the "power" he possessed in kicking a ball and his father developed in him the habit of using the left foot as unhesitatingly as the right. Thus Birmingham fans quote chapter and verse on goals struck with the left after defenders had deliberately tried to force him onto that foot. "My first rule," Francis told American youngsters at a soccer "clinic", "is always try to get the shot on target – make the goalkeeper work. It sounds obvious, doesn't it?" Trevor's father, Roy Francis, says character has something to do with it: "You'll see Trevor shoot, miss, and shoot again; you'll see him hit a 25-yard pass and if it goes wrong, he will try another. Most players today settle for the simpler thing, particularly if the crowd's on their back."

the half volley. Well, it really shifted and sort of curled into the top corner of the net. But my dad will tell you better." He won't; Roy Francis's recollection is virtually identical, except *he* reckons it was 35 – well, 30 yards at very least. "I saw Trev swivel and I remember saying crack it. And just as I said that, the ball flew towards me into the net."

Roy and Trevor Francis have no idea why each of them should think he should take a pot shot at goal from, well, 30 yards. It is instinct, given to those who down the years have preyed on the hesitation of others. That Trevor exploits it handsomely is indisputable; statistics alone put his record of 124 goals in 300 League games on a par with most men in history. He has played nine years in a struggling side, he has been deployed in a variety of roles, yet his average of goals per game is better than Jimmy Greenhoff, Joe Jordan, Peter Osgood, Don Givens, Stuart Pearson, Paul Mariner, Joe Royle and Frank Worthington, all of whom have played for club and, in most cases, country as principal strikers. He is a more consistent scorer than George Best or Bobby Charlton or Kevin Keegan, and level with Geoff Hurst.

And that is pure arithmetic. It takes no account of the degree of difficulty, the quality or spectacle, or the measure of support a man receives. Trevor Francis is as ready as the next man to be judged on his contribution throughout a game, but it is that end product, which boils down to split seconds, that wins games and medals and memories. That, if anything can be, is the £1 million touch.

6
AMERICAN
SUPERSTAR

The $56 million Pontiac Silverdome, in which Trevor Francis was reborn a superstar, beckons the moment the plane begins its descent over Detroit. Before the sprawling plants of Ford, Chrysler and General Motors come into focus, long before the gigantic chemical and smelting chimneys are seen, sending up their deadly smoke signals, the gleaming white dome has caught the eye.

Inside, it is scarcely less a phenomenon. Above the synthetic turf 80,499 seats rise in three tiers of blue and silver to the huge, translucent, inflated cap. The colours are those of the Detroit Lions, the American Football club, for whom the largest domed stadium in the world was designed here in 1975. Together with Detroit Pistons, of the National Basketball Association, and Detroit Express, of the North American Soccer League, the major rent-payers should clear building costs by around the year 2,004. By then, a new roof, costing millions more dollars, will be required.

The Lions can fill the Silverdome on a good day, but right now the messages draped around the arena and bounced from electronic scoreboards herald soccer, the new upstart. "Trevor is – Pele was" reads one banner; "TGIF – Thank God It's Francis" proclaims another. The scoreboard display, around the constant familiar face with its elfin grin, flickers out its commercials: "Come to where the flavour is ... Marlboro Country". "You're gonna love Elias Brothers ... We borrowed some nice ideas from your mother".

Not from Mrs Francis, they didn't. She never made a hamburger in her life. But in downtown Detroit newspaper advertisements and hoardings lure customers to come and watch her boy play soccer. "Don't miss Detroit Express vs. Tampa Bay Rowdies, featuring the world famous superstar Trevor Francis". Inducements include Trevor Francis "Wizardry" T-shirts, courtesy of 7-Eleven Food Stores, free to the first 1,000 youths of 14 and under who attend. And Eastern Airlines will hand out 10,000 bumper stickers, one of which may win you a trip to Disneyland.

Down in the bowl of the stadium, where the spongy green carpet is unnervingly ridged and uneven, the air hangs humid and stale. Leggy schoolgirl cheerleaders in gold-sequined swimsuits attempt to whip up an atmosphere of razzamatazz, and what response there is drifts around in faint echoes from the quarter-filled Silverdome. The entrance of the players is gladiatorial, each running a gauntlet of the "Girl-Guard of Honour" when his name, nickname and number is called. "And now,

The Detroit fans find a new pedestal for Francis.

Nummer Six – Steve 'Iron Man' Seargeant ... OK, Let's hear it for Nummer Ten – the Express 'Mighty Atom', David Bradford ..."

Goalscorers top the bill. Keith Furphy, blond and lean, scorer of 13 goals and seven assists in 29 games, bounds in to a cocktail of cheers and catcalls. He responds by blowing kisses, arms outstretched in a champion's salute. The antipathy is, in part, because his dad, Ken Furphy, happens to be head coach to the Express. And the Express is running downhill in 1979 compared to the heights of a summer ago. The security guards have removed a "Fire Furphy" banner from a prominent position near to the 102 VIP boxes.

The staged climax is imminent. The teams are lined up, except for one player. Drums roll, the loudspeaker manages a momentary hush, then explodes into a high-decibel announcement. "And now ... here he is ... he's hit 13 grreat goals with seven assists in just 13 games for the Express ... it's the WIZ-ZARD ... Nummer Twennee ... TRE-VOR FRAAN–CIS!" The loudspeaker itself leads the applause with a recorded sound loop. Almost apologetically, the quiet Englishman tasting the heights of the American big sell, trots out through the leaping bodies of the cheergirls. A modest wave, and he quickly seeks his place in the line-up.

The players stand politely to attention as the crowd accompanies a recorded rendering of "The Star Spangled Banner". It is a moving ceremony of allegiance to the American flag from two squads of players, which each include the compulsory two US citizens, and otherwise are Englishmen, Canadians, South Africans, a Dane, a German, an Argentine, Brazilian, Yugoslav and Haitian.

We have kick-off. The official North American Soccer League ball, distinguishable by its red stars on white and blue background, begins to roll. Or rather it zips and shoots across the surface. Straight away, you are struck by the pace of the ball on synthetic turf, by its ferocious demands on instantaneous control. A player attempts to trap the ball, it strikes one of those dreadful ridges, and leaps lizard-like over his foot. Up in the seats, it appears to make a mug of him; down on the touchline, you can sympathise.

"It catches them out," admits coach Furphy. "The ball never slows down, and if you haven't enough technique, you're dead in this league." Furphy, once coach to the New York Cosmos, and before that manager at Workington, Watford, Blackburn and Sheffield United, as well as to the England Under-23's, has until now built his Express on British components.

After the 1979 season, however, England closed her doors to the cheap and temporary export of players to the NASL. She annulled the loan system and the spiral of transfer fees put even average British players beyond the purse of most American clubs, whose wealth is superficial. Furphy became obliged to cast elsewhere around Europe and Scandinavia for recruits.

This, he says, may not be altogether bad for Detroit. He may not agree with Austrian coach Hubert Vogelsinger, of San Diego Sockers, that the English are "over-priced and under-talented" and to be shunned like the plague, but he concedes: "We've had First Division players – good players in English conditions, such as Mickey Leach from Queen's Park Rangers – who just couldn't adapt out here."

Francis, meanwhile, was chosen for the NASL All-Star teams of both 1978 and 1979, taking his place alongside Johan Cruyff and Georgio Chinaglia, ahead of forwards like Oscar Fabbiani, Gerd Muller, George Best and Teofilio Cubillas. It is not difficult to see why. His nimbleness, touch and ball control actually thrive in the conditions. His quickness is emphasised on synthetic pitches.

There is no mud in the Silverdome to cling to heels, no treachery underfoot from the effects of rain or ice. Francis wears rubbers which are nearer to carpet slippers than soccer boots and within a minute he has a grip on the game. He darts between two hefty Tampa Bay defenders, judges a spinning through-pass without the need to interfere with its momentum, and clips the ball towards the lefthand post for young Keith Furphy. The Rowdies goal is

It's Wiz-zard . . . It's nummer twennee . . . It's Trevor Francis. Greetings American-style, running on to where the girls are, and where the flavour is, for his debut against Memphis Rogues.

exposed, though Furphy's angle is acute and his run too urgent. He snatches at the ball, slices it wide, and the hecklers are aroused as willingly as any pantomime audience.

To anyone who has not seen the NASL game, the competitiveness comes as a jolting shock. American soccer was reputed to have all the cut and thrust of kindergarten. Not so. There is not the rapport, the interplay of emotions that would pass between an English crowd of 20,565 and the players, but the breakneck speed, the physical endeavour and tight,

Francis (20) celebrates after scoring the winning goal for Detroit Express against Memphis Rogues. Even English team coach Ken Furphy can't keep his feet on the ground.

defensive discipline are familiar enough. Tampa have come to have and to hold, and Detroit is over-cautious, wanting to "break them down without leaving ourselves short at the back".

Heard that phraseology before? Hardly surprising. Ken Furphy is known amongst the players as M.O.D. – Minister of Defence, whilst Gordon Jago, the Tampa coach, cut his managerial teeth on QPR and Millwall.

Where the play falls short of European standards is in cohesion between defence, midfield and attack. They appear to operate in separate units. The running is so scurrying the players look, at times, to be towed along by the sheer pace of the ball skidding along and off this synthetic carpet. Passes are hurried, control is erratic and moves seldom go beyond three passes. Not forward passes, anyway.

The Express publicity machinery describes the play as "Supercharged"; that it is, but it is not super-controlled.

In spite of this – or perhaps because of it – the quality player stands out like an elegant trotting pony picking its way through city centre traffic. He appears to take his time where others rush madly, and yet to get there first simply because his timing is finer. "Trevor Francis is a class player," says Timo Liekoski, head coach of Houston Hurricane, who were Detroit's previous opponents. "A superior individual."

Francis is confirming that at this moment. Perhaps of all the qualities, the one which it is most surprising to re-discover in the States, where Francis himself says the play makes less demands on him, is that his concentration is as extreme as it is in an English Cup-tie. In play, the face loses its boyishness, the skin somehow tightens around the cheeks and the mouth.

It is as if his skin has been tensioned like that of a drum. His eyes are searching all around, looking for situations to exploit, as a jungle animal watches before deciding to pounce. Yet, in contrast, the body and limbs are held slightly languid and loose, suggesting he has a way of putting the mind on full alert without calling on the anatomy to tighten up until he actually presses the button.

All this amidst a defence every bit as heavily muscled as a top European side, against markers at times frantic and painful in the tackle. South African Mike Connell, six foot and a hardened 11 stones (154lb), was voted the best central defender in the NASL, and though Barry Kitchener, on loan from Millwall, carries $14\frac{1}{2}$ stones (203lb), he is experienced in over 500 English League matches. A third defender, Farrukh Quraishi, lies in wait, a swifter, lighter defender put there to match the Francis pace.

Francis's options under such heavy guard diminish with the fact that he is the only out-and-out forward in the team plan. Keith Furphy is just 20, a rangy athlete who alternates with remarkable energy and perseverance between midfield and left wing. He tears upfield like a train; a "Supercharged" train at that. Small wonder that when he arrives in position, his finish is sometimes less than measured.

The Furphy family tale is in itself unique. "I bought our young 'un's contract from Wealdstone (in the English Southern League) for £2,000, brought him across and sold the contract to this club," says head coach Ken. "He was intended as a reserve, but he got in the team and he's not missed a game in two years. Keith does more clinics than anyone. He gets more mail and less pay. It's only an ethnic minority that boo him."

For all his apparent cockiness (which his father says is a response to, and not the cause of, the crowd's alienation), Keith Furphy is the nearest thing to a striking partner for Francis in the field. Reluctant, maybe, the partnership not only provides over half Detroit's goals, but creates opportunities for each other.

It has to do so. The game in America is an infant, weaned on statistical data. The media and crowds pay homage only to goals, despite the NASL attempt to spread the burden of praise to the "assist" – i.e. awarding two points to the goalscorer and one to the man or men who set up the score. This in itself leads to weird anomalies: A man gets an assist if he rolls back a free-kick for a colleague to score with a 30-yard drive; he gets the same point if he weaves past four defenders, draws out the goalkeeper and presents a tap-in goal to a teammate; he gets nothing, however, if that fellow fluffs the chance, nothing for a run off the ball that entices three defenders out of position for a colleague's goal.

Head coach Furphy, and striker Francis, agree that the American pre-occupation with goalscoring promotes selfishness. "I know I'm doing things out here which are contrary to what I've been taught," says Francis. "I sometimes try to beat a man or go for a goal, when in real football I would look for alternatives, see what is right for the team. But the system out here is all about individuals making or scoring goals. That is what I'm being paid to do. Afterwards, I sometimes feel embarrassed when I think back to occasions when I might have given someone else the opportunity to score."

The Express 1979 Media Guide endorses on page 34 everything in that statement. It lists 22 "individual offensive records", ranging from "the quickest goal" to "the latest goal", from "the most goals in a game", "a season", "the most goals in successive games", "in regular time" and "overtime", even "the most shots in a game". Trevor Francis scoops 16 of those awards.

The record Francis cherishes is the double hat-trick against New York Cosmos in March 1979. The Cosmos's international all-stars were travel weary after journeying from Brazil, but Francis himself had flown into Detroit by Concorde and mustered only two hours sleep and a single training session before becoming the first NASL player to score six goals in one march.

It was an exhibition, a pipe-opener to the new season, but opponent Antonio Carbognani took

95

things seriously enough, flattening Francis before being sent off. The 24,000 crowd was whooping at every score, but the final goal in Detroit's 8–2 win remains a special memory. "It was something I'd always wanted to do," says Francis. "I ran with the ball from the centre circle, passed a couple of players, and as I came to the 18-yard box, a Cosmos player shouted *shoot*! It was Beckenbauer ... and I remember the look of astonishment on his face as I let one go with the right foot and it hit the roof of the net."

Francis mentions a couple of opponents beaten; the players and press recall him "going right through half the team." No matter. He had time to reassure reporters that he had scored six "lots of times ... only I always woke up before!", and then he was gone, via Concorde again, back to the reality of Nottingham Forest training.

"Players in the position of Trevor or Cruyff," observes Ken Furphy, "have a tendency – because of the expectation of teams and fans – to go through and shoot from acute angles where they could pull the ball back to make a goal. It's natural, I know that. My young 'un's done the same. Trevor has got to get his goal tally up in such a short time. And he's done it. In our two season's he's exceeded expectations."

No-one is left in any doubt about those expectations. Francis has only to receive the ball for the loudspeaker commentary to rise half a dozen octaves. "Here's the WIZ–ZARD!" Go, Trevor, go, go, go. "I like to try and play nearly the same as I would in England," says Francis. "But I find the *players* are looking for something special from me, as do the supporters. If I don't get a goal, it's as though I've let everybody down." His average of a goal in every game in the bright orange shirt of Detroit Express – a real record unmatched by anyone in NASL history – suggests he has not endured letting people down too often.

Watch him at play in the Silverdome, and you see at once why he is so consistent. The NASL "blue line", which means that a player cannot be offside if he is more than 35 yards from his opponent's goal, is tailored to the Francis gifts of extraordinarily quick turn, of pace and dynamic shot. He stands with his back to two defenders as the ball is played up to him. And everybody knows what he will do. But when? How? From which side?

You watch the faces of the defenders and you see apprehension instead of anticipation. There's no way of telling if he is balanced to control the ball with left or right foot, or if he simply intends to turn

In America, as well as in England, the Francis pace over 15 to 20 yards is crucifying. With apologies to Steve Litt (No. 5) the Minnesota Kicks defender, these pictures reveal in sequence precisely how hard it is to stay with Trevor Francis. Photograph (1) is a deceptive picture because although it appears Litt is nearer the ball, the

pass in fact dissects the two of them and Francis's anticipation is a shade the faster. At 6ft 2 in, Litt has the longer stride, but by the time photographer Gerry Cranham has shot photograph (2) he has lost a yard in three and in the next photograph (3) Francis is well clear, ready to line up his shot. Goalkeeper Tino Lettieri comes correctly off his line (4) but again, in fractions of a second, he is that shade too late to prevent Francis's left-foot chip (5) finding his net. This is the essence of Francis, exploiting the one-on-one situation, his speed and his eye for goal combining in one flowing movement.

suddenly without touching the ball at all, to let it run and beat you in the chase. Suddenly, you see that old, familiar cynicism rising in the face of one defender; he isn't going to try to guess, he's simply going to whack Francis's ankles.

Francis doesn't dive, doesn't feign injury. In fact, he offers his opponent no reaction of any kind. It has happened so often, as you can see from the black scab marks on his knees, the grazed skin on his thighs where he lands on the synthetic surface, that he merely accepts it as a sign that the opponent is beaten. The free-kick provides a goal from 22 yards. Bradford rolls the ball to Furphy, Furphy pushes it on to Francis and the shot is struck clean and straight as an arrow out of a bow. Tampa Bay's Canadian goalkeeper Zeljko Bilecki has organised his defensive wall but left a gap of 18 inches, no more, to the right. You don't do that with Brazilian marksmen, and you don't do it with Francis, either.

A goal. Officially, two points for Francis, one each for Bradford and Furphy for the "assists". Keith Furphy blows kisses into the wind of his hecklers, Francis simply turns, watches the goal replayed on the flashing scoreboards, and blows out his cheeks. Scoring his goal brings a sense of relief rather than elation.

That is the paradox – one paradox – separating US soccer from the mainstream of the world game. In America a player has to be *seen* to be spectacular, and goalscoring is the measure. The spectator is weaned on stop-go sports which can be read almost in balance-sheet form, sports like gridiron football, baseball, basketball and ice hockey.

Even in Europe, where the game has been played for a century, spectators find it easier to identify with a goalscorer. In the States, the tendency is simplified until soccer becomes reported and sold almost as a one-for-one battle between opposing star players, or a striker versus goalminder conflict. The man who orchestrates a side's teamwork, or who subtly dismantles a defence with a dummy run off the ball, will not be recognised nor rewarded by the system.

Beckenbauer's name, but hardly his sophistication, is applauded in New York the way courtiers applauded a king's new clothes. Cruyff's manipulation of men or strategies is subordinated to his direct assaults on goal for Washington. And Francis had to accept that his willingness to work for Detroit colleagues was for their approval only. He arrived repeating the good lesson of English professionalism; he told the assembly-line population in Michigan that he is not purely a goalscorer, that there are

Any time is business time in the States. Here, in the Detroit locker room, Roger Faulkner (executive director, centre) and Dennis Roach (Trevor's British agent for commercial work) discuss the next move.

other things as important in the game of soccer. He was made to realise that in America it is a new ball game; that while he may have to satisfy his coach and teammates on his all-round contribution, he would be judged by the fans on the goals he scored.

"The publicity is embarrassing," he says. "When we played in Memphis, it was as if *I* rather than Detroit was playing the whole Memphis team. It was advertised in the town that the $2 million soccer star was 'leading' Detroit. Well, I told them I don't lead, in England it's a captain who leads. But they said, 'You are the franchise'. It's really embarrassing, but I had to go along with it."

The origins of a Trevor Francis are inseparable from nature and environment. No-one could preordain his emergence as a Birmingham cult figure. But superstardom in the US is a business package invested with the dollar as cautiously as a Wall Street stock purchase.

Detroit's American financiers were guided into the Francis connection by Jimmy Hill, a man who knows the valuation of a footballing public relations exercise better than anyone. Hill's British-based company World Sports Academy put up part of Detroit Express' NASL franchise of $250,000 in 1977, and he is listed as General Partner.

General Partner? Anyone who knows JH could scarcely imagine a more bland or misleading title. The Jimmy Hill who built Coventry City and leads it still from the managing director's chair, who directed the footballing affairs of Saudi Arabia with a budget of millions of dollars, who skims through manifold business interests in sponsorship consultancy, journalism and after-dinner speaking, and whose opinions anchor BBC's Match of the Day, is no "general partner". He is of course the driving force, the boss; five minutes in the Detroit Express "front office" will tell you that the hotline goes through to London or the Cotswolds. To JH.

Hill's "secret" was most succinctly described as long ago as 1968. He was then an executive with London Weekend Television and John Bromley, a fellow executive, said: "Jimmy has one great asset, a feeling for what the public wants."

There was scant evidence before 1977 to suggest the public of Detroit wanted soccer. Cosmos and later Santos were hired to play exhibition games before crowds of 23,000 and 24,689, but these matches drew fans on the basis of the name and association of Pele, the one soccer player most Americans had heard of. A previous soccer franchise, Detroit Cougars, had been kicked into oblivion 10 years before and, the minute the Express rolled, Joe Falls of the Detroit News, summed up: "I look for the stab, and it isn't there. I wouldn't know a good game from a bad."

What the Motor City did crave, however, was a sporting winner and an identifiable figure. Joe Louis, who fought out of Detroit after joining the migration of Southern Blacks in the Thirties, is immortalised in the name of a 23,000-seat downtown arena, but he is a memory. Sport in the city had become as depressed as its industry.

How could soccer, a game they couldn't understand, where they couldn't tell good from bad, fill the void? The start of the Express, the team Joe Falls thumbed down, was worthy, but not exactly memorable; worthy because coach Furphy had put a team together in under three months. Based on the experience of players like Eddie Colquhoun from Furphy's former club Sheffield United and Sam Oates from Newcastle, the team record stood at five wins and six defeats when Trevor Francis arrived in mid-season.

He flew straight from the England international team, and straight into a build-up and a ballyhoo which dwarfed even his Birmingham heyday. Furphy had, rightly, been telling the public that "this is the first time a superstar has come to the NASL

at the peak of his career". Jimmy Hill had predicted: "The youngsters will see in him a hero. They'll see the way the game is played at its best. Thousands of kids throughout the State of Michigan will be inspired to play the game, that's really the magic of Trevor Francis." And John Camkin, a director, added to newspaper reports of a £75,000 contract for 19 games: "He didn't come for peanuts. He knows his name and ability have commercial value and he's keen to exploit it. On a payment per game basis, he will be the highest paid sportsman in Detroit."

Four days after scoring for England against Hungary at Wembley, Francis scored the "overtime" winner in the 97th minute of his first-ever game on synthetic turf, against Memphis Rogues in the Pontiac Silverdome. "I was going to head the ball," Francis told the horde of American interviewers in the locker room. "But then I glanced at the defence and saw I had a split second, so I brought the ball down on my knee and hit it on the volley."

It is doubtful that the reporters had an inkling of the clinical skills Francis had just described to them. "How long have ya bin a superstar?" asked a woman journalist, as he sat with a towel around his midriff.

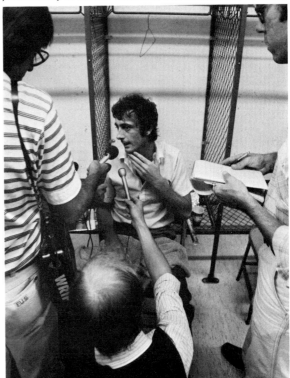

After the match. Say, how long have ya been a superstar, Trevor?

"About three days," he replied. Again it is unlikely any of them spotted the delayed, slow smile as Francis watched the statement dutifully scribbled down.

"I think I can do better once I've got used to the way the team plays," he told reporters. "I was a bit bemused by all the ballyhoo. I expected a fuss if I did well, but the scenes that greeted my goal were amazing. I never had a minute to myself to reflect on my performance."

In a quieter corner of the huge dressing room, the directors and their financial backers huddled together. After meeting Trevor, watching him conduct his press conferences wherever he went, they were already agreed: Get Trevor back for 1979, never mind 1978! If it bothered anyone that the crowd of 9,649 was only a tenth of that for Francis's previous match, word never reached the media.

Fast though their decision had been, the 1978 season did nothing to disrupt the harmony. Detroit won 15 of its remaining 19 games to top the Central Division of the American Conference, and attracted a 32,319 crowd to its final game. Francis scored 25 goals in all, including a NASL record five goals in a 10–nil victory over San Jose Earthquakes, the home club of that American professor whose psychoanalysis had suggested Francis might never mature into a winner.

Small world? You had better believe that. Francis's room-mate, when the team travelled to away games, an experienced defender who advised the newcomer and leant his shoulder whenever press or public demands became too persistent, says this of that first season together: "Trevor's influence, as a creator and scorer, and as a player of immense talent, revitalised the team." Those words came from player-coach Eddie Colquhoun, *the* Eddie Colquhoun who had always believed his tackle at Sheffield four years earlier had threatened Francis's career.

Colquhoun, "A crowd favourite at home and a villain on the road", according to Detroit's media guide, had not spoken about the Sheffield incident to his room-mate. "There was no need to say anything," insists Francis. "We both felt Eddie had done nothing to be blamed for."

Nevertheless, the day Trevor's parents arrived at the Silverdome whilst on holiday in Detroit, the first person to walk up to them was Colquhoun. "Hello," he said, "I'm the feller that did the damage to Trevor." "He wanted to get it off his chest," says Roy Francis.

Meanwhile, there were fans prepared to queue to put Trevor Francis on their chests; and players prepared to try to intimidate him on the field. Jim Smith, the Birmingham City manager, happened to be in the seats in July 1978 when two Tulsa Roughnecks kicked and hacked at Francis. One was cautioned, the other finally sent off, but even Francis admitted in the locker room: "That's the worst physical attempt at intimidation in my career. My marker hammered me in the first minute and kept it up throughout. I was amazed he stayed on as long as he did. At least I proved I'm not frightened of people – what else could I do? I suppose I could have shied away and not got involved, but I'm not paid to do that. I'm paid to get involved."

Smith admitted that the physical abuse worried him. However, a bigger threat to Birmingham rejecting the move for their player to come to Detroit for a second season was the encroachment of the American season into English Football League time. The success Francis helped create in pushing Detroit to the American "play-offs" denied Birmingham his services for pre-season training and possibly for the first matches.

Because of this fear, Detroit held a "We want Trevor back" night, at which 2,000 T-shirts bearing those words sold out in hours. In addition, the usual exclusive Francis merchandise was selling at:

> Coach's cap – $6
> Francis signature T-shirt;
> adult – $7
> youth – $6
> Tapered women's T-shirt – $7
> Wizardry design T-shirt – $7 & $6
> Game replica T-shirt – $8 & $7

Over the two seasons, match crowds increased by 5,000 when Francis was in the team. He arrived late each time, following the completion of the English season. Before he arrived in 1978, Detroit averaged 8,599 for home games and this increased to 13,966 when Francis played. In 1979, the team drew 11,643 without Francis and 16,823 with him per match.

Since tickets sell at a minimum of $2.70 for juniors up to $7.20 for adults, the additional revenue alone would seem to cover the superstar's wage. "No," said Roger Faulkner, the executive director and therefore senior administrator at Express. "In cost terms we have not cut even on Trevor – although he created an identity here, a base on which to build." Faulkner, a Derbyshire man who supported Derby County, played top-class tennis and was personnel director for Burroughs Corporation before helping to pioneer the Express, said it was "not unreasonable when the press said we paid Trevor $100,000 in 1978". And 1979? "More than $200,000 and not as much as $300,000," said Faulkner. "That includes $70,000 for duties with the media." Other players at Detroit received around $20,000 inclusive.

Furthermore, Faulkner conceded that Detroit lost $1 million during 1978 and, towards the close of 1979 was anticipating a loss of $900,000. He believed, however, that a true soccer following had been aroused in the area and that the franchise had substantially appreciated in value.

"The other players accept that Trevor has got to be the attraction," said Faulkner. "Apart from the money, what Detroit has done for Trevor is give him confidence. Jimmy Hill agrees with that. Trevor came here without an ego, and we built him up, told him he is world class, made him believe in himself."

"I think it did help a great deal," agrees Francis. "It helped because I got a lot of confidence from playing amongst players from so many different countries and, even though it is a bit easier to score it makes you feel good to keep on doing it. Football is a funny game; the more you score the more hungry you become to get goals.

"Going to Forest for such a big fee and winning the European Cup, playing in a really good side with good players all around me at Nottingham also obviously helped. What helped as well, was having to do so many interviews, to go out and meet so many people at social events around Detroit."

▬▬▬▬▬▬▬▬▬▬

Surprisingly, perhaps, Trevor's position in the Detroit team appears not to isolate him from the rest of the team, even though he and Helen spent the summer of 1979 in an $180,000, beautifully furnished, ranch-style five-bedroomed house on the sunny side of Detroit. The others live mainly in town houses in Rochester, just outside Detroit. "If we're going to have a superstar," says David "Mighty Atom" Bradford, "Trevor's the best one you could have. On a plane he just sits there playing cards like an ordinary player. You'd never know he is one of the best."

Graham Oates, who has become a personal friend, says: "He's just one of the lads through and through. The thing about Trevor is he'll work for you. Other superstars will score a couple of goals and then stop working. Trevor, though, has the respect of all the players in Detroit. With him around we know something will happen, and we'll all benefit. And when he wins the offensive player of the match

award – often a thousand dollars – he tosses it straight into the players' pool. He says that's the way it should be, it's a team game."

And yet, his position does inevitably remove him from his teammates. "When you have a real star player – and person – like Trevor, you have to use him," explains Roger Faulkner. "It's different here in the States to England because we have to go out and sell the game with no tradition to fall back on. In 15 years as a supporter of Derby County, I don't think I ever met or saw a Derby player off the field. They were invisible. Here the idea is for the players to touch as many lives as possible, to identify with the public in a real sense.

"Obviously the person they all want to meet is Trevor Francis. We have allowed Trevor to go out for an away game four hours ahead of the team to face the press, but we're continually deflecting requests from all the clubs for him to go two days in advance. It's worth 3 to 4,000 on their gates."

Even though training sessions are usually light in the forbidding morning heat and humidity, both coach Furphy and player Francis are adamant he should take part in every workout. When training is over, however, comes the parting of the ways.

The rest of the players sit relaxing on the synthetic grass, sweat dribbling down their bare chests and thighs. Time being of no essence, they eventually amble to their cars, drive to the nearby university shower rooms, and then wind down over a game of cards, a beer or a meal at home. Francis is on a helter-skelter. The rush is on to catch up with himself and the clock. The executive director wants to see him in the front office, the public relations director, Steve Unger, is panicking about a noon radio appointment for Francis downtown, and an English photographer and reporter have arrived to interview him. The all-important public, in the form of 30 small children, wait outside the stadium door.

It is 11.10. Downtown is a 40-minutes drive away. Unger, in his first job since graduating from Kalamazoo College, limits the autographs to a handful, ushers Francis and the two journalists towards a red Tiger V8 sports car, and squeezes the visitors into the back. Trevor looks over his shoulder, unleashes that boyish smile, and then says to the driver: "Don't worry, Steve. I'll be changed in nine minutes flat."

Unger uses the time to fill the car with gasoline and, in roughly nine minutes flat, the superstar re-emerges, looking casual and cool. The 55mph freeway limit is murdered on the drive downtown.

At the wheel, Unger briefs his man. He had phoned Trevor that morning to ask him, beg him, to do this interview. "It's very rare we get a shot at this, Trevor. It's the most important radio station in Michigan, and the club is really gee'd up that they've got a shot."

"What's the programme?" Trevor asks, drying his hair as the car nips through traffic.

"J P McCarthy," says Unger. "He hosts a mid-day chat show. You remember him, Trevor? He interviewed you last year. Went really well . . . he's one of the four most important journalists in Detroit."

"Is there anything special you'd like me to say?"

"Ah . . . don't know for sure. Whatever you do, mention Saturday's clinic just once . . . and Elias Brothers, okay?" The clinic is a soccer teach-in by Trevor, aimed at the kids and sponsored by Elias Brothers, who own restaurants throughout Michigan and a stake in Detroit Express.

"What time is the clinic?"

"Ten-thirty. Just say it's a great educational opportunity."

"This radio show – how long's it take, Steve?"

"Oh, it's 40–45 minutes. But you'll be on first. He usually has three or four guests. You'll be the main part of it."

From a car park, Trevor breaks into a sprint to the radio building. He hates lateness. As they enter the lift for floor 22, a smiling, silver-haired man appears to move out of the corridor woodwork. He makes straight for Francis.

The superstar's experiences in America have taught him to recognise a journalist at 20 paces. He looks at Unger. Steve looks embarrassed, quickly introduces Jerry Green of the Detroit News, and asks: "Is it okay by you, Trevor, if Jerry joins us?" Jerry Green is at least the "second most important sportswriter in Michigan."

Floor 22 – or Catch 22? The red studio light shines above the ident board with the names: Trevor Francis, Senator Don Riegle, Bob Anderson.

The studio is stark and sparse. There is a "live" audience of 12 people, and JP is installed behind a large white, round table. The production team peer in through a large window. "Hi, Trevor . . ." calls McCarthy. "Ya wanna beer or coke? OK. Well, welcome to the show . . . we're on air in one minute." Trevor finds a corner to squat, two ladies from the audience walk through the countdown and thrust pieces of paper at him: "Before ya begin, Trevor, sign it love to Marlene."

JP begins his preamble. "Today we've three of the most successful people in their chosen professions . . . Bob Anderson, one of the most handsome stars in cabaret, Senator Don Riegle, the senior senator for the state of Michigan, and Trevor Francis, one of the most impressive soccer stars in the world right now."

He beckons Bob Anderson to the table. "It's so nice to be on your show at last, JP," purrs the singer. Mr. Anderson has to be one of Detroit's champion name-droppers. Oh yeah, he's worked Vegas with Jones, Tom that is. And Sinatra. And so many more. "But I love all my fellow professionals, it would be unfair to pick anyone out . . . though I have to say it was *some* experience working Vegas when Sinatra was in town."

Francis began by listening politely. "Dead informal, isn't it?" he whispers. But he becomes bored, burying himself in World Soccer magazine, which has a colour front of him carrying his European Cup winners medal.

"Is Tom Jones still a name?" McCarthy asks provocatively. Francis is distracted from his reading. His wife Helen, from Llanelli, had the previous week met Tom Jones at the Northfield Hilton outside Detroit and talked to him about Wales.

The show began at 12.15. It is now 12.46.

Trevor looks at Steve, puts down his magazine . . . and watches the senator walk up to the table. Tall and lithe and immaculate in city dress, Riegle has come straight from the airport with his aide/bodyguard. McCarthy had shaken his hand as he entered the studio, but managed not to break Anderson's flow of party anecdotes with Sinatra.

"What time did you say the show finishes?" Francis whispers to Unger. On the hour. He looks as close as he comes to being piqued. "Shall we go?" he murmurs. "It's an insult, not because I'm a star or anything like that, but because you don't treat *anybody* this way." We stay.

The clock ticks on like a taxi meter running against you. The senator, showing not the slightest sign of feeling short-changed in favour of the entertainer, has some really hot views from Washington affecting 170,000 jobs in the Motor City. He reveals on air some high level correspondence concerning government sanction for a $13 billion loan to keep Chrysler going. He is just into his personal critical assessment when McCarthy interrupts: "Senator, I'll have to stop you there . . . I wanna get Trevor Francis on . . ."

A shuffle of chairs. The senator out, Francis in. Four-and-a-half minutes to go. JP smiles thinly at Trevor. "Say, Trevor, the team isn't doing as well

High time for forty winks. Catching up on lost sleep on the return from Minnesota.

But his voice has speeded up. It sounded like nervousness, but he said afterwards it was pure haste, trying to cram in Detroit's plugs.

To Unger's evident relief, the words are coming from his superstar at last. "The club has a clinic, that's at the Silverdome this Saturday at 10.30 in the morning. It is going to be backed by Elias Brothers and it's a chance for Mr. Furphy, some of the players and myself to help show the kids one or two things about how soccer is played."

That's it. Off air. McCarthy is ingratiating after the show. It sure is nice to have such a fine player come downtown for the programme. Trevor, still polite to a fault, says it is a pleasure. "Have you been to watch us play, yet?" he asks. McCarthy has to say he hasn't but he'd love ... "Fine, I can arrange for you to have tickets for Saturday ..." says Francis. McCarthy squeezes his shoulder, makes his excuses and sidles out. Someone says he really got JP that time. Francis, innocence personified, smiles shyly. He never kicks back, according to his dad.

Within seconds, the mood has changed. Jerry Green is there, having sat through the show for his own interview. He begins with what has become an American cliché, the apology for not having seen or knowing much about soccer. With stunning grace, Francis accepts the honesty of the apology. He says he went to his first American football game recently and understood perhaps 10 per cent of it. But he wanted to get to know it better, so he would be going again. Then he offers long, articulate impressions of how the soccer is progressing in Detroit.

Green is concerned to hear that Trevor Francis won't be coming back to play for Detroit in 1980. "The English League put a ban on loan players coming over to play in America, but it really didn't affect me," Trevor tells him. "I had a contract giving me the option to play for Detroit for three years. My transfer from Birmingham to Nottingham didn't affect that, but one week after signing for Nottingham I changed the contract because I realised that, while Birmingham played 45 games a season maximum, at Forest it could mean 70 games, and that's enough for any player."

But wasn't he losing out by that decision? "Financially I am. I'm losing thousands by not coming back. But I need the rest and my health is more important than the money. It's not just a question of playing the games out here, it's the travel. We went to Pasadena for one trip and that meant eight time zones in 22 hours. And we played the next day."

as last season, what's the position ...?" Politely, carefully and quickly, Francis explains that the standard has risen but the team is not as good.

"Trevor, y'know I don't understand much about your game, but it seems to me with 12 goals in 12 games that's a pretty good personal strike rate ...?"

"Well, you've got that one right ..."

"You score, let me see, twice as often here as you do in England. Now that must mean it's a pretty low standard over here ...?"

"Well, it's obviously not quite the same standard. But in England I don't play purely as a goalscorer, I have other roles, other responsibilities ..."

McCarthy's rapid questions are meant to be probing. Francis, with admirable restraint, isn't drawn into names, isn't flustered by having to defend NASL standards or having to explain the most basic rudiments as time spins away from him.

The sunny side of Detroit. The ranch-style suburban house, the white Cadillac, beautiful wife Helen (and baby son Matthew on the way).

For 25 minutes, Francis painstakingly answered every question and even asked Green to put in his piece, if he could, that "I honestly believe there is a great future for the sport in America. I think this ban on English players might help American boys because it's their game. There'll be more Americans playing. One day I hope I shall come back to play in America, possibly permanently. But I have ambitions to fulfil in my own country first, and anyway it will help if America can move away from the star system."

It is 1.45pm before he leaves the building. He has a signing session in Detroit that evening and wants to get home to rest. He reveals no frustration at the Green interview being sprung on him, but his rapport with Unger is now slightly testy.

"What good," he asks Unger, "was that radio show?"

"Yeah, yeah, okay, they didn't give you time. But you got the plugs in great. And anyhow what you lost on air, you gained by Jerry Green turning up. Jerry's an important journalist; it's important to you and to us that you got an interview with Jerry."

Silence. Eventually, Steve raises the question of another interview – very short, a couple of minutes – he wants to get on tape so he can put it on the answer-phone service for the newspapers. "Okay," says Trevor, "let's do it while we drive. Have you got the machine?"

Steve hasn't got the machine. He should have, but it's gone. They stop on the freeway, which in downtown Detroit is to risk a mugging. Hell, Steve has forgotten his briefcase, left at the parking lot on the ground. He says he will drive Trevor home first, then return to the lot. Francis softens. "C'mon Steve, if we've any chance of finding your case, we'd better go back now."

Amazingly, the briefcase has been handed to the attendant. Eventually they do arrive at the house, Steve tapes his interview and, before he leaves, also tapes a coaching tip for a Detroit newspaper. Trevor dictates exactly what he wants to say about the importance of getting shots on target, making the goalkeeper work. It is 2.25pm. A blue Bonneville car pulls up, a blonde walks over to Trevor, hands him the keys, and leaves in another car. She is the lady from Express returning Helen's car, which Trevor left at the club in the morning rush.

As we drive away, Steve, fair-haired and bearded, 26, feels the need to explain his role. "The club needs to work Trevor this way. It's put the whole of its investment money over two years into him, so he's got to be up front the whole time. He doesn't take to it naturally, but he's fantastic once he gets there. The trouble is, once Jimmy (Hill) is not here, there's no-one dare tell him what to do, so I'm spending five days a week seducing Trevor. But I'll tell you something, in two years he's never once put his foot in his mouth or gaffed. And with our press that's fantastic.''

Back at the front office, Unger works a 15-hour day, much of it in a lather, perpetually phoning the media, trying to place interviews with other players, to arouse interest. ''Trouble is,'' he says, ''they all want Trevor. I try to look at it from Trevor's angle and can see that in his place you'd be driven nuts if you didn't try to take some control of the situation. We did try to pull a few fast ones on him. I did personally, and I'm not proud of it because with Trevor if you put things straight to him he'd do it anyway.''

At the house, Trevor doesn't want a meal. He is a sun-worshipper, and the one thing about the day which has upset him is that he hasn't long before the sun goes down. He has a lager in his hand, stretches out on the sun-lounger . . . and Helen calls from the house. ''Trevor, it's Steve . . . are you in?'' ''No.'' ''I'll say you'll ring back, then?'' ''No.''

Helen smiles, Trevor takes the call. The team is flying to Minnesota tomorrow, but before they leave, there's this important offer to do the Bill Kennedy show on TV. Trevor, look, we don't get invitations to do the Bill Kennedy show every day of our lives. I'll collect you from the house and I'll get you to the airport on time. Oh, by the way, Trevor, there's a journalist from Minnesota asked if he can meet you in the arrivals lounge. Just 10 minutes, okay Trevor?

The TV show turns out almost as bad as the radio show. It's a 12.15 start, Francis is in the studio at 11.55, and Kennedy flies at him: ''Hell, you're late . . . you've almost wrecked the whole thing.'' Trevor says nothing. He realises Kennedy is just nervous about his show. ''I thought to myself, wait a minute, I'm doing *him* a favour . . . but then I just got on with it. It went quite well and just before the end, he says to me, 'Could you do something for me Trevor? When you score a goal tomorrow, would you wave to me like that . . .?' And he shows me this salute which appears to be his own personal sign. We were live on the air. It was a bit embarrassing really.''

At the airport, Ken Furphy is waiting. He looks worried. Francis and Unger should be here by now. The others have checked in and the coach has everyone's ticket. They arrive with time to spare, Trevor buys the drinks. Unger is ecstatic about the

---

Brian Clough wondered if his £1-million player ever got time to relax in America. Here's the proof.

Awaiting the national anthem at Minnesota's open stadium, with real grass beneath their feet. The Express team, from the right: Keith Furphy (8), Sam Oates (5), Trevor Francis (20), David Bradford (10), Roger Osborne (14), Gus Moffat (12), Steve Seargeant (6), Eddie Colquhoun (4), Benny Dargle (23), Mick Coop (15) and goalkeeper Jim Brown (in tracksuit). Spot the Yank? It's Benny Dargle. The rest constitute an Anglo-Scottish line-up.

morning paper. Privately, he'd been a bit worried since someone had shown him the previous day's column, in which Jerry Green had run down Jack Nicklaus as a has-been. "He's in a bitchy mood this week," the informant had threatened.

The column, however, was splendidly partial, displayed on the front page, with a big headline in heavy type saying: "Trevor spreads the word: Soccer has a great future." Jerry Green wants to thank Trevor for coming over. "Trevor Francis," he writes, "has been the finest ambassador soccer could have had in the Detroit area. The town has embraced him. The Express will miss him dreadfully in their third season. More important, it will seriously hurt the Express, struggling to make a buck now, in attendance."

A week later, Green wrote his second front page column on Francis, asking if Los Angeles had bought Johan Cruyff for keeps ("Who is Johan Cruyff?" he wrote) then couldn't somebody raise the three million bucks it might cost to buy Trevor Francis body and soul?

Flying. It's the thing everybody hates most about the NASL. Today's destination, Minnesota, is a three-hour hop, one of the short journeys. But, with at times three and four away games in succession, the team flies thousands of miles. It is bad for the players; worse for a coach. "You play, you fly, you

play and gird up your loins to fly again," says Furphy. "You're up in the air two days in every seven, with no time to work in between. If a bad habit creeps in, you've little chance to put it right."

"It seems strange to be flying to all the away matches," says Trevor. "You can get on a plane, like this morning, and it's 90 degrees. And sometimes, by the time you get off at the other end, it's really cold. Quite often we have a full day travelling the day before we have to play a match, and I don't think the body can function at its best on that kind of schedule. Ideally, I'd like three days to prepare once I've stepped off the plane."

One of the things people in England fail to appreciate is the vast "local" distances Americans travel. Detroit Metro Airport, for instance, is 42 miles from the Pontiac Silverdome. And boredom sets in as the players hang around a small and hot airport, the humidity causing even light casual shirts to stick to the body.

The plane, too, is small and excessively noisy. The moment he sits down, Francis automatically opens a large buff envelope and begins autographing an action picture. Correction, hundreds of action pictures, intended for the kids who write in. "When I was a kid," he explains, "I used to send a big pile of photos to the stars, trying to get signatures. I know what it felt like if they never sent them back. I remember one I really wanted ever so much was Dave Mackay and I couldn't believe it when it never came back to me. Looking back, it was my own fault because I didn't put a stamped addressed envelope with it.

"When the teams came down to Plymouth, I used to go to the hotels where the teams were staying and I'd wait hours for the players to come out and sign.

I particularly remember one occasion when Stanley Matthews was in Plymouth and we all found we'd missed him.

"I found out that he had gone to a cinema, so I followed him there. I paid to go in and got his autograph inside the foyer. The other lads had given up hope, but I pursued the matter and caught up with him. Actually, I met him here at the Los Angeles game and had my photo taken with him at Matthews's request. I was absolutely taken aback; how life can change! There's that photo and three other pictures that really mean everything to me. They are with Pele, Cruyff and Beckenbauer."

Although Trevor Francis has been put on his own pedestal from the age of 16, he retains almost an awe of men who dominate their sports. None more so than Bjorn Borg. "I admire Borg so much, above anybody really. He's a terrific sportsman. He's the best tennis player in the world, as he has proved, but he comes over so well apart from being champion. I like to think I come across well, because it's important to me that the image is right."

Just before the European Cup Final against Malmo, Francis was interviewed by a Swedish journalist and cross-examined the Swede about his own hero. "I know it is a bit of a cheek, like, but would you please get me an autograph of Borg?" The journalist did not forget and, before the Minnesota game, walked up to Francis and said: "Do you remember me? You asked me for an autograph of Borg, and I have it for you."

"I was really delighted. I've always followed his career, especially in the last four or five years. I think he has the best temperament I have ever seen in sport. He plays to win, but he never loses his temper or concentration. If I met him, I'm afraid I'd want to chat about tennis, although it might bore him a bit. I've played myself for about 10 years, not to a good level, just for enjoyment. I think it sharpens the reflexes."

Trevor Francis is not one of the hundreds of footballing golfers, but when the 1979 US PGA tournament was held on his doorstep, at Birmingham, Michigan, he could not resist going along to peek at Gary Player, Jack Nicklaus and Co. "I like to watch anybody who's good, well the best really, at what they do," he says.

During practice, he was genuinely surprised to find himself recognised by spectators. Meanwhile, he approached American golfer Ben Crenshaw. "Excuse me, Mr. Crenshaw," Francis asked him, "Would you mind if I had a photograph taken with you?"

"He was like a little boy, he was," laughs Helen. "You wouldn't believe how much it mattered to Trev to be accepted by the golfers. Eddie Colquhoun couldn't believe it. He said to Trev: 'It's unbelievable. You're a superstar here, yet you get overjoyed about having a picture taken with a bunch of golfers.' But that's Trevor; he's got so much enthusiasm."

As it turned out, Crenshaw, the likeable Texan who was striving for his first major tournament victory, lost on the third hole of a play-off round to Australian David Graham. Crenshaw's putts had twice rimmed the holes, and Trevor recalls: "I liked Ben Crenshaw. The way he came over, the way he was with the kids and signing autographs. I felt for him. I wanted him to win . . . I felt absolutely sick for him when it went against him.

"As he was being whisked away on a buggy, and Graham on another one, I looked at them both . . . one was so happy and the other with his head down. I heard a woman talking, and a man who must have been his brother. I felt as if I was really involved. I know myself that Helen suffers at times more with disappointments than me, and I felt for Ben Crenshaw's wife. She was walking through this huge crowd that was cheering Graham . . . she should have had someone looking after her. She shouldn't have had to walk alone through the crowd."

We sat in silence for some minutes after Trevor had finished recounting that story. Suddenly, the plane lurched forwards and downwards. A glass of wine leapt from Trevor's tray. With a movement so swift and yet so smooth it defied the speed of thought, he caught the glass cleanly in both hands, inches below the side of the tray.

Trevor did not comment on the catch. Perhaps he expects those reptilian reflexes, through which he earns a superstar living, to react like that. Perhaps his mind had not yet left Ben Crenshaw on the third play-off hole. At any rate, he was so tired after only five hours sleep the previous night, he was asleep five minutes later.

Minneapolis airport embraces the players with yet more clammy humidity and more boredom. Time becomes a burden when one does nothing but while it away and 16 players here have nothing to do but wait for baggage and transport. Francis, once more, is the exception. Another interview on his feet, another opportunity to spread soccer's good word,

It hurts, even in Minnesota. Keith Furphy attends to Trevor Francis after a collision with goalkeeper Tino Lettieri.

to carefully articulate views that, in the morning print, will read: "In Birmingham, I get mobbed wherever I go. The problem has gotten bigger and bigger as I've gotten bigger and bigger."

Francis has *gotten* used to the Americanisation of his English, the distortion of his comments. "Most of the time, they get me right," he says, "but not quoting my words. They put it in American terms, which sound pathetic at times. But I have to go along with it."

He extricates himself from the airport newshound to catch up with players at the five-star hotel. Within half-an-hour the team is out training, a loosening session to drive travel fatigue out. They limber up on grass – real grass, because Minnesota Kicks, tomorrow's opponents play on a tough coarse-grained natural grass. Before they disembark from the team bus, the players line up for a quick spray from trainer Karl Glass. A year ago the team had been bitten to distraction in Minneapolis by mosquitos that lurk in the grass but today they are forearmed. Also lurking, around the training grass perimeter, are two television crews and several reporters, but as usual the players, with the exception of No. 20, have immunity from such fellows.

After training, more boredom, spreading out the meal-time. But there is a limit to how long they can chew on steak diane. They wander around the lobby, or watch TV soap-opera – canned boredom. A bellboy seeks Trevor Francis. He isn't there. He has slipped out to dine at the home of Tony Want, a colleague from 1972–78 at Birmingham City, a direct opponent in Minnesota colours tomorrow.

"Just as we sit down for the meal," says Francis, "the phone rings. It's a Tampa journalist wanting to pursue an interview I thought I'd finished earlier. My first mistake was to let on where I was going for dinner. I felt it was a bit of an intrusion, not so much on me but Tony and Elaine, who had to wait to eat the meal she'd prepared."

The interview followed familiar lines: how does the standard here compare with back home? Why wasn't he coming back next summer? Who did he think would win the play-offs? "I rarely see the columns," says Francis. "The distances are so big here, players don't get to know what is going on, and the journalists don't know either. If, for example, Los Angeles win 4–0, I wouldn't get to read about the game.

"I can appreciate why. The press try to build up a game into two individuals – this Tampa guy was asking: 'How are ya gonna shape against Fabbiani?' I had to go along with it. I said it'd probably be quite a tussle, that they'd have home advantage and the benefit of a better team around Fabbiani . . . it was some days before I found out who Fabbiani *is*. He's the top goalscorer in the league with 23 goals from 25 games, but that's the way the game is here. Fabbiani is a star in Florida."

Matchdays on the road provide, in the hotel, something of the atmosphere, without the trappings, of a monastery. Nothing stirs in corridors outside players' bedrooms. They sleep away the mornings, come out for lunch, slope back to air-conditioned confinement. Training is out of the question. The humidity – and heat in places like Florida – drain energy.

At weekends an abundance of televised sport fills out the afternoons; but this is Wednesday, the channels constipated with quiz shows, compared to which Celebrity Squares or Sale of the Century are highbrow viewing. Trevor's passion for popular

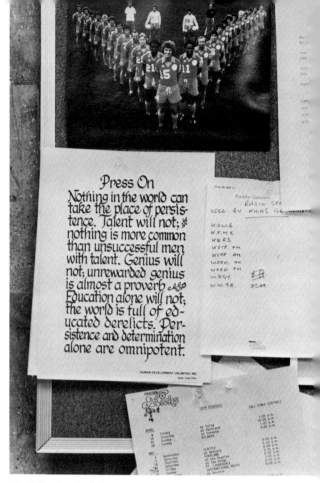

Freddie Goodwin's notice board at Minnesota. A Kicks schedule of two games a week, a heartfelt message that genius without perseverance is failure.

music, his columns written for the English boys' magazine Tiger & Scorcher, insulate him against this boredom.

Once the players emerge from the Sheraton Hotel's purified atmosphere, it is into the late evening air and the smell of barbecued sausage. The farming folk of Minnesota come down from the hills around Bloomington to spread out their picnics. In one car lot, the young gather with their canned beer and canned music; in others, families light up their barbecues behind the tailgates of their cars. There are no vandals, no oppressive police presence.

The Metropolitan Stadium is an open-air arena seating 46,000. It has the flavour of a good European stadium, but its 23 years declare it, by American standards, antiquated. This very night, the Vikings, the gridiron football club, and the Minnesota Twins baseball club who share the stadium, are under a midnight deadline to agree a $35 million budget for a new downtown domed stadium. If they dither beyond midnight, the price will be $71 million.

Ultimately, they all agreed and the new building is due to be completed by autumn 1981.

Inside, two men whose paths keep crossing in life, seek each other out. They meet on the pitch, Trevor Francis and Freddie Goodwin, the player and the manager who guided his early footsteps at Birmingham City. Freddie came to Minnesota after his sacking by Birmingham and, as head coach and now president of the Kicks, has built up a soccer franchise which operates on a minimum of gimmicks. The team attracts a regular gate of 30,000 plus from a population which has predominantly European roots. Goodwin's arm is on Francis' shoulder, his instincts paternalistic still. "We tried to buy Trevor outright for $1¼ million when his valuation at Birmingham was under £500,000," says Goodwin. "But his ambitions are in England and I appreciate that."

Later, as the match begins, Goodwin looks out onto the pitch and says: "Personally, I'd like to see Trevor more relaxed. He'd be a better player again if he could relax, if you could convince him he's not the only player in the team, stop him having to think he's got to be at his best all the time for the team to win. Rightly or wrongly, he has had to feel that most of his career and, just for a change, I'd love to see him settled into a team of 11 good players where he could relax and enjoy his game. At the moment, certainly here in the States, he's too serious; that's the way he is, but there must be a balance somewhere.

"I can imagine how he feels over here. Every city he comes to, builds him up and he wants to please people. It's like a merry-go-round, like a comedian who is expected to be funny every time he speaks. It's a treadmill, never ending; he just can't get away from it."

Minnesota's is a hybrid pitch. The ball drags through three-inch grass, skids over a large square synthetic patch, bounces up off a dusty baseball pitching area. Play is at first inert, with a commentary attempting to brighten up the atmosphere through overlaid organ chimes and recorded applause. The real crowd appreciation, however, is far better attuned to the moments of skill when the match does blossom. In the stands, men in Disneyland monkey costume hand out players' photographs.

Minnesota is by far the better balanced team. It has has Bjorn Nordqvist, veteran of three Swedish World Cups, arranging defence; two wingers, Scottish international Willie Morgan and former Chelsea teenager Chico Hamilton; and a strike force of the strength of Ron Futcher from Manchester City and the niftiness of black South African Ace Ntsoelengoe.

Freddie Goodwin sees all he could wish for on the night. Minnesota run out 5–2 winners and Trevor Francis, who he brought into the professional game, scores a stunning goal. It begins out on the left touchline, sweeps towards the penalty box, holds off one challenge, draws another, and delivers a low cross shot inside the far post from 18 yards. David Bradford, who supplied a five-yards pass on the touchline, is credited with an assist.

Up in the press gallery, confusion reigns amidst electronic gadgetry and piles of statistics. "Who the hell scored that?" "Is that an assist – does any goddam guy know if that counts as an assist?" Somebody, anybody says, yes and it is official. It's in the papers. Each goal is replayed three times on a closed-circuit TV screen for the press, and each followed by a crude line drawing of the directions taken by the scorer, plus data sheets telling how long it has been since the goalkeeper last conceded a goal, since Minnesota last scored five, since Detroit conceded three in one half, et cetera, et cetera. Look over your shoulder for the next info sheet, and you've just missed the succeeding goal. Thank heavens fine outfield moves or good defensive work do not have to be described.

After the match, Goodwin and Furphy must draw deep on their patience. They are being asked to describe moments everyone should have seen, to explain with blackboard clarity elementary points about soccer which no-one in England has ever needed to ask. It is 10.30pm and Freddie Goodwin, whose day in the front office of the Kicks starts around 8.30am with similar reporters' questions, remains patient: "You have to be," he says. "There are still new people, in the media as well as the crowd, being attracted to the game every week. It's our job to explain it to them."

It is the players' job, too. In the Stadium Club beneath the main stand, they mix dutifully with the fans, helping push the new ball game beneath a nation's skin. But there is contact and contact: A pushing American Miss, transformed from her cheerleader kit, seems to be having trouble containing herself in her unbuttoned dress. She just *lives* for soccer; it is so sexy, the players in their shorts an' all. Trevor Francis, who finds it as difficult to wind down after a match here, as in England, shyly excuses himself. The girl moves on to another player who looks as if he might accommodate her nubile advances.

A second girl corners Francis. "Say, which is your picture?"

"That one."

"Really? Well, sign love Debbie, okay?"

He signs. Love Debbie, okay.

"Hey," she says, "didya score tonight?"

"No, not tonight." A fib.

"But ya score every game, doncha?"

"Well, tonight was a difficult match."

"Oh gee, well that's just Tino Lettieri. He's just a real shutout goalminder."

"Yes," says Trevor, that slight smile playing at the corners of his mouth. "I like to score goals, but he made it impossible tonight." She drifts off, satisfied with her goalkeeping hero, oblivious apparently to Detroit's two goals.

Francis finds a quiet corner. Goodwin joins him there, and they chat like father and son. Afterwards, Goodwin says: "The £1 million transfer hasn't changed him, I never thought it would. He's always been an appreciative lad, Trevor. When I left Birmingham he came round to my house and gave me an inscribed silver cigarette case as a mark of appreciation. It was a very nice gesture..." Freddie Goodwin's face can be dour at times; now it is proud and happy.

Trevor is being bundled into a taxi. Chico Hamilton, Steve Litt and Tony Want of Minnesota and Francis, David Bradford, Guss Moffatt and Roger Osborne of Detroit are going to unwind in an impromptu party in Want's house. "A good night," reflects Francis. "Just a sing-song with the players, wives and a couple of guitars. Tony rigged up a little joke on Roger Osborne. He said he was going to practise hypnotism. He lit a candle, held a bowl over it for a few moments, then cupped his hands beneath the bowl and spread his fingers on Roger's face. Roger went along with it in the spirit of the thing, pretending to believe in hypnotism... it wasn't until later he looked in a mirror and realised his face was covered in black soot. We gave him a moustache and beard which he previously didn't have."

Outside the Metropolitan Stadium it was black, too. Black with the aftermath of a modern man's night out. Barbecues had been the outstanding visual image of the night till then. Now it is the wanton abandonment of litter. Cans, bottles, discarded food, cartons, burnt charcoal... the car lots are an endless carpet of debris picked up in the headlamps of a police van which cruises around the car park.

A van drives up. A bearded man jumps out, and begins to load old beer cans and unbroken bottles into sacks. "Find a lot of beer bottles, sir," he says, "don't find much money. There's people like me out

all night long. I'll be collecting till eight in the morning, then the municipal cleaners come along. A *penny* a can, I get... reckon I've picked up maybe 12,000 this summer. I take 'em to the recycling place."

As he talks, he continues sifting through the rubble. "This is the fifth time I've bin here after soccer. I pick up maybe 30–40 dollars a night. It buys a lot of bibles. But I tell you, sir, ain't the same after baseball. Hell, we get a lot of mess, but it's only after soccer it gets so bad. What's really bad is the kids smash up them bottles... Hey, sir, I'd better get goin', else they'll get ahead of me." Out of the shadows, like moles in the night, others are coming out to clean up society's mess, moonlighting for a dime a bottle.

Eddie Colquhoun's Scottish voice rasps brightly down the phone at 9.15am next morning. The players may have got back to their beds by 6am, but

the plane leaves at 10.30. Or should do. Inevitably there's a two-hour delay. Sleepwalking players are bored. Francis, as usual, is up against a tighter schedule. He has to make a personal appearance at a bowling club at 4pm.

At the airport, he jumps into the massive white Cadillac (with red leather trim as he requested) on free loan from a Michigan dealer. As he speeds off, you notice the wording on the nameplate ... A Dalgleish Cadillac. "The other players complain," says Furphy. "I'd be only too happy for them all to drive big Cadillacs, but nobody has offered to provide them."

Later that evening, the Dalgleish Cadillac is parked outside Lakeside Mall, a gigantic shopping precinct north of Detroit. Francis is on duty there to autograph prints of "Night Game at the Silverdome", copies of a painting of himself in Detroit

orange by British Royal Academy artist Roger E. Harvey. The prints are priced at $50 each and available through the Express offices. The signing session goes well ... and not so well.

Francis was due to be there from 7–8pm. He gets away by 10.15pm. But it wasn't so much $50 prints that he was signing, as dealing with the endless queue of autograph hunters. "Kids are great," he says, "and I don't mind signing for them. But some just shove a scrappy piece of paper at you, no pen, and say: 'Sign that'. No please, no nothing. I don't like it. I feel like telling them to come back when they learn some manners. Grown-ups are just as bad. Some of them think because they've paid $50, they've bought the rights to everything."

At the other extreme, Helen, who is six months pregnant, is often overwhelmed by American kindness. Her excess baggage, when they finally leave for England will be bloated by dozens of parcels from Detroit fans, knitted woollies, miniature Express No. 20 shirts, toys and rattles for the baby. Back home the first of 300 Christmas cards – or the last of the previous Christmas mail – will already be arriving from American well-wishers.

The next night, Friday, sees Francis guest of honour at an exclusive banquet for 100 people who have paid $70 a head for an autographed print of "Night Game at the Silverdome" and a chance to rub shoulders with their superstar. Francis wasn't too pleased that the banquet had been sprung on him at five days' notice, when he already had made arrangements to see the Kinks in concert that evening.

But, of course, he went to the banquet. He arrived late after a live radio phone-in involving him went beyond schedule, though he was able to inform the guests of his departure from downtown Detroit over the air. And, of course, it overran by two hours, finishing well after midnight. "I hate being anywhere where I'm the centre of attraction," Francis admits. "I'm like a prize poodle on show for the evening, rented out for two hours by Detroit Express. It's not something I want to do, but it's part of my job. I could find better things to do than just talk about soccer for two hours – I'm doing it practically every minute of the day. And the trouble is, people are going to take advantage of the situation; you know beforehand that they're going to prolong it as long as they can."

Ironically, there is a certain amount of jealousy from other players and their wives that only Trevor and Helen have been "invited" to the banquet. Some players actually asked to attend and were turned down. "They could go in my place," says Trevor. "I don't enjoy being with people I don't know. I realise it's important to put over a good image, but there are so many things I'd put before this . . . number one, the concert. Or going out with Helen for a meal, or sleeping for a few hours."

By 10.30 the next morning, Trevor Francis is on show again. The Silverdome "clinic" has begun. Elias Bros, the restaurant owners who back Detroit Express, have sponsored a soccer "teach-in" which has three main purposes: **1.** to promote understanding of the game, **2.** to show children, especially, that soccer is fun to watch and play, and **3.** to sell Elias Bros restaurants.

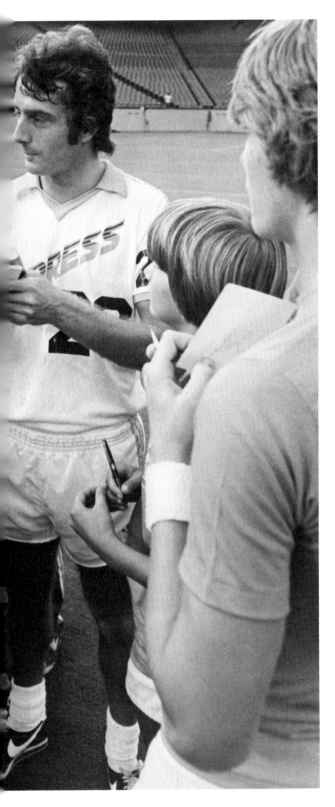

The stadium doors open to fanfares, a vintage car is driven slowly across the synthetic surface, Trevor Francis sitting self-consciously on one side of the open top, and a character wearing the Disneyland-style costume of "Big Boy", an Elias Bros trademark, beside him. The electronic scoreboard urges the boys and girls to eat at Elias restaurants. "We love ya, Big Boy!"

Francis is handed a microphone and told to welcome the 2,500 audience. "I've never done this before," he begins nervously, "so if I make mistakes bear with me . . ." He introduces coach Furphy who will direct demonstrations by Francis and six teammates in shooting, passing, volleying, heading. It is a serious and well-planned exhibition of skills, the like of which Ken Furphy and the players regularly perform to stimulate interest.

Throughout the 1½-hour demonstration, "Big Boy" is walking around the perimeter, shaking hands with the children, reaching up to. sign autographs. In the arena, the part of the clinic which really gets to the crowd is "the nine penal fouls". America really relishes the bodily clash as Steve Seargeant reproduces the "dangerous charge" he presumably learned to perfect in the English First Division. Trevor, of course, is the fall guy.

Now the organisers inject a little more pep into the proceedings. "Dick the Bruiser", a Detroit radio station personality, pot-bellied and dressed in windcheater and jeans, takes the floor to tell Francis: "Trevor – ya might be a star, but I'm gonna teach ya to put aggression into ya game." There follows a pathetic run around, with a world class athlete sidestepping the pantomime efforts of the Bruiser. It was like watching a man trying to catch an eel, and at its most enjoyable when Francis's dummy was so swift, the radio star's nose was blistered on the synthetic carpet.

But it was a fracas in which an authentic sportsman needed great dignity to rise above the schoolboy farce. Francis had no option but to smile and get on with showing the skills which are the purpose of his appearance, and ignore the organised distractions and hard commercial sell. At the end, encircled by a posse of newsmen and TV cameras, he is asked how the game might be improved. "Make the goalposts wider," he says, "it'd be easier to score then." He says it with a smile, but, too late, he realises it has been taken down in writing and will be used in print as a serious suggestion.

What did you say your name was? Trevor Francis, always ready to sign autographs, providing the requests are polite.

The morning clinic lingers on together with just another impromptu television interview.

As the press disperse, Francis and goalkeeper Jim Brown begin to film a TV commercial for Elias restaurants. The idea is for Trevor to shoot a goal past Brown, and while the camera angle and sound quality are being set up, seven successive shots are struck cleanly in. Ready, take eight . . . a perfect take, except for one thing: "I blew it," admits Brown. "I forgot myself and caught one. Great save, but we had to redo it." Francis's part in the commercial is covered by his contract; Brown's reward is $50 worth of vouchers, marked LB. They are Elias restaurant vouchers, lettuce and bacon sandwiches only.

There were two pairs of eyes observing Trevor as the television crew pandered to him and the auto-graph hunters waited outside around his Cadillac. Each, in their way, saw what made Trevor Francis an important figure in the Detroit Express launch.

"You know they chose Trevor as the second sexiest athlete in Detroit last year?" says Sharon, a medical student who worked at the club during summer vacation from Michigan University. "Look, I'm not a groupie or anything, but, gosh, NASL is so exciting partly because you see real men – human beings of human size performing out there. I mean, look at Trevor out there. He's not a blown up 180–200lb freak or anything; he's not a giant, just a human guy playing with a lot of skill and emotion. I love it, and I play too. Lots of women do.

"But, you know, I worry about Trevor. I mean he's expected to do so much, you can see the strain on him. You wonder how long he can last out."

Ken Furphy, meanwhile, looks on from the inside. He knows for example that the strain the girl has spotted has in part a physical root – the niggling pain in the groin which Trevor Francis has felt obliged to play with for much of the summer. It needed rest, but his commitment to Detroit sched-uled no rest period.

"Trevor's been a better player for me here than Pele was when I coached at Cosmos," says Furphy with no hint of bluff. "He's younger, you see. Trevor was 24 when he came here, Pele was 31 when Cosmos got him. But off the field, where Pele could sell it, we only get Trevor for 10 weeks – and who can sell anything in 10 weeks?"

Having lost the star, Detroit's fear was they might lose the audience. They made brave statements, they said Trevor Francis had created the awareness, they were Francis fans but now they were Detroit fans too. They tried, and failed to sign Argentine World Cup player Rene Houseman, but even that would not replace the presence of a player built into a super-star, and embraced by the city on and off the field.

"I appreciate it is a letdown," says Francis. "I really have enjoyed myself over here. It was a special feeling, particularly that first year, to go out to play and know that the crowd wanted you to do well. But my circumstances have changed so much, I realised something had to give. I was playing more games than ever, with Nottingham Forest and with the possibility of an extended run for England, that I felt I just could not give my best both in England and America. There are people who suggest that I could just come to the States, not play so hard and use it as a holiday, but that would be cheating people of money, and I hope I would never do that.

"I made the only decision I felt I could. I have

The style and movement is familiar but the balance is even more pronounced as Trevor Francis, the Detroit superstar, demonstrates his soft-shoe shuffle on synthetic surfaces. *Above :* Tampa Bay Rowdies defender Farrukh Quraishi attempts to head off Francis's route to his goal-a-game average. *Right :* All alone and demonstrating a balletic agility.

It is definitely a different scene in the USA. Beneath the $10 million inflated roof of the 80,000 seat Pontiac Silverdome, the cheergirls do their thing. Trevor Francis does his with the inevitable microphone and, with Willie Morgan, late of Scotland, Manchester United and Bolton (No 7), he takes time out for a quick refreshing drink. *Overleaf*: Away from it all Trevor and Helen Francis are sun-worshippers for whom American summers are irresistible.

From the Trent to the States, they'll believe in miracles.

always said that I feel soccer has a great future in America, and I hope I can at some stage be a part of that future. But to be honest, as a professional footballer, I need to play in the best League in the world right now. There are things I have to try to win in England, and hopefully for the national side, which must come first.''

After the 1982 World Cup, Trevor Francis will be 28, an age he is more likely to be tempted to move full-time to the States. He is not one to consider the future beyond his present three-year commitment to Nottingham Forest, but Detroit Express is not the only American club with designs on his long-term future. Down on the Florida coast, the name of Tampa Bay Rowdies has been linked with his ever since Francis experienced the sunshine there, the almost English nature of the grass pitch and the

enthusiastic 30,000-plus crowds.

But even Tampa might face competition. Over the New Year of 1980, Steve Unger, the public relations man at Detroit Express, was being installed in a similar job with Fort Lauderdale Strikers. And virtually his first instinct in the job was to send a greetings card to Trevor, saying: ''This is a great club we've gotten here . . . we should keep in touch, 'cos I'm right where you'll want to be.''

Make no mistake, America wants Francis back. And if that happens at the end of his Forest contract when he becomes a free agent, the £1 million transfer fee is likely to dissolve into thin transatlantic air.

117

7 A
CONVERSATION

On the stroke of the hour, the white Jaguar XJS arrives with an unhesitant sweep into the driveway. The two men step out beneath the Georgian porch of the West Midlands house. There is no sign of friction between them, nothing to betray the intense pressure of the morning's two-hour snooker session. Sensibly, they had decided beforehand which one of them should make the coffee.

Side by side in the hallway hang symbols of success, clues to the identities of the two. On the left, a gold disc presented to the Electric Light Orchestra in 1975 for the million-selling album *Face the Music*; on the right, a plaque awarded to the Detroit Express Player of the Year, won by the house's chief occupant in 1978 and 1979.

Jeff Lynne and Trevor Francis are buddies who have made it in public life, supports to each other in private. To call Lynne a pop star is as inadequate as to say Francis is a footballer; Jeff literally orchestrates the ELO, being originator, writer and conductor of the cocktail of electronic beat and strings sound that sells records by the million, in America even more than Britain. In demand also as a composer of film scores, he was commissioned to write the theme music for the American TV coverage of the 1980 Olympics.

He and Trevor share an appreciation of the rewards and pitfalls – the real pressures – of working class lads made good. They find relaxation in the other's world, Jeff in football and Trevor in music. They unwind through snooker or tennis at Lynne's country home, where there also happens to be a full-sized soccer net. And their wives keep loneliness at bay in each other's company while the men are on tour; each had their first child in the space of one month last winter.

When all four are in the country together, they share a simple social exchange, well out of reach of the back-slapper and the hanger-on, the champagne boy and the spiv. A meal at home or a quiet restaurant plus conversation nourishes the friendship and provides relief from professional demands and the tensions of marathon snooker duels.

And yet, as they step out of Trevor's Jaguar and into his elegant home, the separate paths of their worlds are immediately apparent. They dress differently. Trevor Francis is unmistakably the footballer – clean-cut, clothes casual but tapered to fit and bearing the inevitable manufacturer's motif that sportsmen parade at all but formal gatherings. Jeff Lynne, permanently hidden behind dark glasses, sports shoulder-length, frizzy hair and a wispy d'Artagnan beard and moustache. His T-shirt is a rainbow of colours, his boots cowboy style.

Their sense of humour, however, is as one. One word will set them both off. Lynne might deliver it in his meaty Brummie accent, or Francis might let it roll out in his slight Devon burr. While a stranger struggles to get on the wavelength, they are giggling away. With that warning, here are some moments from a conversation with them:

Where did they meet?

Trevor Francis: "Before we start ... is the coffee okay?"

Jeff Lynne: "Is this the first one you've ever done?"

TF: "Er, no .. I did one back in '66, when I was 12."

JL: "I knew you'd had some practice. Well, actually we met at the Blues. It was in 1970 ..."

TF: "You've been rehearsing this."

JL: "No, I know the date because I'd just joined The Move and you'd started in the team in '69, you'd just started to shine and I'd just started going back to the Blues. Between 1966 and '70 – when I was 18 to 22 – I'd lost interest in football but suddenly I became more involved again. I think it was through John Lines, the Blues photographer. He'd taken some publicity shots of our group and he happened to say: 'Why don't you come down, I can get you to meet the players.' What? Meet the *players*? I couldn't believe it, never thought I'd actually get to meet one."

TF: "Funnily enough, when I first came to Birmingham The Move was one of my favourite groups as well ... It certainly helps, knowing somebody and also liking their music. I've often thought that I like Jeff not because he's with the ELO but because he's a friend . . . but I think, blimey, wouldn't it be embarrassing if I didn't like the music? I mean if I really hated it?"

Has the mutual appreciation of each other's skills helped sustain the friendship? Or could the friendship have survived without that?

JL: "If I could just tell you from the beginning. The team was in the Second Division wasn't it Trev?"

TF: "It was *always* in the Second Division ... not really."

JL: "Well, with me I just wanted to meet any player. In fact, it was Trevor Hockey I met first and, as an excuse to sort of get behind the scenes at Birmingham, I asked him if he wanted to do a song because I knew he was a bit of a singer. I got quite friendly with him, but he went to Sheffield United about a month after, and so that was the end of that.

But it had got me in the back door of the Blues, which I always wanted to do. Just to meet the players, actually hear them talking about matches when they had finished. It was like magic."

Had you had ambitions to play football yourself?

JL: "Not really, no. I was never really interested in playing, except at school."

TF: "Were you in the school team?"

JL: "Not really. I mean I used to play after school. It's a funny thing that all footballers would like to make a record, and all members of groups always want to play football. I don't know why it is."

TF: "I don't want to make a record, but I love music. It's my hobby. Jeff said he would teach me the guitar but I'm not too good at learning. It's like coaching at football, I just can't be bothered with it really. I think it would be the same with music. If for instance I could get hold of a guitar and play it, I'd love to do that, but I'm sure it would take such a long time for me to learn."

JL: "Well, that's always the thing. Everybody says 'Oh, I'm sure I could do that' and, like you say Trev, you obviously don't want to learn because if you did you would."

TF: "It's the same with tennis. I could be better at that if I wanted to, but I'm happy now just to go out and have a knock-around, go out on court and enjoy it. I don't *want* to have lessons. It's like driving. I never really wanted to have lessons at driving, it's just that I had to if I wanted to pass my test. But it's the same with all games for me. Snooker, I could get better at that – I've had the opportunity to go to a professional for lessons, but I just can't be bothered. I just enjoy giving Jeff a beating..."

JL: "Like I was saying, I suddenly got this open door into the Blues. At the time, though he wasn't playing regularly, it was funny – Trev was so far above the rest of the team. You know, all the crowd used to shout: 'Give it the kid! Give it the kid!' And nobody passed to him or anything at first. It was quite funny. He was 16, and everybody could see how good he was – all the crowd could. I suppose the manager's thing was he didn't want to rush him into the big-time and all that stuff... y'know, the big-time of the Second Division!

"Anyway, I got talking to Trevor occasionally and he was always shooting off somewhere. You couldn't actually pin him down. Eventually I got the chance. I didn't know whether he was shy or just a bit stand-offish at first. Then I saw him in the tea room at Birmingham – it's not very conducive to conversation but later I saw him at a testimonial for Ray Martin, the Blue's captain.

"I was really pissed. I'd had a load – oh, about 10 pints or something. I'd been there all night, sort of helping Ray get this testimonial together. At the Dolce Vita, it was. We had to do an appearance and stuff, and I was like a drunken yobbo when I met you Trev."

TF: "That was when you started thinking of forming the Electric Light Orchestra, wasn't it? I can remember, as far as music was concerned I was rather naive at that time. You said you were going to start the group off and asked if I fancied joining it. I thought you were serious at the time!"

JL: "Well, we were looking for somebody then."

TF: "I should have packed in football and joined, shouldn't I?"

JL: "After that we lost track a little bit. I moved to Worcester for a couple of years, went up to $13\frac{1}{2}$ stones, then came back to Shard End in Birmingham."

TF: "He couldn't afford the bus fare to watch the Blues..."

Neither of you is financially insecure, but does the insecurity of being rated as good as your last game or last composition help you understand each other?

JL: "I think so, it's almost like that. We are both in artistic professions. Trevor has this thing where he can't sleep after a match, he keeps reliving the moves. That's the difference. With us, when we're finished playing, we're always in a position where there's a bar and we can have a laugh and unwind afterwards, whereas Trevor's profession doesn't allow him to do that. But there is still the same sort of feeling, whether you're going out there to play football or up on the stage... you're playing before people."

TF: "Actually there was one time when I did go up on stage with Jeff and shared the feeling of singing – or trying to – in front of 40 or 50 people. It was a New Year's Eve party the year Alberto Tarantini came over. There were four members of the group over at Jeff's house and we set up the amplifiers after 12 o'clock. I can remember there was Alberto, myself, Keith Bertschin, Gary Pendrey, Malcolm Page from Birmingham and John Richards from Wolves (he's a pal of the drummer Bev Bevan).

"Anyway, I was on wine that night and I think Jasper Carrott must have slipped something in my drink! The group started with Auld Lang Syne, then Alberto requested Telephone Line, which was the only ELO number they did all night. Then, with me sharing lead vocal with Jeff, we did Get Back by the Beatles. It seemed to go down well, but I still haven't received a contract from them, so they couldn't have been that impressed."

JL: "It's just that we never had time to put one in the post, Trev. But it's funny, you mentioning Alberto being at that party. Do you remember when he left we had another little party and gave him the album Discovery? He must have been doing his stuff because it's just become the No. 1 in Argentina."

TF: "With a bit of luck you'll be able to thank him personally. He's hoping to come over to Wembley when Argentina plays against England in May."

Presumably it helps your friendship, insofar as other friendships, casual friendships are harder to form because people try to wheedle their way into your company – sitting close to your fame or your money?

JL: "Oh, yes. Exactly. I always have a barrier, all the time. It's very hard for me to meet new people. It takes a long time before I'm able to say he's a good friend."

TF: "I've noticed that – you're a bit wary of people, aren't you?"

Can you put into words in front of each other what makes you compatible?

JL: "Yes, basically. I'm just going to stay friends with him long enough to beat him at snooker."

Do you argue?

JL: "No. It's just that he misunderstands my skill."

TF: "We've never ever had an argument, have we?"

JL: "It's just that sometimes I'm very fast and he fails to move the scoreboard along. He hates losing, y'know."

TF: "I do, because I love to win at snooker. There was one time when I'd been winning 2–1 and Jeff equalised. In the fifth frame I was so confident that I'd win, but Jeff took it and, you know, I didn't even stop behind. I said, 'Well, I'd better be off now, lads' and went out of the house, shouting 'Bye Jeff', trying to put on a smile. But I hate facing people when I lose. I don't know if it was Jeff's idea or Sandi's (Jeff's wife) but just to make it worse a telegram arrived through the post the following day . . ."

JL: "It said: 'Many commiserations on your defeat at Walsh Hall.' That made it all official and got him even madder . . ."

TF: "Yes, I was really, really mad about that . . . I go a bit quiet, don't I, after games if we get bad results?"

JL: "Sometimes you are horrible, yeah. Moody. Can't speak to you . . ."

TF: "Remember that game at Manchester City when I was trying to get my 100th League goal? Joe Corrigan made some incredible saves and finally I got through, knocked it around him, and he dragged me to the floor. We got a free kick just outside the box. I hit it and it was going right in the corner when he dived across and got it. Unbelievable. I wasn't in too good a mood after that. Funnily enough, Manchester City was the only club I hadn't scored against in the First Division."

JL: "Didn't Corrigan say after he should have been sent off for that?"

TF: "That's right, yes."

JL: "Just to rub salt in the wound . . . 'I should have been sent off for that, shouldn't I?' He just sort of walked off whistling . . . big feller, isn't he?"

You are both from similar backgrounds. Do you find any difficulty in the leap from what you used to have to what you can afford today?

JL: "Not at all, no. I find I still like exactly the same things as I did, but I manage to spend fortunes now."

TF: "We've still got the same values."

JL: "The greatest thing I could ever have done was buy me Mom and Dad a nice house in Castle Bromwich. They had a hard time of it, and the one great thing I've been able to do is put them in a position where they don't have to worry about money. They were still at Shard End – that's a council estate a bit like Trev's home in Plymouth, only not quite so pastoral. There was just a sewage farm instead of a field over the back to play on. Actually, I was there myself until about three years ago."

Have you been to Trevor's home in Plymouth, Jeff?

JL: "Yes, we were playing at the Guildhall, I think that's what it's called. We'd just started the group and it was a bit of a grim do. I think the Francis family filled up most of the place, and that was about the 10 seats we sold. Actually, the hall only holds about two hundred . . . it was about half full thanks to Trev and his folks. But I really enjoyed it; I had a kind invitation to stay with Mr and Mrs Francis and while the other lads were roughing it in the Holiday Inn, I had a great day. We went down and had a game of football on Pennycross playground and stuff."

Friends from different worlds: Jeff Lynne of the ELO, Trevor Francis of Nottingham Forest, and the European Cup, symbol of the game which brings them together.

TF: "He's quite good, got a good shot with his right foot. What he likes most of all is to get a goalkeeper and for me to make a few crosses. I've got to time them perfectly so he can hit them on the volley, and I'm only allowed to hit them from one side. If I do it from the other, he can't hit them at all . . . he'd take the ball and leave."

JL: "Just another facet of my skill . . ."

TF: "Jeff's got this full-sized goal with a net set up on his tennis court and he hates playing unless there's a net. He can't see the fun of scoring unless there's a net."

JL: "We've had a couple of really big games out by Elmdon Airport, where Birmingham train. One day there was Brian Jones, our roadie, Garnet, my mate, and me – the three of us – against Trevor and Alberto Tarantini. We had a full-sized goal and they had a five-a-side goal. It was really great, it was getting so close and then they suddenly started getting serious because we were winning and they suddenly panicked."

TF: "At first we gave them a few chances, but suddenly Alberto started to get in block tackles. He was shouting, play harder, play harder."

JL: "It was really very funny, because we weren't even trying. Just a good laugh, great fun – and it was the coldest day of the year. Our roadie, Brian, has got really long hair and it froze stiff on his head. You could tap his head and watch the cracks . . . it's cos he sweats like a parrot."

TF: "The other occasion was also at Elmdon. There was Jeff and the lads, Keith Bertschin and myself and we seemed to be playing on for ages after the normal training. Eventually, Jim Williams, the physio, said that's enough for me because I'd been injured. I said bye to the lads, Jeff said 'Oh, great, thanks ever so much' and I went in for a bit of treatment, then a shower. When I came back out, it was almost dark and they were still out there kicking about."

Obviously when Trevor was trying to decide his destiny there was a short, concentrated period of pressure on him – did you, Jeff, experience anything similar with the ELO?

JL: "I don't think so. It's built up so gradually for us, getting better and better each year at a gentle kinda pace. We've never had any real drastic decision to make cos our manager has guided us in what we've done up till now. I'm 32, and haven't had to make a decision in my career yet. The manager's done it all for me."

TF: "I often think Jeff's under pressure because he writes everything for the albums and he's under pressure to keep improving all the time. Each album that he's done has gradually got better, and I keep thinking I can't believe he can possibly improve with the next. He did the double album Out of the Blue, and I felt sorry for him having to do another one after it."

Isn't there a parallel there? Couldn't Jeff feel the same about your performance in the 1979 European Cup Final, or the five goal performance in Northern Ireland?

JL: "Exactly – how do you top that, Trev?"

Another pressure on the athlete that doesn't exist in the same way in music is that for Trevor there'll come a time when age will decide the peak, whereas with music presumably you change as you mature?

TF: "Yes, Jeff – Do you know when you reach your peak?"

JL: "Yeah, I would think so . . . it's when you can't come up with any good tunes. But, really, you can write songs for ever, any style you want, whatever you choose to do. But I think I'm getting better now, I think my creative ability is increasing at the moment. I'm going to reach a peak eventually, but I can't see it coming. I've got a lot more ideas just this last couple of months . . . I usually work them out on the piano, but I can do it anywhere. The phone might ring and I suddenly get an idea and have to say – hey, hang on a minute, I can do some stuff here."

That's one difference, isn't it? Whatever Trevor invents he attempts in front of a critical audience, whereas your audience sees the polished version.

JL: "That's true, but in the same way he has got to rehearse as well – some of the moves at least. Although he has a lot of things that he will invent on the spot in a game, I'll also invent stuff on the guitar at a show. Most of that's done backstage though and I agree with what you say – Trev's is more instant because no game is the same. Ours is basically the same except that you get so used to it you start ad-libbing bits here and there, whereas Trevor never gets two balls coming at him the same."

Part of Trevor's value is the ability to improvise – can you actually do things off the cuff during a show?

JL: "You can only do subtle things, really. You've got to stay within the framework of the piece because there are seven of us and the others are still playing it exactly the same. So the only way you can do it is within the same chord structure, just improvise through that. Even then, they're saying 'What's he doing?' Sometimes we've had disasters. On stage I have to count a lot of gaps. I have to cue people in occasionally through difficult pieces with a quick one-two, sometimes on complicated time changes. And some nights I've perhaps been having a great laugh, or I'm thinking about something else and I forget to count and the whole thing collapses in a big heap. Then we have to pretend it was a thing that was meant. It's horrible.''

TF: "In football, even though I like to do unusual things, I still can't be too individual. If I'm told to play on the right, I've got to stay there or else it affects the balance of the team. And obviously, even up front I can't just continue doing things because I want to. I have always had to be sensible about it and play as a member of the team.''

JL: "That's true, but the great thing about Trev is he's always striving to be better. One thing you sense with him that you sense with very, very few players – it's like a sigh of relief when he gets the ball, you sense something's going to happen. You can't predict – it might be something totally outrageous or a fabulous pass... but it's rare he actually fluffs it.''

TF: "Sometimes it's luck, you know. Sometimes you don't plan it and it works out.''

JL: "You see, at Birmingham a couple of years ago, you'd suddenly see Trevor shoot off on one of those runs. He had a spell of doing these solo efforts... you'd see him dive into about a hundred and fifty defenders by the corner flag and there'd be a horde of people around him and he'd come out the other end still with the ball. Then he'd either cross it or have a shot. That was what used to draw gasps – the fact that he could emerge out of this big collection of bodies still with the ball bobbling around his feet.''

Those days might be over – at Forest he's in a more disciplined set-up.

JL: "Exactly. At Birmingham, Trevor was at one point a one-man team.''

TF: "Obviously if players want the ball, and if they are good players and they get into more positions to receive it, then you pass it to them. But it depends which area I'm in – if I get the ball in an attacking area and there's space, I always do expect myself to attempt something. I suppose I put pressure on myself to create things, but you don't feel pressure on you like I do, do you?''

JL: "Not that sort of pressure, no, basically because I've got a passion for recording.''

TF: "You have to keep churning out great stuff all the time, but you don't feel any effect. Once an album's done, all you want is to get back and do another.''

JL: "You used to be a lot worse. It doesn't get to you so much now, you shrug a lot of it off.''

TF: "That's right. I can't put my finger on it, but I've changed somewhat since I've been at Forest. I think I've hardened.''

JL: "Definitely – he's really flash now!''

As the discussion continued through three hours, Jeff Lynne periodically lit a cigarette and Trevor would get up and open the door to allow clearer air to circulate. Neither commented on the fact. Eventually, each offered their favourite anecdote in relation to their friendship, each story being told to a background of laughter from the other:

JL: "Me and two mates decided we were going down to see him play one night at Bristol. This is not so much a funny story as stupid. Anyway, we made up our minds very late and it was about 7 o'clock when we saw a sign saying Bristol City football. We didn't read the rest of it. We just parked the car and started off walking towards this glow in the sky, which was their floodlights. We went on and on. Bloody hell, where is this place? We'd seen the name of the ground and everything and we could see this glow in the sky, but we didn't seem to be getting there.

"We go down this back street, through this factory yard... it's total darkness, all derelict. We come to this canal which is impossible to get across, no bridges anywhere. So we find this great lump of old wood, like a tree trunk it is, lay it across the canal and tip-toe across. We can see the ground now, it's getting nearer. We cross over some more wasteland ... it's all to see *him* play football this... We're nearly getting there. Next we come to this big dip down an old railway siding. Can't find a way through, so we climb under these old trucks, over them, round them. Then we come to this motorway with a flyover across it. Down the grass embankment, run across the motorway – still in this terrible darkness. But the lights are getting nearer. By now it's half-time. We've been walking, running 45 minutes. So we carry on like idiots, me and a bloke called George and our roadie Brian. Finally we get to the ground, covered in muck from the puddles and swamps and all sorts of things we've come through.

"They're out for the second half by this time. There's this bloke on the gates. 'C'mon,' I say to him, 'let us in... I'll pay.' 'Can't come in 'ere mate', he says, 'you'll have to wait till we open the gates to let them out.' '*Whaaat*? C'mon, honest, I'll pay yer'. He says 'No, can't open these gates'

"There's old dossers about, and little kids that

don't want to pay, waiting for the gates to open. So we stand there, all this roaring coming from inside. I'm so mad; when you're locked out of anywhere, it's so frustrating . . . we go round all sides of the ground, trying to find a gate that's open. Nothing. So eventually we wait till the scroungers are let in with about 15 minutes to go. We climb up this pile of dirt that leads to the grandstand, and as we're climbing up there's this great big roar. We jump up and see the Bristol goalie taking the ball out of the back of the net. So its 1–0, we miss everything. Can't go for a drink with Trevor in this filth so we turn around and walk back to the car and drive home.

"The end to it is this: Trevor phones up and says: 'You didn't come to the match then?' *Whaaat!*"

TF: "My story's in America. When I was over there in 1978, Jeff came out on tour and was playing down in Cleveland. I didn't know about it till two days before, but I went next door to get a road map to see how far it was from Detroit. It was about five hours, a bit too far really, not knowing the roads. So I went down and asked a mate of mine, Graham Oates, if he'd fancy going with me by plane.

"We trained Saturday morning but we weren't required in after until the match, which was Sunday evening. We didn't mention our plan to anybody. We finished training, drove straight to Detroit Airport and got the plane to Cleveland. When we arrived, Jeff had fixed up a limousine to pick us up. Graham and myself went to the hotel, saw Jeff, had a good chat, and went off in the limousine to the concert. It was as if we were in the group. We went down to the baseball stadium and there were 63,000 people there."

JL: "I was really glad Trev saw us there because he'd only seen us before in places like the Plymouth Guildhall. We'd gradually been getting bigger and bigger in America and Trevor had read it in the papers and charts and stuff, but never seen it for himself."

TF: "Anyway, I'm not finished yet. We watched Jeff tuning up and things were delayed while this other group called Foreigner was going on a bit. We'd got all the badges so we could go wherever we liked. We walked through the crowd to where the mixing machine (a sound balancing unit) was because this was the best viewing spot you could wish for. It was really embarrassing, wandering for about five minutes through all these bodies, people lying down, smoking pot, drinking . . . all out of their minds."

JL: "And that's just the group . . ."

TF: "There's a few heavies on this mixing

machine, and there was such a big fuss. 'There's no way you can come up here!' The feller with us says the group says we can . . . a really bad scene, it almost came to a fight. Eventually we got up on this mixing machine and watched the concert.

"Great concert it was – hour and a half. Afterwards we went back by the limos again and at the hotel there was a little reception . . . a few drinks. We went

to bed at about two or three in the morning. In the morning, Jeff and Bev, the drummer, decide they'd like to come across to Detroit, so we all flew back, had a bit of salad in the house, and had about two hours to spare before the match. We went off in limousines again and played against Houston. Graham reckons he had his best game of the season. I scored a goal, so it went really well.''

On stage: four members of the Electric Light Orchestra with the strings which distinguish their type of music.

JL: ''That was a real exciting thing for me, to see you playing in America.''

TF: ''Nobody knows about it. It was the one time I stepped out of line.''

JL: ''They will now.''

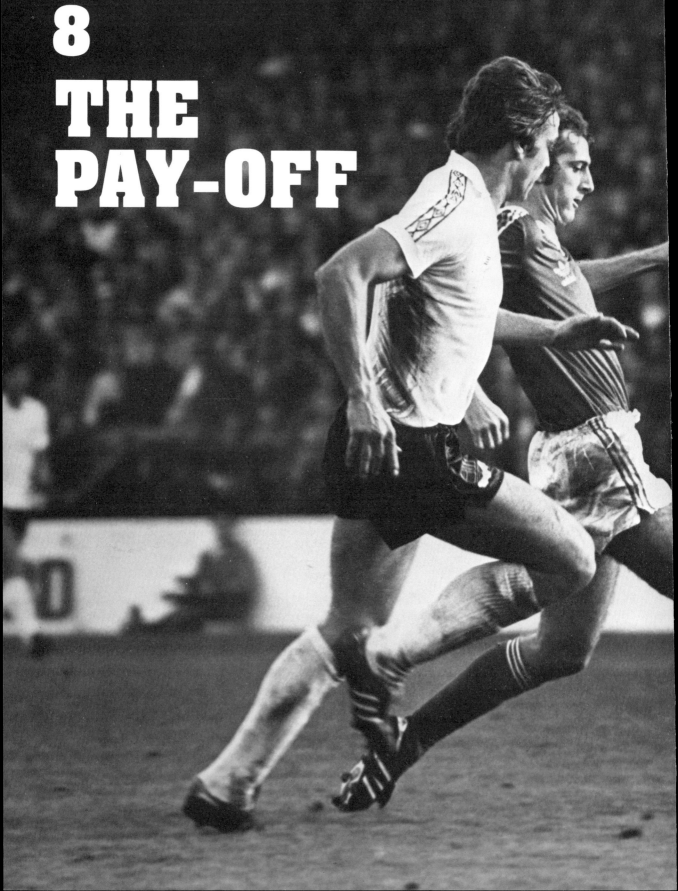

8
THE
PAY-OFF

The days and long nights of the first £1 million transfer in British football took more twists, more diversions, more false leads than an Agatha Christie novel. More moves, perhaps, than even Brian Clough and Peter Taylor cared to follow.

They knew they were bidding an historic amount for a player who makes things happen on the field quicker than opponents can think, though they were to discover that his strength as a man is to hesitate, to stay his hand and ponder all offers before signing away his future.

That strength had been guided by Trevor Francis's father when the boy resisted the first tempting offers to sign schoolboy forms. Now the young man was being showered with advice from so many angles, he must have felt like Jimmy Carter besieged in the White House. And who could detect that the voices he was mainly listening to were those of a Birmingham policeman and an international pop musician?

"Normally, I try to keep everything close to myself," Francis says. "But on this occasion – it was the biggest thing that had happened to me – I found myself wanting to discuss the whole move with Alan (police constable Alan Cooper) and Jeff (Jeff Lynne of ELO fame). Before Nottingham Forest came on-to the scene, there was an unbelievable package offer from Coventry City and Detroit Express, but in the background there were other teams I kept hearing about. There was another team from America – Washington. Then Everton were always in, trying to arrange an exchange deal. I think West Brom were always interested. Manchester United were there as well. I kept hearing things, little things; every day something new would be happening."

Francis continues: "Some of it, I'd hear from the club, from Jim Smith (the Birmingham manager). But there'd be other people as well. I was forever on the phone. People were ringing me and saying 'Don't do this ... don't sign for any English club, there are Spanish and Italian clubs very interested.' There were agents, journalists, so many different people phoning it was driving me crackers. I was just trying to think that I'd got to make the right decision. It was a big decision *for* me."

Days blurred into sleepless nights, the only relief coming from morning training sessions out in the harsh February frost near Birmingham airport. "I don't think he knew which way to turn," says Jeff Lynne. "He was getting journalists all night long. All day and all night he was being called to the phone. He and Helen were both knackered and I knew what it must have been like when he actually did sign for Forest. He came round to my house for a couple of days, just to play snooker and get the actual decision off his mind. He'd had nothing but pressure from all sides and I felt that the best thing Clough ever did was to tell him not to speak to the newspapers when he signed."

Jeff Lynne admits to being something of a recluse from his own musical press, and it was his Warwickshire country retreat, his snooker table, that provided some refuge as the week of February 5, 1979 began its climactic auction of Trevor Francis.

Tuesday, the sixth, was the afternoon and evening of the marathon snooker duel. "We played about six hours non-stop," recalls Jeff. "And I was letting him win. He thought he was going to have to make a decision that night because Gordon Milne of Coventry City was coming round to his house for a private meeting.

"He played lousy snooker that day, but, like I said, I let him whitewash me. He was a bit down, kept asking: 'What shall I do?' I was saying stop at Birmingham, stay with the Blues – and helpful stuff like that. It was ridiculous, he was getting a different offer coming in every five minutes. He was making a list of them on the wallpaper. It's still there, actually.

"Seriously, what Trevor really wanted was some medals, and I didn't think Coventry were too likely to win anything just yet. But with the American club, the money was a bit special, and I remember his pal Alan Cooper was saying that he ought to go for the money, pick up the security Coventry and Detroit were offering."

Francis was double-booked that night. He stayed behind at home while Helen went for a drink with Jeff and his wife Sandi and Alan and Maria Cooper. They expected him to join them, but the meeting with Milne was still going on after closing time. "We rolled out of the pub, and went back to Trevor's house," recalls Jeff. "We'd had a few pints, and were boisterous and that. So we steam in, thinking the meeting is over, and I'm yelling 'C'mon, Trev, forget it! Got any more of them lagers?' And the meeting's still going on in the next room ... all these big secret discussions about the costliest footballer in Britain and his future! Gordon Milne must have loved it."

Alan Cooper, the policeman who had befriended the teenaged Francis by offering him a lift to the ground in pouring rain nine years previously, says: "Trevor came out and invited us for a drink and a chat with Gordon Milne, which was a very brave gesture in the circumstances. I mean, Jeff and myself were really ardent Birmingham supporters and, for purely selfish reasons, we were hoping deep down that he wouldn't leave.

"Gordon was extremely nice about the situation. I don't think he intended to talk football while we were there, but he wanted to convince Trevor. 'There'll be no problem when you sign for us,' he was saying. 'People have short memories, people will forget very quickly that you were ever a Birmingham player.' I can see Trevor to this day looking across at us and smiling. It was the most traumatic thing anybody who had followed the club could imagine; there'd never been anything like a Trevor Francis at Birmingham in my father's time, let alone mine. He was the Great White Hope."

After Milne left, with high hopes but still not the signature for which he was pressing, the three friends continued the finer points of discussions they had shared for days. "I was advocating that it was better to be financially sound, and that the money from Coventry and Detroit was on the table," says Cooper. "There was the possibility of success at Forest – assuming they agreed Birmingham's figure – but no guarantee. Anyway, you can't spend medals, or safeguard your future through them. But Trevor's answer was: 'Don't you think it would be better to *achieve* something, rather than go for the money?'"

Later still into that night, Trevor and Helen Francis were alone with their thoughts. She, contrary to what the gossips in the front office at Detroit were saying, was determined to play only a supporting role, to help her husband make up his own mind. "It was such a good offer from Coventry," he says. "And I like Gordon Milne so much. He's a great, great feller. Jimmy Hill had also been good to me with Detroit. The Coventry and Detroit deal was unbelievable. What's more, another thing going for it was that I'd just moved into a house, which we'd spent months and months looking for, and it was even closer to Coventry than Birmingham. Gordon was trying to convince me that Coventry was the team to play for, but I was very much aware of the fact that if I did go there, I'd be open to criticism because my main reason for wanting to leave Birmingham was to further my career and look for success. I'd have left myself wide open.

"Still, I felt a little disappointed in many ways with Birmingham for putting a million on my head. February was a bad time to transfer, anyway, because by then a lot of teams may have spent any money they had – such as West Brom who'd paid half a million for David Mills. It was one thing

The crucial voice on the end of the line ... policeman Alan Cooper, whose friendship and advice helped Francis through the traumas of the biggest transfer in history.

knowing you'd got admirers, but I felt in pitching the price so high they had really cut down the clubs who could pay it. They hadn't really thought too much about me. By insisting on the million they narrowed it down to two clubs ... and the greedy devils got it!

"I know I was lucky in many aspects that Nottingham Forest was one of the teams that could afford me. I could have been in a situation where I desperately wanted to leave Birmingham and, like Andy Gray and Steve Daley, found that only one club was willing to pay the money. They didn't have any choice where they moved. Still, I suppose in my position they were all better teams than one that was going into the Second Division, as Birmingham was at the time."

At that stage, in the early hours of Wednesday, February 7, the Forest alternative was not even concrete. Clough and Taylor had, so far as Francis knew, stuck at a bid of £950,000. "I had made up my mind Coventry was going to be it," says Trevor. "I had already told Gordon Milne there was no way I expected to get a better offer ... the next thing I knew, the telephone started ringing. At three o'clock in the morning!"

It was Alan Cooper. "I'd been lying awake with a blinding headache," Alan remembers, "when Maria woke up and asked: 'What's the problem?' I just said I'd got to phone Trevor. I told him to cancel everything I'd said beforehand, I wanted to clear my own conscience. Knowing him as I do, I lay there thinking that the most important thing to him and the people around him was to show all the doubters in the world that he *can* play. Everyone in Birmingham knew this, but with Birmingham not being a successful club he wasn't getting the opportunity to display it to the world.

"I got to thinking that Coventry was in the same boat; they're not winners either. So in this phone call I was telling Trevor that I felt he should sign for Forest – or Everton if Gordon Lee could manage a deal – and that even with Brian Clough I felt certain he'd get the money anyway if he stuck out for America as well. In the end, I felt that Forest could offer him the platform to prove he is the best player in the country."

The following day was strangely quiet. The lull before the storm. Francis trained at Birmingham in the morning, taking in good part banter about where he might finish the week. At 7.30 pm he was settling down to watch England's European championship game against Northern Ireland on television when his phone rang again. It was Jim Smith, telling him Forest had agreed to pay Birmingham's million; Brian Clough and Peter Taylor wanted to talk to Trevor at the City Ground in Nottingham on the Thursday.

"He came mainly out of courtesy," Peter Taylor says. "I'm sure he believed he was signing for Coventry. When he arrived, he confirmed what I'd hoped. He was nicely dressed, well spoken, polite, determined. He produced a typewritten list of questions and ticked them off when we answered them. The character came through loud and clear. We didn't have to spend a lot of time on him from that point of view."

Clough's interest came as no surprise to Francis. In 1977, the Forest manager had presented Trevor with the ATV Midland Player of the Year Award with the words: "You are undoubtedly a very talented player. I wish I'd been your manager when you were 18." But Francis learned that day how Clough is apt to temper praise with criticism: "I wasn't too pleased when Brian Clough also told me to take my hands out of my pockets," the player admits. "I didn't think remarks like that are called for on live television."

Now, however, Brian Clough was paying Francis the ultimate compliment, bidding more for him at a stroke than he had paid for nine previous Forest signings – Peter Shilton (£325,000), Colin Barrett (£40,000), Larry Lloyd (£60,000), Kenny Burns (£145,000), David Needham (£145,000), John McGovern (£60,000), Archie Gemmill (£130,000), Garry Birtles (£2,000) and John O'Hare (£25,000).

The Forest managers may have felt they had to queue jump Coventry, with its lucrative American connection, but their persuasion began in conventional challenging manner: Show us your medals – sign for us and we'll guarantee you one. If you're really serious about wanting to win something, there's only one choice. You're now 24, nearly 25 years of age . . . for a man with so much talent what have you got to show for your 10 years in football? If you want to be a regular England player, sign for us and we'll guarantee it. It'll be no bed of roses here, but we'll make you a better player, put you on the level of a Kevin Keegan – with more goals.

The contract was on the table. The offer to Birmingham – £1,150,500 including taxes – was then worth three times Trevor Francis's weight in gold. His cut, wherever he went, was around £50,000 spread over the length of his contract. There remained one delicate matter: the contract Francis already had, to play during the summer in America for Detroit Express. It was a contract which, whether people believed it or not, he felt some obligation to honour, quite apart from the huge financial implications it held for him.

Clough and Taylor, however, were fundamentally opposed to any player working the two-way Atlantic stretch, with the obvious demands such 12-months a year stress imposed on the human physique. "I don't think a player with a successful English club needs America," said Clough. "At our level, if you are not tired at the end of the season, you should be." More than that, if Detroit was only moderately successful, if it merely qualified for the American play-offs, Francis would not only miss Forest's pre-season training and its first matches of the new season, but would return too late to qualify for the first two rounds of European competition.

"I didn't think for one moment that Brian Clough was going to allow me to go to America," admits Francis. "When I first mentioned it, he immediately said no. We were there for five hours. He knew I'd been talking to Coventry and he felt I would be joining Coventry if he didn't let me go to Detroit. To be honest, I'm not sure what I'd have done if he had said the deal was off unless I broke the Detroit contract.

"I would probably still have signed for Brian Clough because I wanted success and because, apart from Liverpool, Nottingham Forest was the best team in the country. The Coventry package offer did keep going through my mind, but I was also very much aware of the criticism I might get, particularly from Birmingham fans, if I joined Coventry. In the end, Brian Clough virtually made my mind up for me when he said I could go to America in the summer."

Trevor Francis is a master at disguising his feelings on the pitch; and if he had betrayed in that interview the merest suspicion that he could have been talked out of his American moonlighting, it is unlikely Clough and Taylor would have missed it. Both were convinced that they had to sacrifice the issue. Taylor admits he could not blame Francis for standing up for himself, so high were the stakes. And Clough – could he or anyone else have turned down that opportunity of playing in the States?

"I know full well the difficulties of a young man turning that type of money down," confides Clough. "We all crave for security in football. I still do now at 44, having gone through the mill as player and manager, and though not being short of a bob or two, I myself still crave for this so-called security. But y'see, *he* was craving for it before he'd achieved anything, and that's what's happening to the modern-day footballer. They're looking for a security that can only be built on a foundation."

But wasn't Trevor Francis possibly losing heart of ever achieving that, having waited almost 10 years to be part of a successful team?

"Possibly," agrees Clough. "But that was his own fault because I'm certain if he'd wanted to get away from Birmingham that much, he could have got away earlier than he did. I'm absolutely certain."

Might you, however, have had to change his personality to get him to do the things necessary to get away?

"I think he could have got away," retorts Clough. "I'm not too sure about this young man's ambition. You've got to have ambition to do things in life, particularly in football, particularly when you're up against it."

But didn't he sign for *you* because of his ambition above all else?

"Pardon? I think the fact he signed for us indicated he thought we were the best thing whereby he could realise other aspects of his footballing life. I'm not sure whether he had the ambition to do it. And I'm not sure that he doesn't think it's very hard now he's with us."

The day before Brian Clough answered those questions, Helen Francis gave birth to her first child, Matthew. Clough, very much a family man, used the event to illustrate his feelings: "That young man had a son yesterday, and he'll want to tell his

son, to show his son, and prove to his son what a good player he was. The best way to do that is not by showing him a big house and not by showing him 15s-6d in the Co-op building society, because a lot of people have big houses and fifteen and six in the Co-op. But he can say, well y'know I did play in a European Cup Final, I did help to win a League, I did play in a cup-winning side. Any player, not just Trevor Francis, needs to get his priorities right. And money isn't top priority, though it's a great comfort at all times."

It is history now that Francis made Forest his priority that February day, history also that by joining Nottingham he turned his back on a 10-year testimonial at Birmingham which would have rewarded him with between £70,000 and £100,000. It is well known, too, that apart from the 5 per cent entitlement of the transfer fee, players often demand and receive money from clubs who sell them. "Birmingham got a million for me," reflects Francis, "but I never asked them for a penny. Not a penny. I just didn't feel I wanted to. I had had a nice nine years there, a good contract, and was always well looked after moneywise.

"Money was never a factor in my leaving. I wanted to go for the simple reason that, year after year, I had played with relegation worries and I felt this was restricting my development as a player. There was no other reason and if people start to think otherwise, they can think it."

If his conscience was clear over Birmingham, he demonstrated that he felt an obligation to Gordon Milne. Francis had shaken Clough and Taylor by the hand on their deal that Thursday, but he requested 24 hours before he either signed or the decision was publicised so that he could personally explain to Milne. "It wasn't easy," says Francis, "but I rang Gordon that evening and told him I'd decided on Forest."

En route from the City Ground to making that phone call, Francis was taken to Peter Shilton's house by Peter Taylor, Shilton being a familiar face and an England international colleague of Trevor's. "Peter was just back from the England game," recalls Francis, "and he was having a lie down in bed. The next minute Peter Taylor with Helen and myself were knocking on the door. Taylor left us there, and Peter (Shilton) opened up a couple of bottles of champagne."

In retrospect, that impromptu celebration could have turned dreadfully sour. The £1 million headlines were written for Saturday's papers ... and where were the trio who had created the story?

Making their separate ways to a Nottingham parks pitch, where Trevor was to make his debut for the Forest A team against Notts County.

The day began with a phone call at 9am, this time from Trevor to his policeman friend's home. "He told me he was going to play for Nottingham in the third team, and asked if I would go along with him," says Alan Cooper. "I also had to go round to St. Andrews, the Birmingham City ground, to collect his boots. It was a funny feeling for me as I went up to the boot room and asked the chap for Trevor's boots; a sort of mixture of elation that he was at last going to play amongst players of class, and soul searching that here I was, a Birmingham supporter all my life, taking away the boots of the best player we'd ever had.

"When we arrived in Nottingham we drove up in Trevor's Jag right into the middle of the park. It was an absolutely bitter, freezing day ... and there was Trevor, the £1 million man, elated at the prospect of playing for these people, but being stuck in the middle of a park deserted except for 40 spectators around the pitch and a dog. Even I knew he wasn't eligible to play and I felt embarrassed. I felt they were knocking something out of him.

"During the game, I felt they were playing him for no better reason than to put him in his place, and it was not what the chap needed. He was the last person that needed it. I've always felt since that if Forest had taken the attitude Wolverhampton did with Andy Gray, built him up, made the signing public and so on – and if Wolves had taken the attitude with Gray that Forest did with Trevor it would have worked out right."

Typically, Francis interpreted events of that Saturday morning with less offence than his friend. "Many people might have felt it was demeaning," agrees Francis, "but I didn't think so at all. If, for example, I had been put in the A team because I'd had a bad game, then I might have. But in fact I had only played once for Birmingham in five weeks because of the bad weather, and Brian Clough asked me if I'd like to play and I said yes.

"I think it was the coldest day I'd ever known, but Clough, Taylor and the chairman, Mr. Dryden, were there on the touchline. I remember I had a shot at goal that didn't go on target, and a spectator shouted 'Got to do better than that, Francis'. Clough ran half the length of the pitch to tell him off: '*Trevor* is his name,' he said.

"Then at half-time, we went over to the side of the pitch. Clough came over and I thought he was going to discuss some aspect of the game, but in fact he gave me a lecture about (shin) pads and from that moment I've worn pads in every game. I always felt they inhibited me but you never see a Forest player without pads on. If I had a choice, I'd still sooner play without them. I didn't wear them in America. I always think if you're going to get injured, you'll get injured anyway. Only the other day at the City ground a young apprentice came up to show me this great bruise on his shin. I said he should have worn his pads and he replied he did, the kick went straight through them."

Since Clough had himself been finished prematurely through injury, he obviously had every right to ensure his players – his investments – took every precaution. It was ironic, therefore, that Nottingham had risked Francis in that A team game before he was registered as their player with the Football League. "It didn't dawn on me until the afternoon," Francis says. "Alan and myself drove straight from Nottingham to St. Andrews to see the Birmingham–Leeds game and we just missed the start. As we were walking through to one of the private boxes, people seemed amazed when I said I'd just played in the A team.

"The Forest secretary was there that afternoon with the registration forms to sign, and I remember people asking what if I'd been injured? Whose player would I have been then? Looking back on it, I did have a collision with the goalkeeper that could have caused an injury." Ultimately Francis became a registered Nottingham Forest player a week later.

At that time, too, he decided without pressure from anyone to cancel the final two years of his contract to play in America. "When people talk about money," he asserts, "they never mention the fact that, although I felt committed to Detroit for 1979, I opted out of the next two years. You don't have to be an idiot to work out how much I threw away. But I felt that with Forest I was likely to play about 70 games a season instead of about 46 with Birmingham. And that, with England internationals as well, is enough for anybody."

Awaiting Francis in the Forest dressing room was a face even more familiar than Peter Shilton's ... a face unmistakable to him. There were plenty on the outside prepared to wager long odds against Trevor Francis joining Forest because of his past clashes with Kenny Burns; indeed, one family friend down in Plymouth lost money on the bet. What he failed to appreciate was that the two players had matured, each to put a healthy respect for the skills of the other above their long-suffering and often mute partnership at Birmingham City.

Francis says there was no need for discussion about his relationship with Burns during the five-hour interview at the City ground. "It was never a factor," he insists, "except that Kenny, like Peter Shilton and Tony Woodcock, was a person I'd played with before and this helps a player to feel he can settle into a new club. I was aware that so many people – the press again – were questioning whether it would be a stumbling block. Everybody reads the papers and things get blown out of all proportion. It's not just with Kenny; recently I introduced Stan Bowles to someone who said afterwards: 'What a nice fellow, I couldn't imagine Stan to be like that.'"

Peter Taylor, the half of the Forest management who assesses the backgrounds of intended newcomers, agrees that the friction between Burns and Francis in Birmingham prompted no fears about reuniting the pair. "Never," he says. "No, I got all the facts, such as you can in this situation. I'd seen them together, y'know? It was incredible. They were playing as a double spearhead at Birmingham and it seemed they'd go through matches without speaking one word. Unbelievable. But it's a case of the devil you know. Here, it's been no problem at all. Burns doesn't dictate who we buy and who we don't."

Nevertheless, Taylor undertook to inform Kenny Burns of the impending transfer. "Of course. I told Burnsie: 'We're bringing your friend, Trevor.' I said it would be a great help in his household. Yes, there had been friction, they don't deny it. But there is so much difference now, difference in Kenny I mean. He's so gentle, it's unbelievable."

"It's true that Kenny and I had moments on the field when we were not speaking to each other," says Francis. "We'd also had arguments on the field but the next game I could get to the touchline and pull the ball back, he'd stick it in, and we'd be seen hugging each other. I could never explain why: it just seemed part of the game. Nowadays we can have a game of snooker and not even get upset over that."

The low hurdles – Francis steps over a tackle from Brighton's Mark Lawrenson.

Kenny Burns himself is now able to rationalise those Birmingham days with surprising clarity: "I was 22 and still a babbie when I left," he reflects. "Deep down, I'd been envious of Trevor since the apprentice days. He had everything so young. He was the star doing great things while the rest of us were still in the A team, and any apprentice who wasn't jealous should not have been there. I wanted to prove so much *I* was the best in the world."

Burns can penetrate deeper than anyone else into those feelings, and express them in material or personal terms: "Trevor was driving a TR6," he says, "while I had an Austin 1100. He had a smashing family coming up every week from Plymouth, while I miss my mum and dad even today. My dad died before I was born and my mum when I was 13 . . . and it's only now I have a wife, a young daughter and a nice house of my own that I realise you don't need much excitement."

Now he has that home, Burns insists, nothing is going to take it from him. "Trevor was always level-headed and couldn't go wrong," he admits, "but I was a tearaway. I'm a natural moaner all the time and I gave the managers some stick, particularly Willie Bell who was so weak he couldn't manage a Sunday school outing. But at the end of the day, it's excuses isn't it? Okay, so Trevor had the praise from his family and I didn't . . . but it works the other way. I could have faded out and nobody would have noticed, I would have let nobody down, you know. But now we're here, and we've both battled through I think we have both realised football is a career just to go out and enjoy."

Curious, isn't it, that it takes a £1 million transfer to recreate a pairing that seemed unmanageable in another dressing room four years previously? So what had changed – they were, surely, the same players from the same background, the Glasgow tearaway and the placid Plymothian? "But they're not the same," insists Don Dorman, the Birmingham City scout who signed both as youngsters. "The first time I met Kenny Burns after he'd gone to Forest, I couldn't believe it was the same person. He was like a lad who'd just come out of Borstal – that's Borstal in the old days – a completely changed character. I was never more proud in my life than to see the two of them together in the European championship side.

"All the frictions came from the youth stage. They're men now. But I'm still convinced we could have done more in that respect at Birmingham. I'd never witnessed such a change in a feller as when Kenny Burns came up to my office a month after

he'd gone to Forest. Can I come in *Mister* Dorman? I was shocked. And he conducted himself so well . . . I'm a great admirer of Cloughie and Peter Taylor; they obviously heard all the tittle-tattle, yet they thought they could manage the two in one side, and the proof of the pudding is in the eating."

Both Francis and Dorman have stated (in Chapter Four) that they felt a lack of strong managerial discipline was the root cause of Burns's problems at Birmingham. To know Peter Taylor's feelings, we must momentarily go back to 1975, when Forest took Burns off Birmingham's hands for £145,000. "I'd done my homework," says Taylor. "Kenny Burns was at the end of the road – domestically, playingwise, weightwise. I'd made enough enquiries to know he'd a good streak in him, and Brian and I told him straight: 'You are in the gutter. We are prepared to be mother and father to you, to sort you out and put you up there a winner. But you've got to do what *we* want.'"

"I wouldn't say Kenny Burns is the brightest man I've ever met," Taylor says today, "but he had enough in him to see what we were saying. He couldn't grab it quickly enough."

Whatever else Trevor Francis was watching from afar he could not have failed to see the apparent transformation of Burns, the 1978 Football Writers' Association Player of the Year. If Burns possessed a video recorder that year, he might not have recognised himself in the player who turned the other cheek, who walked away, arms innocently raised above his head, after an opponent had clearly punched him in the face. That incident alone may have told Francis of the effectiveness of Nottingham Forest discipline, convinced him that, if a dressing room is sometimes a family at war, he and Burns could live alongside each other again.

Indeed, if Burns was pushed up from defence to centre-forward tomorrow, Francis would relish the partnership. "I've always rated him as a forward," explains Francis. "I always feel there are so many who can play midfield or defence, but not too many who want to play as striker. Kenny prefers the back four, but he proved on many occasions that he is a successful target man – he's good on the floor, good in the air and he can score goals."

Peter Taylor admits a special satisfaction at combining the temperaments as well as the talents of a Trevor Francis and a Kenny Burns. "That," he observes, "is what management is all about. Brian and I took a risk with Burns, and eventually we bring Burnsie and Trevor together again . . . and the outcome's superb."

True as that may have been, the absorption of a new player is not a marriage of two, but at least 12 personalities. Kevin Keegan walked into more than a language barrier in Hamburg, where he admits the initial resentment was so profound it almost broke him before he overcame it.

Francis, a Birmingham cult figure and a part-time American superstar (reaping summertime payments no Forest player was allowed), arrived at the City Ground with headlines inevitably as bloated as Keegan's. He was aware of, and embarrassed by, his media image as an individualist who had grown bigger than his club. And he knew that, whatever relationship he developed with Clough and Taylor, the £1 million fee guaranteed him no acceptance with new colleagues. He had to win that.

And the winning is on two levels. Even in the days of the squad system, only 11 play. So a newcomer must prove better than the man he replaces. Tony Woodcock, Martin O'Neill and Ian Bowyer had helped Forest to the League championship and League Cup double; they, and not Francis, were eligible for the 1979 League Cup, FA Cup and next two rounds of the European Cup. And if they reached that last final, would one of them give way for the £1 million man?

None of that was discussed in front of Francis but is it not human nature to look over your shoulder?

The second level of acceptance is equally important: would the team embrace Francis as a man? Footballers are sometimes couped up in the artificial atmosphere of hotel life for longer than they see their wives. And when the games are played at the heights Nottingham contests, the long hours are interlaced with tension. Trevor was immersed in that but the 60-mile drive between his own home and theirs curtailed his wish to socialise, to share more relaxed times with the players. His England international appearances, his American commitment and his wife's pregnancy, added to Forest duties and commercial business, meant it was a full year before he found a house nearer to Nottingham to which he could move.

In a curious way – or perhaps in a designed way – the unorthodox managerial style at Forest probably helped Francis's integration. He was asked to pour out the tea at half-time, to collect players' shirts after matches he couldn't play. Clough and Taylor say they expected him to resent these menial tasks; they looked for it and when they thought they saw it, they took Trevor to one side and explained this was not to slap him down or humiliate him in front of the team. It was the way they did things at Forest.

Anyone, from the chairman down would pour the tea if necessary, and a million-pound player was no different from anybody else.

Francis agrees he was "surprised" at first, though resentment is too strong a word. And he was later to learn that it was not unusual for John Robertson to be asked to pour drinks at the boss's behest on the coach journey home, or Peter Shilton or anyone to be seconded to similar duties. And in retrospect, in the climate created at Forest, was there an easier way for Francis to be shorn of any £1 million misconceptions in the eyes of the team than to pour the tea? And if he became the exception to the Forest rule, would that have helped the others to like him?

"The way I was accepted, it was as if I'd gone on a free transfer," says Trevor. "That's how much help the lads were. There were one or two jokes, such as on pay day when the lads pick up their wages in the office. They said I'd have to bring Securicor round for mine. But that is the humour you expect in the dressing room, and which I like."

There was a lot of humour about at Forest. All complaints about the authenticity of that statement, or of the following caricatures, should be addressed to Francis's England colleague, Viv Anderson. Some months after Trevor arrived, Anderson provided in Shoot magazine a stylised "dossier" of the team-mates Francis could expect to share the next years of his life with.

Shiltsie and Tommy, for instance, are quiet in company but row in their room. Translated, that means Peter Shilton and David Needham (Tommy because of a resemblance to singer Tom Jones) share hotel life and an argumentative tendency on their journeys. In Nottingham, Shilton has never kicked his teenage habit of staying behind at the ground to practise his lone pursuit of perfection, while Needham slips off to his Leicestershire farm.

Scottish left-back Frankie Gray tells jokes, "mostly old", with a dry delivery. Larry Lloyd is the chief bookworm, who reads anything, while winger John Robertson reads everything from Playboy to the Rise and Fall of the Roman Empire. Robbo is a film fanatic, fan of Roxy Music's Bryan Ferry and of Clint Eastwood. His renderings of Bryan Ferry numbers are less appreciated than his leading role in the comedy trio of Robertson, O'Neill and Bowyer.

Martin "The Squire" O'Neill studied law at Queen's University, Belfast, impersonates Benny Hill's "Fred Scuttle", and laughs (according to Anderson) like a leaking gas cylinder you can't shut off. Ian Bowyer, "Bomber", distinguishes himself

by putting his home, his kids, his shirts and his cups of tea at Anderson's disposal.

Tony Woodcock, before he flew off to Cologne, was "so quiet you sometimes have to shake him to make sure he's awake – and that's when he's standing up." Garry Birtles never took to the nickname Hitler, so the lads changed it to Charlie Chaplin, though that seems equally inappropriate for a trendy dresser with a passion for pop records.

John McGovern, the skipper, received Anderson's vote as the gentleman of the side, with a taste for Lowry paintings, champagne and good food, and a diplomatic air. It was no small triumph for democracy when he was persuaded to wear one of the ELO tee shirts brought to the ground by . . . guess who?

Francis, of course, knew all about Kenny Burns, whose "wild man" image Anderson decided was tamed by Brian Clough and Kenny's wife Louise.

The halo slipped slightly, later in 1979/80 when Burns was twice suspended, but even then the aggression was more in line than in the bad old days.

When Anderson penned his enlightening column, Francis had scarcely popped his head round the Forest door. But that was enough for Anderson's assessment of him as "another quiet, but friendly sort." Modesty forbade Anderson to reveal more than his "Spider" nickname, but his wit was written into the column and his name in the history books as the first black player to represent England.

The laughs could not altogether ease Francis's apprehension at joining Nottingham for such a huge fee. "I was nervous," he admits. "I wondered how the rest of the players would react. I didn't feel nervous in running and the exercises, but once we got into 5-a-sides, I suddenly started to think how to play, as if everybody was watching what I was doing. It was like going back to St. Albans for that

The moment that launched countless thousand boots. The European Cup winner. "A goal I'd have been disappointed if I'd missed."

schools' trial. It lasted the first few days, but fortunately the Forest lads were tremendous."

There was still the public to satisfy. Francis's first full game for the first team was at Ipswich on March 3. "I think that's when the pressure really hit me," he recalls. "I didn't have a particularly memorable debut. I didn't play well and I suddenly found I was making a few mistakes, trying too hard to live up to my price tag. The crowd was obviously making it as difficult as possible, shouting 'What a waste of money'. When it's echoing around the ground it gets home to you; it's not a nice moment.

"I was given permission by Brian Clough to speak to the press, but I was that disappointed I didn't want to speak to anyone. I was heavily criticised on

the Monday for not giving interviews. Also, unknown to me, Match of the Day was analysing my every move – my passes, shots, bad shots, headers, et cetera. And I didn't come out too well on that, so the pressure got through to me.

"I felt that I'd got to try to forget that I am a million-pound player and just attempt to play my normal game. The press made it hard for me; every time I played, they suddenly didn't judge my performance within the team, they judged me on the basis of £1 million. If I played as well as the other players in the team, my rating wasn't as good because they were trying to put it on the level of a £1 million player.

"The pressure eased for about 20 seconds after I scored in the last minute against Bolton to preserve Forest's unbeaten home record. The next home match was Aston Villa. There the Villa crowd got at me during the warm-up. 'City reject' and 'What a waste of money'. I looked at Martin O'Neill and said: 'I must be having a terrible warm-up!'

"It had its nice moments, like when kids wanted to touch me. But the best moments were when Steve Daley and Andy Gray went for £1¼ million and £1½ million. From that moment, the pressure was off. I don't think the pressure on Steve and Andy was as much as on me, being the first ... but I did feel I lifted a lot of the pressure off myself when I scored the goal in the European Cup Final."

There was at once an aura of destiny, and yet fantasy, about the night of that European Cup final played in the magnificent Munich Olympic Stadium. All that had gone before, in the 15 weeks of the union of Forest and Francis, had quite deliberately denuded him of the cult image ... but now he would not be denied his stage.

Trevor Francis began the day of May 30, 1979, as a curiosity to much of the football world. He had fetched a million pounds, he had never played in a European club match, and now he was to appear in *the* final, the blue riband event for 80 per cent of the world's 22-million registered players. He had complained before that the British press and public judged his every move by the grandiosity of his price tag; now the pre-eminent European judges would do the same, and beyond them the coaches watching on television around the world.

He responded. He won the match. His performance, and not merely his winning goal, was irresistible. It was as if Roy of the Rovers, that mythical hero, had burst from the original pages of the Tiger children's magazine. Francis was continuing to write for the magazine a quite informative

TRANSFERS—THE INFLATIONARY SPIRAL

February 1905	Alf Common	Sunderland to Middlesbrough	£1,000
February 1922	Syd Puddefoot	West Ham to Falkirk	£5,000
October 1928	David Jack	Bolton to Arsenal	£10,890
June 1947	Billy Steel	Morton to Derby	£15,000
November 1947	Tommy Lawton	Chelsea to Notts County	£20,000
October 1950	Trevor Ford	Aston Villa to Sunderland	£30,000
September 1958	Albert Quixall	Sheffield Wednesday to Manchester United	£45,000
March 1960	Denis Law	Huddersfield to Manchester United	£55,000
August 1966	Alan Ball	Blackpool to Everton	£110,000
June 1968	Allan Clarke	Fulham to Leicester	£150,000
June 1969	Allan Clarke	Leicester to Leeds	£165,000
March 1970	Martin Peters	West Ham to Tottenham Hotspur	£200,000
December 1971	Alan Ball	Everton to Arsenal	£220,000
August 1972	David Nish	Leicester to Derby	£250,000
February 1974	Bob Latchford	Birmingham to Everton	£350,000
August 1977	Kenny Dalglish	Celtic to Liverpool	£440,000
February 1978	Gordon McQueen	Leeds to Manchester United	£500,000
January 1979	David Mills	Middlesbrough to West Bromwich	£516,000
February 1979	*Trevor Francis*	*Birmingham to Nottingham Forest*	*£1,150,500*
September 1979	Steve Daley	Wolverhampton to Manchester City	£1,450,277
September 1979	Andy Gray	Aston Villa to Wolverhampton	£1,562,500

OVERSEAS SALES

June 1957	John Charles	Leeds to Juventus	£67,000
June 1962	Denis Law	Torino to Manchester United	£116,000
June 1977	Kevin Keegan	Liverpool to Hamburg	£500,000
June 1979	Laurie Cunningham	West Bromwich to Real Madrid	£900,000

NOTE: In the 40 years between 1939 and 1979, football transfers multiplied 90 times. In the same period, the cost of a house in London rose from £685 to £51,250, an increase of 75 times. Thus the trafficking in human flesh only slightly outstripped the cost of inflation in bricks and mortar. However, in 1979 the transfer record was doubled by the £1-million purchase of Francis, and then raised a further 50 per cent by the Wolverhampton–Manchester City transaction.

column whilst the rest of the British media bemoaned an apparent embargo on his views.

Malmö FF, it has to be said, was a wretchedly sterile and negative opposition, but where other Nottingham players froze under the burden of being made the favourites to win in Munich, Francis (who had less right to be on the pitch than any man) emerged as a bird released into flight. His was the fastest movement on the field, the most graceful, the most free. He was not in his best position – or at least not where he likes to be – yet his performance surprised and satisfied even those at Forest who had publicly questioned whether the individual bought from Birmingham City could so swiftly accept the responsibility of playing for the team.

Strangely, Trevor Francis speaks of that triumph in Munich only when spoken to. Or is it so strange? The goal was replayed on Match of the Day every Saturday for 36 weeks, the football he created from a deep right wing position spoke volumes for itself, and the unanimous acclaim of the world's premier coaches affords no room for doubt about the accomplishment. "So much has been said and written about my performance," he says openly, "that I'm happy to leave it at that. I felt, anyway, that the goal was one I ought to have scored; I'd have been disappointed to have missed it, and I remember some of the other moves with as much pleasure, if not more."

Helmut Schön of West Germany, Cesar Menotti of Argentina, Enzo Bearzot of Italy, Ron Greenwood of England ... any one of them will testify to the effectiveness of Francis as an international performer, and a team player, on the evidence of that night. Francis, however, would settle for the after-match quotes from the two managers:

Brian Clough of Forest: "John Robertson's cross was perfect and when it reached Trevor Francis it meant we had a talented lad on the end of it. Trevor was the best player on the pitch. It was his first European match at club level and he handled it superbly. He showed great pace, good control and good vision. He looked well worth £200,000!"

Bob Houghton of Malmö: "If a Forest player had to win this game, I'm pleased it was Trevor Francis. He must have been under enormous pressure, but he showed how good he is in the first half: three strikes on goal, three hits on target. He was the best player on the pitch."

Yet Trevor did not even register the moment, the single word of praise he would have cherished most on that night of nights. "We were waiting outside the dressing room after the match in Munich," says Roy Francis. "When he came out, I shook his hand and told him: 'Brilliant'. I couldn't say more." As he looks back on it, Roy Francis's mouth curls into that shy, almost elfin smile his son uses so often.

Brilliant. It was the word both of them knew Trevor had always wanted to hear from his Dad. But when it came, he did not even hear it; he is surprised, now, to be told it was actually said. "Yes?" he says with an expression of total disbelief.

"I'll tell you why," says Phyllis Francis, his mother. "It's because our Trevor was looking at his medal when he came out ... ooh, it was lovely to see his face, the best moment I've known. He came across and said: 'I can't let you have it now Mum, I want to take it straight home. But I'll bring it down to Plymouth, so you can show my aunts and uncles.'"

Roy and Phyllis Francis offer clearer memories of the night than Trevor will. "We were late getting there," says Roy, "and Trevor had left the tickets with a friend. We didn't see him till he walked out on the field. He looked tired, as if he hadn't slept, but as soon as I saw Trev I knew it would be all right. He wanted to go, he was in the mood. I had seen young Tony Woodcock in the corridor before the match; he looked like he was shaking with fear, but when Trevor had spoken to his Mum the night before he just said he felt that tired. He said that was a good sign. She couldn't make it out." Trevor confirms it; he did feel tired, but not really nervous, sort of serene and ready.

"Before we left Trevor that night, you know what we did?" asks Phyllis Francis. "We went out on the pitch, about five or six of us. A security guard let us on, and we just stood in the goalmouth. Then, coming home, the purser on the boat couldn't believe we were Trevor's Mum and Dad. When he did believe it, he gave me a beautiful box of Swiss chocolates ... You know, I sometimes think if it wasn't for Trevor's profession, I don't believe we'd ever have seen how the rest of the world lives."

The professional performance of their son that night had two delayed-action spin-offs, one personal and the other highly commercial. The personal moment happened at Trevor's Warwickshire home and is told by his mate Jeff Lynne. "I can tell you how much this European Cup medal means to Trevor," he says. "I came rushing round here, thinking, 'Oh great, I've got to have a look at this.' He comes down, and it's like a really big production. He's at the doorway with this box – and I'm really looking forward to it – he hands it to me, and I open it up ... and inside there's this broken crisp! An old potato crisp. Anyway, he got the medal out in the end, tossed it over from about 10 feet away. I think he was getting used to it by then, he'd had it for about a week."

When he recovers from the hysterics the memory brings on, Trevor says, suddenly serious: "I didn't do that to Jeff because I was underplaying the thing. I think so much of that medal I've hidden it away."

The second direct but delayed result was strictly commercial. "The European Final convinced not only football coaches but also advertising people that here was a world talent," says Dennis Roach, his business agent. "We became inundated with all sorts of offers. American companies, European companies ... suddenly they all wanted to know. Adidas (the giant German sportswear manufacturers) jumped in to offer him their No. 1 football equipment merchandising role to replace Beckenbauer and Müller. They'd been offered him for two months previously by their English people, but they were hesitating. They didn't realise who he was; it didn't mean much that he'd been scoring goals to keep

Birmingham in the First Division. Now they're marketing three Trevor Francis boots with his name on around the world on a royalty basis."

For how long, you may ask, does the danger exist of even a sensible player resting on his laurels in reflection of that peak performance? "It's not even a problem," answers Francis. "I want to be part of a team that wins things. I shan't be happy until Forest win the League, League Cup and FA Cup. Then there's Europe again and things to try to win with England. Football isn't just one day or one medal. You have to keep on achieving things. It's like I said about goals: the more you score, the hungrier you get. It doesn't end with the first."

Yet the first medal had come so swiftly, in just four months and 20 games with Nottingham, he might have been overwhelmed by it. No chance. The euphoria of Munich began to evaporate the very next day, as the team flew home. In one section of the plane Francis was being put on a pedestal by the national newspaper photographers; in another their reporters were writing up comments by Peter Taylor on which to pin the most derogatory headlines of the player's career.

Thus, when *The Sun* came next morning, it was topped by a banner headline "*CAPTAIN MAR-VEL!*" beneath which was a pose of Francis with a pilot's cap on his head and the European Cup in his lap. And next to that, a side heading declared "But Trev was 'just a disgrace' when he arrived."

The story was no exclusive. Taylor's comments echoed throughout Fleet Street, though there were more versions of what he actually said than camera angles of Francis with the trophy. Francis chose, as usual, to suppress any offence he felt, but supposing he had wanted to confront his bosses, which paper should he have tucked under his arm?

The contradictions defy a definitive version, but here is a summary of what Taylor said in the majority of reports:

> "In a footballing sense, we've made a man out of him. When he was at Birmingham, Brian and I thought he was a disgrace to his profession. They called him a superstar and he wasn't even a player. Trevor would not have become an England regular in a million years at Birmingham. Once we've finished with him England will have an asset for years. We've not finished polishing the product yet.
>
> "But we have sharpened him up. When he came to us and got his first rollicking, he looked at us as if to say 'But I'm Trevor Francis'. He thought he had a stamina problem. We've got rid of that nonsense. Now he actually heads the ball and gets back to challenge people.
>
> "We bought potential. We knew all about his pace and control, that's why we paid a fortune for him. It was something to work on, something to build on."

Francis, who was to join the England squad as a substitute for the game in Bulgaria a few days later, said on the plane from Munich: "I didn't do anything much different against Malmö than what I used to do for Birmingham. The difference was having the right stage to do it on." He added that playing in midfield for Forest increased his awareness (as it had in his early Birmingham days).

Birmingham City's response to Taylor was less cautious. "Those remarks are a slur on me and my predecessors," said manager Jim Smith. "They are completely untrue and for Taylor to suggest they paid £1 million for potential is ludicrous and right out of order."

From a neutral corner, Hugh McIlvanney, The Observer's respected correspondent, wrote: "With his head and his game in such disarray, how the hell did Francis ever manage to score all those goals for a Birmingham side that was often abysmal during his time there? And, if a footballer's standards can be raised so dramatically in four months, why didn't more of the Forest players, all those who have been around the club for years, perform as well as young Francis did on Wednesday night?"

Subsequently, sharing with Sir Alf Ramsey a paid interview spread in the *News of the World*, Taylor reiterated some of his views on the improved Trevor Francis. Although the main headline read "Francis – the £1 million headache", and although a provocative second headline was "Why we'll knock spots off Trevor", Taylor's reasoning proved far more restrained and favourable to Francis.

Later, Brian Clough and Peter Taylor gave us considerable time to discuss things. Moreover, they did so expansively on a day of a League Cup replay which became complicated by a proposed £600,000 transfer of Brighton's Peter Ward. For lunch, Cloughie was reduced to a brandy or two; Taylor to nothing.

Clough's taste is as refined in brandy and holidays as it is in players. He himself had not returned with the team after Munich, travelling instead to rejoin his wife and children in Crete. But he says he would have endorsed Taylor's comments, though "possibly it came out better second time around. The first was an instant few words in Munich and, y'know, we don't get to European Cup Finals very often."

In Taylor's office, the mood is cautious at first, as if he is parrying shots like the goalkeeper he once was. "Tell me what I did say," he challenges. "Yes,

---

A pain in the . . . for Trevor from Bolton's David Burke.

The Pay-Off

yes . . . still stand by that. What's more important to me is what I said, rather than the way I phrased things which probably hurt Trevor's pride. We're not blessed here with picking our words, y'know. It's content. I'm more delighted that Trevor's been a happy member of our staff – which I know he is – than him being slightly annoyed by how things come out.

"Our attitude to Trevor Francis is no different to the others, including Garry Birtles who cost £2,000 from Burton Albion. Ask Trevor, ask any of the others. If we have to bawl out Peter Shilton because of something he's done wrong, we do it. Nobody's too special here. I was wary of people thinking that, having paid a million, we'd got the finished product; we hadn't at all. All we'd bought was brilliance on the field, and everything we did was blown up in public because of the £1 million tag."

Peter Taylor says he and Clough had always felt Trevor's publicity had gone ahead of his achievements. He accepts words like derogatory and hurtful about his Munich statements, and says: "Blow me, they weren't accusations. No, I felt, having signed him and lived with him for a period I was in a position to comment.

"I felt he was a young 25 mentally. I saw him not totally committed to the game, I saw him having too many outside interests. I saw his phone on tap to all and sundry – you people, the press, agents, businessmen. There was too much selling of Trevor Francis and I had to tell him politely that wasn't worth a bean unless he produced the goods out there. We didn't want to stop his commercial activities, but we wanted to channel them and get the very best out of him because we looked at his record and there wasn't a lot to show for a player we were reading about daily. There wasn't a medal."

Trevor admits he felt uneasy at the start of the relationship, as if Taylor was needling him, trying to find faults with his lifestyle that didn't exist. "Exactly right," says Taylor. "We thought, on the evidence we had, the character was right when we signed him, but you can't be sure till you've lived with somebody. You look for the flaws. After five or six weeks, I knew he'd turned out to be far superior – as a character – to anything we could have anticipated. I could see then we were onto a bigger winner than we'd thought, even having paid a million."

Clough and Taylor were out of sight and earshot during Francis's American summer, though not entirely out of mind. The only communication was a cryptic telex asking when they might expect their

player back, but the irony of the Francis situation – shepherded away from the media in England and thrust towards it in the States – was piquantly observed by Freddie Goodwin, his first manager. "In some respects this is Birmingham all over again," said Goodwin. "There the individual had grown bigger than the team. It was the best thing that could have happened for Birmingham and for Trevor when he left.

"The only place for him was a really good club, like Liverpool, or like Forest where Cloughie is the dominant force. But I'm sure Trevor will respond to Clough. Now he is having to adjust himself to the needs of the team he will benefit from Forest's discipline – I'm positive."

Trevor doesn't argue about the position at Birmingham, although he insists: "It was no fault of mine if that happened. You have to look at the managerial situation and remember I had been fined more than once for saying to the press that I hoped Birmingham would sign good players. I wanted to play in a better *team*."

At Forest, he was undoubtedly in a better team, but as Clough had warned, he had not fallen into any bed of roses. Maybe Francis felt he had made the ultimate gesture in forsaking his final two years of the Detroit contract. It did not save him the wrath of Clough when he arrived home from the States with a groin injury. Another field day for the headline writers – "Tough Clough! £1,000-a-week Francis warned: No play, no pay." "Francis pay freeze – Clough orders: No wages for the £1m man."

The salary was newspaper conjecture. "I'm not correcting it, either," says Francis. "I don't feel it is anybody's business." He then jokes: "Not that it bothered me, they only mentioned the tax anyway." Clough, however, was perfectly serious when he announced that Francis had arrived back from Detroit with a groin strain and would not be paid until he was fit to play for Forest.

The circumstance developed into such a full-scale row, that at one time it appeared the only people not arguing were Clough and Francis. "Being Honest Joe, I'd told Brian Clough straight away about the injury and where I got it," admits Francis. "Others would have said nothing, played on it, and had to come off. I played into his hands but that's the way I am. I would only have been doing the lads and myself an injustice by trying to cover it up."

When he told Clough, the manager immediately replied he was stopping the wages. "I laughed," recalls Trevor, "then he laughed. Then he said:

144

'Hey, son – I mean it!' To be honest, I came out of the office not knowing whether he did or didn't. Then I read the papers and a couple of days later Peter Taylor said to me: 'Brian should never have said that . . . he can't do it anyway.'"

Meanwhile, it festered in public. The Professional Footballers' Association made contradictory statements that it was a breach of contract, that Clough knew Trevor was going to the States when he signed, that Detroit should be responsible for any lost wages. Detroit coach Ken Furphy answered in a radio interview: "Our legal obligation ended the moment we were out of the play-offs, which was 3 o'clock on Sunday. By 5 o'clock, Trevor was aboard Concorde, that's how eager he was to get back and play for Forest. Frankly, it's not as serious as it sounds."

Clough's retort to that is unprintable, but a Sunday newspaper drew one conclusion by phoning Detroit to try to suggest that maybe the injury was bogus, maybe it was Cloughie's way of getting rid of Francis? Detroit didn't bite on the suggestion.

Nothing, literally not one word more, has passed between player and manager about those wages since then. It festered in the press, through comments from Clough such as "We've 13 games under our belts here; Trevor's only got a money belt". But by last February, with Forest committed to the hilt with League, League Cup, European Super Cup and FA Cup games to play, Francis was getting by with the help of the odd shot of cortisone into the groin. And the "missed" wages? His accountant was chasing up the *insurance*. Yes, the player was insured against injury in the States.

Clough looks back on the affair and says: "It's no secret that that young man went to America for money. He didn't hide it, we don't hide it and all that type of thing. And it's no secret also that I was incensed because he came back injured. And I was even more incensed when I found out he actually got the injury in the first few weeks of going over there!

"Being such a nice lad – and he is, y'know – and feeling morally obliged, I'm certain he wanted to earn his 60 or 70 thousand quid, whatever it was he was getting. He hid the injury, played on . . . and *I* had to carry the can because he came back to me injured. There was no way he could play for me. It wasn't a case of my standards being higher than the Americans – that young man came back so injured that at one stage it reached the low ebb of morale of him asking me if I'd mind if he got a second opinion.

"Second opinion! We never take second bloody opinions on anything in this club because we employ experts in every field. We were quite happy with the treatment he was getting; over the moon with our specialist and our club doctor."

Clough agrees that it is a dangerous and difficult task for a manager to decide when to try to "talk" a player through an injury. "Or the other way around," he warns. "I had that experience in the European Cup Final. We'd had Archie Gemmill injured since the semi-final, and Martin O'Neill injured several weeks before the final. We sat around the perimeter of the Munich stadium, and I'd got three players injured. I'd got Frank Clark, Archie Gemmill and Martin O'Neill.

"We went round them individually, Peter and I, asking are you fit? And everyone said they were. People might think it's a stupid question to ask, because nobody's going to say he's *unfit* for a European Cup Final. Nevertheless, we went through the formality. I then had the job of saying to Martin O'Neill: 'I don't believe you're fit. Even if your injury has healed, you're certainly not mentally match fit.' And I had to say that also to Archie Gemmill.

"I made the other decision with Frank Clark. I said: 'Frank, you are playing'. Fortunately he got through the full match remarkably well. So I was right on him, I was right on Martin because within a few days of getting back he had to go off injured in an international match. The doubt, obviously, was with Arch. I felt sure he wasn't match fit, even if his groin was better, but Archie never forgave me for not playing him. That decision had to be mine, nobody else could make it . . . so you see, it's an extremely difficult problem, and not only with a million-pound player."

That Munich fitness "test" is the more significant viewed against Clough's BBC television comment that "Francis won a medal by fluke". It is one of the few statements that did upset Francis; it hurt and surprised him where much else dropped like blarney off the stone. Yet Clough insists: "I told Trevor – and I *meant* it – there's no way he'd have played in a European Cup Final if we'd had a full side. Having sat on his arse and watched us battle away in bloody Cologne and Liverpool and Athens . . . that would be going against my absolute first rule of picking the best side. No, he would not have played if Martin and Arch had been fit."

As it was, O'Neill and Gemmill were on the substitutes' bench in Munich. Now there is nothing so vulnerable in sport as an injured athlete. He is like a eunuch. His weeks are held together by matchdays and intelligence offers no insulation to the deprivation of being sidelined. Clough, having had his own career stunted in his prime because of a knee injury, knows this better than most. The loss is still with him and, although it is seldom part of the image that comes across, Brian Clough's warm encouragement to a player cut from the action is at least equal to the provocative printed judgment.

Indeed, there were times during Francis's six weeks' absence with that groin strain that the very moments of Clough's understanding were so totally misinterpreted in the media that one wonders why the manager, with his experience, left the damaging flow unstemmed. The answer, he says, is that if he ever started to try to correct every version of every story printed about him or his club "the floodgates would open and I don't know where it would stop. In fact it wouldn't. I'd be talking to your lot all the time. And I've a job to do, a very difficult and demanding job of work."

The trouble is, silence merely encourages speculation. At a time neither Clough nor Francis was meeting the press, journalists were under pressure to write something – anything – about the £1 million man's return from Detroit. And when one piece of guesswork went unchallenged, the wrong conclusions were drawn.

When, for example, Clough and Francis were seen in intense conversation outside the Forest dressing room after having to sit out another match, against Coventry, the printed word was that there had been a "clash", a "feud", and that Francis might soon be on his way out of Forest.

"What a load of nonsense that was," says Helen Francis. Clough privately dismissed the report as typical rubbish, Trevor Francis thought it laughable but sometimes it takes a woman to read the danger signals. "Do you know what Brian was telling Trev after that game?" she asks. "He was concerned that Trev was trying too soon after the specialist had said he must rest. 'I don't care how long it takes,' he was saying. 'Get it absolutely right before you play on it. There's at least 60 games to go over a season. *I'd* far rather we clear the injury up completely and get you properly fit than make things worse by playing on it now. We don't want a thing like that fellow at Derby.'" (The last remark a reference to Roy McFarland who never recovered completely after a torn Achilles tendon.)

The rest of the conversation concerned Clough's usual questioning of Francis about Helen's health. "How's that baby? Is it kicking yet? Tell her I was asking after her ... don't forget. And young man, you like cricket don't you? Get sat down and watch

the television. Take Helen out for a walk, take it easy. Don't get driving over here for treatment tomorrow ... rest is what you need."

The very nature of the groin strain perplexed and exasperated Francis and all around him. "One day it hurt so much I could hardly play at all," he says. "The next I could play five-a-side without much pain and then, just as I'd think it was going well, it suddenly started to hurt so much I could hardly walk. It hurt in three places at the top and side of the groin, and I suppose looking back people might have seen me looking depressed and thinking I was fed up for other reasons. But when they were insinuating I was fit, I just wished they could have called on our club doctor or physiotherapist. We'd tried cortisone injections, resting, playing through the pain, heat treatment ... nothing seemed to work.

"Brian Clough was coming up to me the whole time, asking how it felt. The one good thing was that it taught me a lot about Brian Clough and Peter Taylor and how they feel towards me. They wanted me to play. After one match at Bristol, the boss phoned me at home and he was on for 20 minutes, encouraging me and saying there were so many chances I'd have scored a hat-trick on one leg. He used the word genius and he and Taylor couldn't have been nicer. It was almost worth all the bother when the boss came over to me after stories had been

The non-aggressive Francis creates an illusion of determination.

receive the honour (particularly since Adidas had designs on his marketing value). He travelled with the club chairman and secretary.

Meanwhile, at their home in Warwickshire, Helen Francis received a huge bouquet of flowers with a card which read: "Thanks for the loan of your husband for two days to stand in for me. Hope you are well, love Brian."

That, says Helen, was typical of Brian Clough. "Right from the beginning, he's been so nice to us, and always the same," says Helen. "My friends and even family would read things in the paper and assume he didn't get on with Trev, but as far as we were concerned he was a man we took to, an honest man who proves all the time that he cares about people and not just players." There were occasions when Helen would drive to the City Ground and wait in the car for Trevor so they could go out house-hunting. And Clough would not have her sitting there alone.

"Hey, kid, you're looking radiant. How's those twins, still kicking?" he would say and then insist that she waited in his office, used his telephone for privacy rather than the corridor phone. "Mind you," she laughs, "*he* was listening. I was fixing up to view one house and he said it sounded lovely, if we didn't take it he might. And he told Trev once: 'My daughter is 12, but if she has got to go out in life one day to wed, I would *hope* she finds someone as pleasant as you.'"

So which is the true Cloughie – the authoritarian who forbids his players to pass the time of day with a journalist, or the warm family friend? Jekyll or Hyde? "Hey, I'm riding under a façade of being a bully. I will bully if there's a need to do it, but really I'm a reasonable bloke trying to do a job."

Is part of that job to withdraw a man's freedom of speech? The whole football world is convinced that Francis is gagged to such an extent that Kevin Keegan has referred to it as an "East German" type of insult to a player's intelligence, lowering his dignity; and Ray Wilkins has said: "I'm sorry for Trevor Francis. Freedom of speech is one of our fundamental rights in a free country, isn't it?" Even George Best, hopping over from the States, commented in a newspaper column that he felt Francis's "fine for saying no comment" treated the player with contempt.

The press gag on Francis was not all it appeared. It is true that the player was told to make his telephone ex-directory and to abandon a system he once had where his calls were intercepted by the operator who then rang to ask if he wished to take

bandied about that he was going to sell me. 'You know what I think of you as a player – I think of you like I think of Peter Shilton as a goalkeeper. I've spent eight bloody years chasing you, you'll not be leaving Nottingham Forest Football Club while I'm manager here.'"

Eventually, after an erroneous article claiming Francis had been fined £50 for saying no comment to a reporter, and after the inevitable back page flyer that Clough was preparing to get rid of the £1 million man, a press conference was called at which Taylor and Francis attempted to dispel all the rumours of disharmony. "There has never been a moment since I came to Forest that I have regretted the move," said Francis.

Four days after that conference, two newspapers carried the story of "Francis, the £1m messenger boy", sent by Clough to Paris to collect the European Team of the Year Award to Forest at the France Football–Adidas Golden Shoe Awards. The simple truth of it was that Brian Clough and Peter Taylor were with the team for a League Cup game in Middlesbrough; Francis, as the European Cup matchwinner and a player ruled out of training through injury, seemed the logical person to *ask* to them. By that time, Clough asserts, the player is already disturbed, the "freedom" everyone talks about is ruined for a £1 million star by the continual interruptions.

"Trevor didn't have the ability to say no," says Brian Clough. "And if he did refuse a phone call, being a reasonable young man and a nice young man, he'd spend half the night worrying about letting the journalist down. Because he's got a job of work to do as well, the journalist, y'know. So he might as well have taken the call in the first place."

Clough insists that no-one, not himself and certainly not an athlete, could possibly be on call to the demands of the media all the time and turn up fresh for work. But there are times when Francis tells the press: "Sorry, I'm not allowed to say anything, the boss won't let me." Isn't that a denial of a human right?

"Look," says Clough, "I do tell players to say no. There are very few people who are brave enough to say no sometimes; most of us say yes. Trevor Francis in particular is a young man who finds it hard to say no, so I've given him my back, Pete (Taylor) has given him his back, to lean on till such time as he can stand on his own two feet and say no. I've said use me as the excuse, let me appear the villain of the piece, but say bloody *no*.

"We do that for all the players. I understand that every sports journalist in the country – and not just this country either, in Europe he's absolutely top priority – wants to talk to the man who cost a million quid. It's the most natural thing in the world. All I want to do is confine the areas while we're working. I want him to be able to leave this ground and know that his work's finished, and to go home and lead as normal a life as we all try to lead. And then get in this bloody ground in the morning and be totally prepared to work. I don't want players coming in and saying 'Oh, I'm up to there with it . . . all the pressure.' I'm as keen as the next man on so-called rights, but one of those is to do a job without being drained of energy before you start."

The system at Forest is not a total ban. Players are told to inform the management if they are requested to do an interview or a television show that appeals to them. In Francis's case these were few and far between. When it mattered to him, he was allowed to make appearances or give newspaper interviews and, moreover, Clough at no time objected to any business or advertising venture put forward by his agent.

But there was yet one more element to the press relations over Francis. Several national journalists

began goading Francis to respond to some of the unkind statements by Clough and Taylor – was he a man or was he not? "The truth was," says Francis, "that the things that were being reported bothered journalists more than they did me. They were annoyed because they couldn't speak to me. As for my image, I did feel once or twice that it had been somwhat tarnished in the newspapers, but I also came to the conclusion that I couldn't fight it. Whatever I might have said, they would only come back stronger.

"I was in a bad position anyway because I had come back from America, where it's true I did earn a great deal of money, with an injury. I understood people being annoyed about that. I just didn't see what more I could do about it than say I would not, for the time being, contemplate going again. I made that sacrifice, and I only hope that I'd built myself a reasonable image over nine or ten years that people would not read too deeply into the headlines at the time."

In saying that, Francis is aware that the more publicity a person gets, the more commercial he becomes, the more some people will construe misleading ideas. He had seen it with Jeff Lynne, whose rise to the top was buoyed up with superb press and public encouragement and, who now he is there, finds that some of the same people never have a good word to say for him. The higher you get, the more shots people will take at you.

However, where Francis admits he does tend to jump to the Forest managerial orders, is on the field. "We're *all* conscious of the dugout," he admits. "After a move breaks down, you'll be walking back to the halfway line and suddenly a voice from the dugout makes you break into a sprint to get back into position. They expect so much, and it gets through to you when you're playing."

His master's voice bellowing from the dugout . . . could that be the carrier of the *fear* so many outsiders assume makes Forest run like men possessed? Francis smiles thinly at a well-worn suggestion. "The talk of fear is completely wrong," he asserts. "There's so much flair produced by the team, it would never come out if players were afraid to express themselves. The only thing we're frightened of is giving less than 100 per cent."

Furthermore, the flow of expression is encouraged by preparations more relaxed than any Francis had experienced elsewhere. "For example," he explains, "we often have a glass or two of wine, or even champagne, the night before a game – sometimes on the day itself. When we played at Liverpool in the

League Cup we had six bottles of Chablis on the table at 12.30 pm, and by 9.15 pm we were celebrating another appearance in the League Cup Final. And the night before the European Cup Final in Munich some players had three or four glasses.''

Who was counting? Certainly not Clough and Taylor. ''They put complete trust in the players as professionals,'' says Francis. ''I went through a period at Birmingham where Freddie Goodwin sent the trainer round knocking on hotel doors to tell us to switch televisions off at 11 o'clock the night before a match. There's never been anything like that here.

''The amount of time we get off at Forest is another example of trust,'' adds Francis. ''It's not unusual for us to train for an hour on Monday, play a game on Tuesday, have Wednesday and Thursday off, and do an hour on Friday. I feel some managers are reluctant to give days off either because they don't trust players to be sensible, or they think they are paying them so well they should be seen at the training ground.''

It is well known within football that Clough and Taylor themselves are not too often seen at training. Jimmy Gordon, their faithful old trainer, had the job of ensuring that players are fit enough, but not overworked in view of the demands of 70 or more matches and fatiguing travel successful sides experience in a season. When the bosses are seen at training, however, the players are on their toes.

And bosses is the right term. ''Peter Taylor has exactly the same authority on all matters as Brian Clough,'' says Francis. ''The only difference is we call Taylor, Pete, and Clough, boss.'' But what is the pre-match chemistry, the great motivational factor with which the pair bless their teams? ''Players often ask me that,'' says Francis, ''and I think they feel I'm being secretive when I say we often don't see the managers until 2.45 when they enter the dressing room.

''Sometimes Pete takes the team meeting alone, more often they are together. But we rarely discuss the opposition, and never go into it in depth. We don't complicate things, we have no set routines with dead-ball situations. The majority of our play is off the cuff ... if we feel there's something on, say a short corner, or a free kick, maybe Frank Gray or myself will have a direct shot at goal or John Robertson may fancy a bender if the wall's not properly set.''

An observer watching Clough and Taylor in the dugout might sense that they are right to keep pre-match ritual to a minimum, to lessen the impact of managerial neurosis on the team. From the bench,

however, comes a constant tirade of communication; Clough the more vocal and Taylor gesticulating. ''Mainly,'' says Francis, ''they'll hammer us if we fail to exploit situations, say a two-against-one advantage. After the match, we all know that the managers might criticise players in the press, but they have the ability to put their arm around the player next morning and have a laugh and joke. They seem to be able to do this with everyone, not just myself.''

After Francis had been even temporarily cut off from this through injury, you could see when the jauntiness was returning to his stride, sense when Helen's life and his family and friends' lives were all going to move out of the depression. Six weeks is a short enough period, but every day had seemingly been illuminated by one rumour or another, by one pressure on top of the other.

Last autumn, following the groin strain in America, the morning of the match against Wolves, the comeback, arrived. There was a note of urgency as well as apprehension in his voice that morning. It was his first English League game since Munich, and he admitted: ''I'm more nervous than I was before that game in Munich. It's like starting all over again. It isn't all the criticism I've been getting, because that wasn't the truth. But it's very strange, as if I'm making my debut. I'm telling myself that the main thing is to get through the 90 minutes, but I'm hoping for something more than that.''

He didn't hear, as he walked into the dressing room, a spectator catch the mood of the day: ''If Francis doesn't play well, Cloughie'll have his guts.'' Clough in fact was feeling and saying ''Despite Francis's talent, he will need help. We are flying in a few yards of Astroturf to make him feel at home and if he gets an assist we will flash it up on the scoreboard. And he can have a hamburger at half-time if he wants it.''

Despite the banter, Clough knew the strain on his player. ''Hey, my mate,'' he called in the dressing room, ''just concentrate on getting in a few shots.'' The trace of uncertainty was visible in his mate's stride as he took to the field, but the Nottingham crowd, not noted for its vociferous activity, at once welcomed him with choruses of ''One Trevor Francis, there's only one Trevor Francis ...''

''Brilliant, that was,'' said Trevor afterwards. The start of the match was neither brilliant nor ordinary. But it was memorable, as Shilton saved from Andy Gray in 30 seconds and from Willie Carr after 62 seconds. Direct from the corner, Nottingham broke down the left and John Robertson's

thrusting centre struck Francis on the chest to ricochet into the net. Time: 1 min 31 sec, his first touch of the season.

For an instant Trevor looked in absolute disbelief. Then the reaction triggered through his body. He ran towards Robbo, right arm raised in salute. He looked embarrassed, surprised ... relieved. Later someone told him it had been a brilliant header, just like the one in Munich. Francis grinned. He didn't spoil their vision, but later he said: "I was just glad to be there. It happened so fast I knew it had struck my chest, but I didn't have time to direct it. Still, as Peter Taylor said in the dressing room: They can say it was a fluke but it counted on the scoresheet."

It counted deeper down, too. It lifted something off the burdens of the comeback, it helped him continue to want the ball even when he felt weary. "I was gasping for a time," Francis admits, "but I never felt I wanted to come off and the boss told me afterwards he could see I was knackered but if he had taken me off the press would be on my back.

Anyway, towards the end I was feeling stronger, really thinking I was through the worst at last."

There was a sense that some pressure had diminished for his manager, too, now the player was restored. Clough was quoted afterwards as saying "If everybody on the Forest staff was so concerned about the club's affairs as Francis is we would win everything in sight."

Certainly the first 12 months in Forest red won more for Trevor Francis than the entire nine years in Birmingham blue. The anniversary of his transfer was celebrated in victory over Barcelona, which added the European Super Cup to the 1979 Champions' Cup. There was pain, however, in the satisfaction of that night; Trevor had begun to run at Barcelona from deep positions as effectively as he had against Malmö nine months previously, when the usually constructive former Spanish national captain Juan Manuel Asensi buried his studs into Francis's shin.

That Spanish thrust required six stitches, includ-

Forest players are always conscious of the bench. A voice rings out . . . they move.

---

ing two deep sutures into a damaged ligament. Yet a fortnight later, this time in a forward role against Manchester City, Francis claimed his first hat-trick in Nottingham colours.

Francis was, in effect, responding in the only way a player could, to the challenge (both public and private) from Peter Taylor to "prove me wrong – show me you can turn a defender the way, say, Tony Woodcock did for us." Throughout the year, Nottingham had never resolved Francis's true position, alternating frequently between striker and midfield. He began the 1980 League Cup Final in midfield and was blamed for defeat. Four days later, released to attack, he rescued Forest's European life against Dynamo Berlin, scoring first with a brave, sharp thrust and later with a brilliant turn and an emphatic shot beneath the crossbar. A clinical response to management.

Brian Clough said at the start that he hoped Nottingham Forest would prove the most important years in that young man's life . . . "and I'm not just on about what he will achieve footballwise."

He recognises that Trevor Francis's make-up contains a degree of sensitivity, that this quality is part of what makes him a player apart. But is there a danger of bending the player to too much conformity, a danger of driving out the sensitivity and with it the touch and vision?

"We won't eliminate the sensitivity of any human being," asserts Clough, "because we think sensitivity is part and parcel of the make-up of a human being. I don't want to dismiss it as far as Trevor is concerned. And I hope I don't knock it out of him. But I do want him to curb it, because you can't go through life, let alone be a superstar as he wants to be, without taking what comes along with it also.

"If he wants the billing, then he's got to take the straight talking as well, and he's had more of that in a year at Forest than he's had in six years before that. I swear to you, by the end of his three year contract you will see a mature man for a start. A *man*. That's what we're all aiming for, being bloody men in life. In three years time we'll have cracked it to such an extent that if Trevor Francis decides then to finish his contract here and go somewhere else, he'll go out there with his shoulders a bit straighter. He'll face the world with a bit more direction in his eyes, because in actual fact we're hoping to educate him in life not just football."

However, since Brian Clough himself says that part of the package he and Peter Taylor ventured a million pounds of Forest's money on was the good character of Trevor Francis, isn't he afraid that he might knock something out of the player, something that is particularly nice?

"No, no . . . I'll enlarge what he's got. In all areas. I'll do it by a bit of encouragement, bullying, cajoling, teaching, opening his eyes. Isn't that what we all got at school? Players are not treated like gods here, they're flesh and blood like most of us trying to earn a few bob. They must never stop learning their craft, and I sometimes think Trevor hasn't learnt his. I genuinely feel he looks a little bewildered on occasions when I'm talking to him.

"But it's up to him to listen to people, to me talking to him. He's got to assess whether I'm talking sense, he's got to reject the rubbish and so on. And at the end of the day, if I've got even some of it right, he ought to finish up the better for it . . . Hey, that would be some player, wouldn't it, if we could improve on *him*?"

9 ASPECTS OF SUCCESS

If fulfilment is a glass cabinet brimful with England caps, a contented home, and a lifestyle enriched by the trappings of success . . . then Trevor John Francis is there already. Yet so much more has always been demanded of him, *will* always be demanded until he and his country actually win something together. And that, in a way, was where Francis came in.

He was the hub of two apparently vintage young England sides which won the European Youth Tournament, the so-called Little World Cup, in Prague at the end of May 1971 and again in Barcelona the following spring. Trevor was then a teenager so slender you feared he was a sapling that might bend in the wind or be broken by the ferocity of tackles hurtling towards him, from eastern Europeans especially. He did neither. And on a parched and dusty Spanish evening in 1972, it took a foreigner to translate into words the hope that ought to have matured into success for English football.

"You have now the boys who will be most difficult to beat in the world after Munich in 1974," observed Yugoslav youth coach Vasa Stojkovic. "This No. 8, he is your special player, no? Give me this boy, give me perhaps five of your strong, disciplined team, and I think in six years I build world class team."

History shows that six years later England was in the confused hands of Don Revie, failing to qualify for the World Cup, as it had the European Championship finals. Francis, the "special" player, was never nearer than the fringe even of that failure. He was the 49th player fielded by Revie in the manager's 22nd international, too late to be influential.

It was 1979 before Ron Greenwood, Revie's successor, granted Francis a sustained run; 1979 when, following his transfer and his winning European Cup Final display, Trevor Francis, the international at last, justified Yugoslavian impressions of his potential. True his achievement was against Northern Ireland, but it was in Belfast and it did transcend every other English player's on the day. His two goals were, whether he accepts comparisons or not, reminiscent of Jimmy Greaves, and his searing pace, his vision in creating two other goals in the 5–1 victory, were acclaimed as the qualities essential to English aspirations for the 1980 European Championships and 1982 World Cup.

Why, oh why was it so long in coming? The answer is a compound reflection of the ills of English football in the Seventies: of the lack of continuity between youth and full international level and the preference for work-rate over flair. In Francis's own case, the backlash of pulls and strains which were legacies of the stress pumped through immature muscles at 16 and 17, strains which surfaced with sad regularity when Revie initially selected him.

In fact, Francis was a jaded youngster when Stojkovic laid eyes on him. He journeyed to Spain with the wear and tear of Birmingham's promotion struggle in his bones, and it was Stojkovic's own national boss, Miljan Miljanic, who astutely observed he would rather play England in May, when the tired players are shadows, than autumn when they are lions.

Not that we can take precocity as a good recommendation in football. Only Liverpool defender Phil Thompson established a permanent international future out of that 1972 youth side, whilst the 104 England international schoolboys between 1964–70 produced one permanent face, Peter Shilton – and only another three – Dave Thomas, Tony Towers and Steve Whitworth – who achieved full honours. And remember Kevin Griffin, the boy who outscored Francis at school and who then frittered away in Bristol City reserves? A similar fate befell Derek Forster, whose goalkeeping debut for Sunderland in 1964 made him the youngest post-war League player at 15 years and 185 days, but whose career disappeared as he waited seven years in the shadow of goalkeeper Jim Montgomery's record 537 games.

Yet, says Francis, "I have always believed if you are good enough, you will get the opportunity. It's just that some players at 15 are already as good as they ever will be, while I for example improved so much between leaving school and 18."

Sir Alf Ramsey, before he was sacked as England manager and before of course he joined Birmingham City, had shown clear indications of his awareness of the blossoming Francis talent when, in April 1973, Trevor played, scored twice and enjoyed a 9–0 win for an English FA side in Gibraltar. Small beginnings, perhaps, but Trevor was a week off his 19th birthday and it was Sir Alf who had given him the first of five Under-23 caps.

However, Francis was to fret almost four years more to graduate to full honours, despite the Birmingham clamour, despite Don Revie's quarter-million pound offer to buy Trevor as a 16-year-old for Leeds, and despite the fact that Paul Madeley, Revie's man at Leeds and England, openly regarded Francis as the most difficult opponent he had faced. Revie had chosen Francis in his first England squad in 1974 when that knee tendon deprived both of the

• That's one in the eye for the one-man-team critics •

ENGLAND manager Ron Greenwood professed himself 'delighted' with his five-goal team yesterday and he added:

'That's certainly one in the eye for the critics who have been saying we're a one-man team' that man being Kevin Keegan. Kevin had a quiet game this time but we showed we had plenty of other match-winners.

'Admittedly Francis and Woodcock scored the goals, but it was the service from behind from Brooking, Wilkins, Coppell and Kevin that

— GREENWOOD

made them.

'Our first goal was particularly well-executed. It was a decisive, positive, delightful goal.

'We also showed we'd learned a lesson from the Austrian match because we didn't allow the Irish to settle and quickly put them under pressure.'

Greenwood's only mild criticism . . . 'We could have scored even more.'

DANNY BLANCHFLOWER was not bowled over by five-goal England.

The Northern Ireland manager said: 'We didn't concentrate. It was present's day. We handed England three or four goals. They certainly deserved to win but their goals were more our fault than a result of their good play.

'I'm still puzzled about this England team. They looked more uneasy than they should have been when we came back at the start of the second half.'

Both Blanchflower and Greenwood made Manchester United's Sammy McIlroy Ireland's man of the match.

TOO EASY . . . Trevor Francis beats Pat Jennings for England's first goal.

Five-star Francis

	P	W	D	L	F	A	Pts
England	6	5	1	0	18	5	11
Rep. of Ire.	6	2	3	1	9	5	7
N. Ireland	7	3	1	3	7	14	7
Denmark	7	1	2	4	13	14	4
Bulgaria	6	1	1	4	3	12	3

PREVIOUS RESULTS : Denmark 3, Rep. Ireland 3—Denmark 3, England 4—Rep. Ireland 0, N. Ireland 0—Denmark 2, Bulgaria 2—Rep. Ireland 1, England 1—N. Ireland 2, Denmark 1—Bulgaria 0, N. Ireland 2—England 4, N. Ireland

Northern Ireland ... (0) 1   England ... (2) 5
Moreland (pen).   Francis 2, Woodcock 2
25,000   *Nicholl o.g.*

TREVOR FRANCIS yesterday began England's transformation from a nation determined enough to reach Italy into a team dynamic enough to be genuine European Championship contenders.

A different class of striker and just the ticket for England

pounced to make an exceptional save from McIlroy.

Relieved, Wilkins, Brooking, Keegan and Coppell picked up their rhythm again in midfield and just after the hour Coppell swayed past Nelson, crossed on the run and watched admiringly as Woodcock lashed the ball into the goalmouth and Francis applied a deliberate finishing touch.

Blanchflower, whose own position looks less secure than

---

fulfilment that might have been; he encouraged Francis by letter and public word throughout the long rehabilitation.

When he came back, Francis was further encouraged by Revie's requests to play in a succession of testimonial matches, but three Under-23 games in 1976 were ruined by injury or illness. Finally, with even Ramsey publically canvassing for his inclusion, it appeared Francis had to play 89 consecutive League games and score 44 goals to prove to Don Revie that he was no longer prone to injury. In the middle of it all, when his gaunt face revealed the disappointment at not being chosen for another England squad, his controlled comment was no more than: "If I'm not in, then it means I'm not playing well enough. I shall just have to play a little bit better."

Finally came the month. In February, 1977, England had a friendly international against Holland, and Revie had virtually promised that this was the match for Francis. In training near Birmingham airport that week Trevor Francis was unmistakably the man grown out of the youth who so impressed Vasa Stojkovic five years before. There was a carpet of snow and ice under his feet rather than dusty dry grass; the slender frame had transformed into a sturdy athlete, and the acceleration was leaving men, not boys now, in his wake. It was amazing to see his appetite, so close to the England promise.

The headline that says it all about Trevor Francis's game for England.

On the field he was free, but his mind was cautious. There were newspapers offering him cash to give his views about the coming debut, but he said no and he actually told them why: it was because he didn't want to say or do anything that might even remotely harm his chance. And yet he did unburden himself freely over a long and memorable lunch to a journalist he had never met "simply because I felt the approach was constructive. My manager (Willie Bell) gave permission and from the start there was no question of sensations."

Trevor Francis that lunchtime cut a remarkably clean and open figure. When he realised the location was a licensed restaurant, he phoned Bell to inform him of the fact and the really striking aspect of the conversation after that was that here was a player who had been put on a pedestal, at least in the Midlands, throughout his career, here a young man about to play at the highest level in the world, and yet he was genuinely modest. More than that, he appeared to be reaching out, to a virtual stranger, for what seemed like reassurance.

Looking back to that lunchtime, Trevor says: "It wasn't that I had any doubts about my ability, but I was in awe, if that is the right word, of the other players. People like Kevin Keegan and Mick

Channon were established internationals, and suddenly, after all the waiting, there was a possibility that I might play alongside them – or even be asked to replace one of them.

"If I seemed to lack confidence, it was because I'm not one that sits down beforehand and analyses a game, or where I'm going. You see, I don't know what is going to happen next week. Looking back, the best start I could have had was being chosen for England youths; it was probably a pointer for the future, but there is so much that can go wrong." The England debut almost came into that category.

Of all places to contest a match before an international debut, Francis found himself at Liverpool against the champions. The match was a stampede, Birmingham being slaughtered 4–1 despite a 78-second goal from Kenny Burns. Keegan had predicted beforehand that Liverpool would give Francis special attention, and Keegan it was who willed and ran Liverpool's charge, demonstrating the work-rate which Francis had resolved to copy if he was to convince Revie of his manhood.

Francis had what Keegan described as "a magic half-hour". But suddenly he began to look taut and distressed ... then you noticed the limp. He played through the pain but came off at the end into the hands of the club doctor. He had badly bruised several toes. "I felt my injury jinx had caught up with me again," says Francis.

Birmingham physios worked throughout the Sunday to ease the bruises and finally Francis joined the England squad in their north London hotel at 6pm. He roomed with Butch Wilkins, but saw more of Emlyn Hughes and Trevor Cherry, the other "walking wounded" and eventually the three of them had fitness tests before the team could be announced on the Tuesday. "There I was, less than a day before the match, being tackled by the England manager. Eventually the decision whether I was fit to play was left to me. Five minutes later Don Revie announced the team. I was in, at No. 8. As soon as I got back to the hotel I phoned Helen, then my parents, but it really sunk in after lunch when I was taken by the boss to meet the press. That was more of an ordeal than the match; there were about 20 newsmen asking all manner of questions."

Revie took the brunt of the conference, saying "it will be very interesting to see if youngsters such as Francis can do better against top international teams than the likes of Keegan, Bowles and

Rising to the occasion: Don Revie once told Francis to challenge more in the air for England.

Channon ... If Francis is going to be an international player he must give a performance to 75 per cent of his ability in his first England game."

Francis was overwhelmed by the reception Birmingham supporters created for him outside Wembley stadium: "Incredible, when the coach arrived there were hundreds and hundreds of Blues fans outside the entrance chanting my name and carrying banners. Then, after the game, there were once again hundreds of fans saying congratulations for being picked. I had 92 telegrams, 65 of them waiting in the dressing room ... if I'd stopped to read them all, I'd have missed the kick-off. Then, afterwards, I was invited for a meal by a coachload of Birmingham D Club members: they had even baked a special cake and when Helen, my parents and myself walked in they all stood up to applaud."

Trevor Francis says that coming out of the tunnel to face his first 90,000 crowd that February night was "an emotional experience. I was so happy and proud for my family and friends I was nearer to tears than panic." Phyllis Francis may have been near to tears as well; she was in the stands with four broken bones in her ankle, the result of a fall on Boxing Day (And the Francis family still deny they are prone to injury!).

England was comprehensively beaten by the Dutch. Masters that day. And although Francis had a shot saved off the goalkeeper's legs, he summarised: "My debut got mixed up somewhere between Holland's 2–0 win and the acres of column inches devoted to opinions about the so-called state of English football." He admitted he was astonished by the close control even the Dutch defenders possessed and said: "It wasn't the easiest of debuts, but if anything good came out of it, at least I got a close-up of what a fabulous footballer Johan Cruyff is. He is able to create terror at speed, as well as slow down the game to his liking. I found this inspiring."

A month later, in his second international, Francis was played wide on the right in a 5–0 thrashing of Luxemburg. He had a hand in the opening goal scored by Keegan, scored the second himself with a sharp, left foot volley from seven yards, and had a classic winger's game. Don Revie made him the player of the match; Denis Law said "Francis was the difference between one-nil and five-nil" ... and then he was promptly dropped for the next two games.

Consolation was swift, however, when he played in June, 1977, probably his best game for England before the one in Belfast. The opposition? Brazil. The location? The world famous Maracana in Rio de Janeiro. The result? 0–0. It was the first time he had been selected in his club role – alongside the centre-forward. Francis ran assertively at the Brazilians, was paid the "compliment" of cynical fouls by ZeMaria and Rivelino, and though he missed a scoring chance, was "thrilled to bits" by his performance and the reception.

The late Les Cocker, the assistant manager, had been in charge of the team that day. When he remarked to Francis as he played tennis before the next England game, against Argentina, "Take it easy, you've a game on Sunday", Trevor excitedly phoned Helen to tell her he had a birthday present for her: he would be playing for England again. However, Don Revie, whose absence we now know was because he was negotiating his Saudi Arabian contract, returned to take Trevor aside and say: "I hear you had a good game in Rio . . . but you're on the bench tomorrow." Mick Channon, with his greater experience, was preferred.

"I had a raw deal there," says Trevor. "I remember going back to the hotel, into the room of Ray Kennedy and Phil Neal. I said something there I'm sure would have been wrong, but I was so upset that I contemplated flying home to England. Later I went to see Jack Wiseman, a director of Birmingham and an England committee member on the tour. He advised me not to do it, but that evening I still couldn't believe it: we were playing putting and bingo which Don Revie always arranged for the lads, but my thoughts were still on the fact that I was left out after my best performance for England, so when we finished and everybody went to bed, I stopped behind and asked Don Revie if I could have a word with him. I had been to Les Cocker first to ask if he minded if I went to see the boss - I was very much aware of the fact that I didn't want to put him in an awkward predicament. Then I explained the situation to Revie, who said he wasn't sure what Les Cocker had said to me; he told me I was a part of his plans.

"It never got to a serious shall or I shan't I position because of my ambitions to play for England and I remember sitting on the subs bench for the Argentina game, just hoping to get on. After that, the lads did well for a draw and it didn't surprise me that I was sub again for the Uruguay game. If I'm not playing, I always look for the reasons why, and I could see that he would keep faith with the lads."

When Ron Greenwood took over, therefore, his task was clearly to rid the England camp of the uncertainty created by Don Revie. Greenwood built a settled squad, he established an impressive record

of only two defeats in his first 23 games and, although he acknowledged his players' first true test was the European Championship in Italy, he firmly reconstructed the playing emphasis, so it was towards creative football. Kevin Keegan's enthusiasm bore the flag, but Trevor Brooking's subtlety was the real mark of change.

And Trevor Francis? For a year it looked as if Greenwood was not entirely convinced. He chose Francis in most squads but at one time appeared to view him as a substitute for Keegan alongside Bob Latchford.

"There was never the worry with Ron Greenwood we felt under Don Revie," says Francis. "He is easy to chat to and creates an atmosphere where we can relax and express ourselves; he leaves more to the players. Whenever he talks to me, we chat about the England-Hungary game which we won 4–1 in 1978. That obviously gave Ron Greenwood a great deal of satisfaction and from a personal point of view it was something new, the first time the boss tried a new formation with just Kevin (Keegan) and myself up front. He felt we could alternate – if Kevin was up, I'd drop back and vice versa. Ron still regards that as my best performance for England."

Later, Greenwood used Francis wide on the right, and eventually sharing a mobile striking role with Tony Woodcock, with Keegan in support. The true understanding, pace and quality were devastatingly apparent in Barcelona last March, where Woodcock scored through supreme acceleration and then Francis's instant control and instinctive finish completed a 2–0 victory. Here, enthused Greenwood, were players with character to withstand quite brutal physical intimidation, skill to punish opponents with goals. Suddenly, England had three match winners, Keegan and Woodcock, whose techniques were improved in the West German Bundesliga, and Francis, a talent made and matured in England.

That was the formation which dismantled the Northern Irish defence to consolidate England's position in the European Championship. "We want people who can be different, who aren't always settling for the obvious, the orthodox," Greenwood said approvingly.

The effectiveness of England's performance that day was the more laudable for the reason that the players spent the eve of the match in an undisclosed hotel near Belfast, a short time after the murder of Lord Mountbatten and the apparently increased IRA bombing activity at that time. In the light of that, it is interesting to eavesdrop on a Belfast to

Plymouth telephone conversation the night before.

Trevor: "Hello, Mum, everything all right?"

Mum Francis: "Yes, how are you?"

Trevor: "I'm feeling tired."

Mum Francis: "Never! It's only a 45 minutes trip across. How can you be feeling tired?"

Trevor: "They have two detectives in the hotel..."

Mum Francis: "Only *two*? I'd have thought they'd have been more than that."

Trevor: "I've got a boot at the end of the bed."

Mum Francis: "What for? That won't bring you good luck."

Trevor: "It's in case anybody comes into the room."

Mum Francis: "Don't be so silly!"

Trevor: "You know where we are, don't you?"

(It was 9.45pm and Mrs Francis had been waiting for a call since 7pm. Not even parents were told the name of the hotel.)

Mum Francis: "Yes I know."

Trevor: "Aren't you worried? Helen's petrified."

Mum Francis: "No, I'm more concerned what you're going to do tomorrow afternoon." "I think it's now or never, Trev."

Trevor: "What do you mean...?"

Mum Francis: "I think you've got to stamp your mark on the international scene. And I hope it comes off for you. You've got to pull something out of the hat... ...Trevor? Are you listening? You still there?"

(Silence.)

Mum Francis: "Trevor, I feel sure you've just got to make some justification to get into the England side. The *public* want it. We know what you can do... I only hope you can do it on the night, or the afternoon, whatever..."

Trevor: "Am I under pressure from you, mum?"

Mum Francis: "*Yes* – get your bloody finger out!"

There are bursts of laughter. Afterwards, Mrs Francis admits: "That's very unusual for me talking like that. I always just say 'I hope everything goes all right, Trev.' I think I've put my foot in it, haven't I?" She giggles.

The following morning, the day of the match, Trevor phones again. Mrs Francis daren't chance her luck again. Trevor's in such a lovely mood, wanting to speak to Ian and Carolyn and dad about records and driving lessons. She contents herself with wishing him all the best, and leaves it at that.

The tension hangs visibly around the council house in Plymouth as the kick-off nears. Mrs Francis is alone, feigning indifference, preparing the evening meal. She has Radio 2 on, listening for score-flashes. Suddenly she throws open a window: "One up! He's *scored*. A goal from nowhere the man said, a superb start by Francis!"

She sits down. She stands up. Sits down again, smokes. Plucks at grapes. A chocolate in one hand, a grape in the other. She looks exhausted. She lights another cigarette: "Trevor hates me smoking, you know?" she says as if she does it for that reason. "He has a notice in his car, No Smoking, but I always do." The phone rings. It is Helen. She says it's 2–0.

Apparently Helen had turned to Radio Telefis Eireann and was getting a running commentary. She had heard the score on the motorway as her dad drove her home from Wales, had a whim to stop a police patrol car and ask them to get a message to Trev's dad at the gasworks. She didn't, though. Now she'll clean the silver while listening.

Trevor's 21-year-old sister Carolyn walks in, beaming all over her face. Trev got one and Tony the other. The phone rings again. It's Aunt Doreen calling from the hairdressers to find out the score.

John Bennett, the BBC commentator, says: "The speed of this man Francis... carved the goal out with the precision of a brain surgeon, even though it's wet and slippery." However, in the second half, England come under pressure. McIlroy grazes the bar, Shilton saves. Penalty. 2–1. "Come on ... pull your fingers out, the lot of you," says mum. The phone interrupts. Aunt Dolly. By the time Phyllis returns, it is 3–1, but the commentary isn't clear on who scored. It's either Francis or Woodcock (it was Trevor). "Trevor Francis is making all the difference," comments Jimmy Armfield, the former England defender and Leeds manager. "He's looking very sharp today. England with three quick men up look as dangerous as I've seen them for some time..."

A good man, Jimmy.

The tension eases, the consumption of chocolates levels off. Ian, 23, arrives, accepts the news calmly, takes his own transistor upstairs. Goals four and five are anti-climactic in the Francis household, even though he's involved. Later, there's a bit of laughter when Malcolm Macdonald says over the radio: "I've known Trevor for many years now. He's a very shy, quiet lad. It takes him a long time to get settled into a group. He needs to get a little bit on the egotistical side."

Enter Roy Francis. Two radios are going, but he

knows the score. The smile tells you he's walking on water. "Nice for Trev to score a couple, and Tony (Woodcock) . . . The opposition sounded rubbish." They look at him and smile. He says nothing more except later, when the sports news repeats a summary, he comments: "Scored twice and made two . . . can't ask for more, no matter what the opposition."

The real relief of the night doesn't come till 9.45pm when Helen phones to say Trevor is back in Manchester. He wants her to book a table at their "little restaurant". He had a meal on the plane but he wouldn't sleep anyway tonight.

Some days afterwards, Trevor is discussing his Mum's phone call. "She *thought* she was putting pressure on me," he says. "She tried it again before the Forest-West Brom game and, since I scored again after a lean spell, she must have succeeded."

Lighthearted, it may be. Yet there is a serious intent in the way people inside and outside the family constantly look for something more from Trevor. Something that perhaps doesn't exist. From Roy Francis to Don Dorman to Don Revie, Bill Shankly and probably Uncle Tom Cobbleigh and all, they are looking for Trevor to "take the game by the scruff of the neck . . . have a bit more aggression in his play."

They all applaud the fact that he can be viciously fouled, get up, show no anger, and decide he must be getting the upper hand if his opponent resorts to fouls. Trevor is reminded of it every time he plays for England. There is always a telegram from Don Dorman, the scout who signed him for Birmingham. Even when he had his heart attack, he sent a telegram: "All the best, Trevor. Get hold of it and go at them."

Dorman sums up what they are saying when he comments: "Maybe what he needs is a bit of Kenny Burns inside him. Trevor's too nice, a nice West Country person. But for me, I agree with his dad: he's still to do it all in internationals. Y'see he allows himself to be dominated by players around him, players on his side with not half his skill. Once he realises he *is* Trevor Francis, once he gets out there like Kevin Keegan, full of the flowers of May, he will become *the* outstanding English player. Kevin Keegan is a good player, but Trevor Francis ought to be a better one. He can be a world-class player and he should be one now."

Bill Shankly says if he had signed Francis for Liverpool – "which I would have if he had been available" – he would have told him what he told Denis Law at 16. "I couldnae teach Law to *play*,"

stresses Shankly, "but I was teaching him to talk. Go on son, talk out there. And he'd go out, he'd be pushing a colossus, the size of Ron Yeats, back and goad him a bit: How the hell did *you* ever get a cap? Trevor could do this. You've to knock the shyness out of them." Shankly, for a split second confesses that John Charles never suffered from his shy gentleness. "You picked a good comparison there . . . a unique man, aye. But I'll say this: He was nearly the greatest player that ever played. If he'd have had the outlook of a Denis Law or an Alan Ball, he'd have gone down in history as the greatest that ever played."

It begins to have a familiar ring. Wasn't that what men like Joe Mercer used to say about Bobby Charlton? That he had so much talent, if only he would go forward, tear them apart . . . ?

And didn't Bobby Charlton react with the same tolerant, shy smile? And didn't he then beat his man in his own way?

What people are calling for it seems is a personality change. "The same thing happened in my case," says Kevin Griffin, the schoolboy chum who got left behind. "I don't know whether it's a characteristic of Plymouth, but it does take a hell of a lot to rile people there. In Bristol reserves I was knocking in 20 goals a season, and they were saying if only you were more aggressive! But I feel that you use aggression in different ways. You don't need to be knocking people over in the penalty box to prove you're brave, but that's what they faulted me on, same as Trevor."

Francis himself says: "People talk about aggression, but I think its aggressive to go at people, take them on, score goals. I like challenges, they drive me on, but it would be very difficult for me to adopt a ruthless attitude. It's not part of me or my upbringing. I've never been the sort to do a dirty about anything."

He takes comfort in the smaller, but equally convincing group who insist that he should be himself. "Jimmy Gordon (the 65-year-old Forest trainer) took me to one side the other day and said he'd noticed I was trying to rush everything, even where I'd got time. He told me I should relax more."

And that is precisely the message from Jackie Milburn, Wor Jackie of Newcastle fame: "Tell Trevor he's got to slow down. You know, there was a time Bobby Charlton tried to do everything at top speed, we all did. But, y'know, Bobby when he first started, same as me, he'd just crack 'em. What happened to Bobby I've seen happening to Trevor: Instead of just cracking 'em, you start trying to pick your spot, or trying to do things with that bit more aggression. And you lose a bit of natural ability. You're trying to live up to what the papers make out, and you've forgotten what you did in the schoolyard. And it's a funny thing, the older you get the more you realise – if only you could go back to them younger days, recapture what you did then without thinking about it.''

Milburn listens to all the advice to Francis to instil more aggression, more tackling back into his play, and says: "The only thing that worries me about Trevor is that *he* worries. And it shows in his play. I know Cloughie, I've been brought up in the same area, seen him at coaching courses. If he could, he would bring 15 men back. So now Trevor's worrying about chasing back. I'm not saying he should stop working, because he's not the sort to be out of a game for too long, but he should conserve enough energy to turn it on in those 60-yard runs. Why, if he came within 10 yards of his own half in my team, I'd fine him a week's wages.''

One area Roy Francis says his son got things exactly right is his marriage. "Helen's No. 1 now," says Roy. "She's perfect for him. He's always been looked after and she looks after him right."

The pursuit of Helen was a classic Woman's Own romance, and indeed it was published in the magazine in 1979. They met on holiday, had a wonderful time, and he took her phone number. But he lost it and all he could remember was that she worked as a hairdresser in a Llanelli salon. With the help of the Welsh player Gary Emmanuel, from Swansea, he began ringing every salon in the district and found her "on the 15th call". Of course, Helen, a steelworker's daughter, was never taken in by the line that he was a professional footballer . . . not until she found she had to do the travelling to keep the relationship going, and found dates subject to lengthy postponements for such things as treatment for injuries and cup replays. Not, though, that there were many of those at Birmingham. Helen was previously a rugby fan, a friend of Phil Bennett. She had only ever heard of George Best and Geoff Hurst, but is now a constant spectator at football (soccer in the States) because Trevor likes her there.

Priorities began to change in the footballer's household in November, 1979, when Matthew was born. He proved of independent mind when he arrived two weeks ahead of schedule and Trevor just

Trevor Francis, the international style.

The Francis body-swerve unbalances Bulgarian defender Ivan Iliev.

managed to keep his date at the delivery after rushing back from a testimonial match, coincidentally at Plymouth. The young man who found it highly embarrassing whenever mothers plonked baby James on his lap to be photographed with the £1 million man is now prone to waking up his young son to play on the floor. There is no truth in the rumour that his position has already been designated; indeed, with Helen's background, it is not certain which ball the lad will excel with.

One thing the boy is sure to learn very quickly, if there is a choice, is to eat his mother's cooking rather than his father's. When Trevor shared a house with goalkeeper Gary Sprake, even he admits the cooking was close to disastrous. Helen, on the other hand, is a superb cook and her specialities include a variety of Tarantini dishes – specially garnished steaks which she was taught to cook by Alberto Tarantini, the Argentine international who spent a season with Birmingham. In return, Alberto has gone back to Argentina with a strong Devon accent, so often was he with Trevor, who befriended him as he seems to any outsider.

And one day, if Trevor's boy like everyone else Francis seems to bump into, asks: "Do you think you were worth a million, dad?" Trevor will look at him and say (assuming circumstances do not change): "Son, I look at my car which is probably worth £18,000, and I think no way is it worth that; and I look at our house, a hundred grand, and I think no way is that worth what it cost either ... but if you want something and you have the money, you'll pay for it. The greatest honour Brian Clough paid me is that he wanted to pay the million. With the record he's got, he's no bad judge, so I must be worth it."

Whether or not the fee is out of proportion isn't for Francis to say, although he asks: "How can any player be worth a million? How can you put that kind of valuation on anything, how would you compare it?" You could begin perhaps by equating the fee Forest paid for one man to the £1 million which the Government injected through Sports Council grants to inaugurate a new concept amongst 18 League clubs to develop grounds to serve the surrounding area with its facilities, developing football stadiums as the fulcrum of the community.

The advantages and disadvantages to Mr and Mrs Trevor Francis of that £1 million tag divide quite evenly: the advantages into commercial deals which grew in proportion to the enormity of the fee, and the disadvantages into the cost to their private lives, a cost which spread around them like a plague.

First there were the begging letters. One arrived from a lady in Cornwall who said her husband was out of work, would Trevor please send her money to provide him with a meal to celebrate their golden wedding? Another from a man who wanted £5,000 to enable him to give up his job so he could concentrate on writing his poetry. Francis happened to open that one at the club and his teammate Ian Bowyer said: "That's absolutely ridiculous ... send him £3,000, five's a bit strong."

Helen had nasty letters, such as the one telling her: "I see you've already spent your husband's money. That coat you had on on TV obviously cost him a packet." Helen says the trouble is, everybody thinks Trevor was paid the £1 million himself.

Strictly unfunny was the occasion when some

162

unsavoury Birmingham City supporters asked for his autograph and, while he went into the club offices, smashed huge dents into the top of his Jaguar. This, apparently was in retribution for the fact that he did not have a pen to sign autographs. The car also proved a Halloween target when somebody decided to break half a dozen eggs over the £1 million man's motor.

Neither Trevor nor Helen could go out for months without being pestered in streets, shops, restaurants. "When people came up and politely asked 'How are you Trev?' it was no problem at all. But I'd answer politely, and then they'd suddenly say: 'What's Cloughie like then as a motivator?' Oh, brilliant really, I'd say, he does ever so well . . . So then they'd go into 'What's he like as a tactician then?' And it would go on, usually ending up with them saying that I should tell the boss what he's doing wrong and so on. It's so rude: can you imagine me going up to Jack Nicklaus and asking him how the hell he missed that putt?"

For Helen it was just as bad. She would get women coming up to her in supermarkets, saying they knew she was pregnant because they'd seen it in the papers. That it was disgusting that Trevor sent her out shopping. There was one man who followed her around, a crackpot who eventually rang the doorbell and said he was the police, he knew who she was, she was Mrs Francis. People also asked what they intended to call the baby so they could call their own children the same, and even asked Helen what she was going to do about Peter Taylor's remarks in the papers.

Neither could the families in Plymouth and Llanelli escape. Trevor's mum was sitting at the hairdressers when a woman asked sarcastically: "What's it like having a son who's a millionaire?" And Helen's dad, who can be a bit fiery if pushed, came close to "laying one on" a bloke who sneered: "New suit, have we? I expect Trevor's bought you that?"

If Trevor and Helen wanted to buy anything – anything at all – they found it best to let Helen go in and pay for it while Trevor waited almost as a fugitive outside. "If they saw my face, the price went sky high". Even negotiating for their new home in Nottingham proved testy because Francis felt at a disadvantage once the vendor clearly knew who he was.

Against all that, there were the more welcome moments. The letter from a young boy in Africa saying "I'm the Nigerian Trevor Francis, can you send me your boots so I can really play like you?"

The power and the balance, the left thigh takes the strain as Francis keeps the ball in play.

The wholehearted response from radio listeners who enjoyed his two-hour Star Special presentation of pop music, fans who wrote long appreciative letters concluding: "PS. I hear you are also quite a good footballer".

And then there were the commercial spin-offs. Helen was asked down to London to model clothes and Trevor's agent Dennis Roach was inundated with firms wanting to use the £1 million footballer in advertisements. "Apart from the big Adidas break-through, we had Nike, an American shoe firm offering to match it dollar for dollar. The tag of

being the first £1 million player seemed to open up avenues not previously available to footballers. They were after the £1 million image,'' said Roach.

"There are two television adverts in the pipeline, one on a hosiery line, ('If a million pound player is prepared to wear our socks . . . ') and another on hair shampoos which is a tie-up with Helen. We are considering offers from British Airways and a bicycle company and when Helen finds more time after her involvement with the baby we are keen to promote the His and Her image.''

Roach has no doubt that Francis will eventually become a millionaire, and points out that Trevor himself is insisting on taking few contracts and quality work only. "Brian Clough is advised of everything in advance and I can only say that he's co-operated 200 per cent, in every way, on Trevor's endorsements. Mind you, we don't tell him about the contracts we turn down . . . such as the stocking manufacturers who had a sexy His and Her idea of their own. They offered a contract worth a minimum £5,000 a year and Trevor wouldn't even listen to it. He has turned down even bigger sums because the proposals do not fit a healthy and clean image or because they would make too many demands on his time. People have got the idea that Trevor is a placid character, but behind that surface image he is very strong and won't put up with any nonsense.''

The agent, who was introduced to Francis by Johan Cruyff for whom he had acted in Britain, says he has been surprised by the way Francis can walk off an aeroplane in the States and deal with the media for 45 minutes at a time and never appear distressed. "I find myself hovering there, waiting to jump in . . . but he never seems to need it.'' He found that Francis knew exactly what he wanted to do and how long he was prepared to spend on things. One of Roach's priorities has been to organise a fan club for the 200-plus letters arriving every week from Scandinavia, America and even Asia.

"He already had an accountant and a solicitor whom he totally trusted and he virtually put the deal to me – he wanted all three of us to work in harmony.''

Trevor Francis might have a shrewd idea of exactly where to draw the line. He has learned to accept that he is fair game for such radio programmes as "Hello Cheeky'' which delight in such quips as: "Britain's first million-pound footballer Trevor Francis slammed his locker door too quickly today

Pas de deux – Francis and Bulgarian defender Georgi Dmitrov in perfect symmetry.

23/2 PHONPICHAI R.D.
HAADYAI SONGKHLA
THAILAND.

DEAR .. TRAVOR FRANCIS

THIS IS MY FIRST LETTER TO YOU, I AM A THAI BOY WHO LIVE IN THAILAND I AM THE GREAT SUPPORTER OF NOTTINGHAM - FOREST

I LIKE THE MANAGER AND ALL PLAYERS OF YOUR CLUB BUT - YOU ARE MY FAVORITE PLAYER.

WOULD YOU MIND GIVING ME YOUR PHOTO AND NOTTINGHAM - FOREST TEAM GROUP IN COLOR & SEASON OF FOOTBALL MATCH, MANY THINGS OF YOUR CLUB, TEAM KIT OF YOUR CLUB AND YOUR STORY PLEASE. THANK YOU VERY MUCH.

I HOPE TO HEAR FORM YOU SOON.

LOVE YOU
CHAT CHAI CHAI VIVUT

I AM NOT GOOD AT ENGLISH

PLEAS PARDON FOR ME TOO.

From Scandinavia to Africa, from the USA to Thailand, the fanmail pours in. This, and two hundred letters a week from all over the world, prompted Francis to start an organised fan club early in 1980.

and cut off 38 quid . . . doctors say the fingernail will grow again.'' Yet there is one inevitable question he, in common with so many professional sportsmen, has never dared look into: What comes after football?

It was in fact Anthony Dowell, the ballet dancer, who best put the dilemma shared by all performance artists and athletes: that the agony of their existence is that as experience mounts, so the body is going in the opposite direction. There will come a time when the touch deserts even a gilt-edged player, so what is Francis preparing for that day?

"I learnt the mistake of trying to predict things in this game when I was 16,'' he says. "I was asked to make a prediction on radio and I boasted I'd score 30 goals the next season. Freddie Goodwin heard the tape and said: Edit that out, then he told me that I was leaving myself wide open to criticism.''

But preparation for the sporting "afterlife'' is surely different? Does he not want anything or dread anything?

"I can't think of a single thing I desperately want,'' he answers. "And I never look on the black side of things. Well, I know already that when I do finish I shall be disappointed . . . that's the only thing I dread.''

The lifestyle of the successful footballer . . .
Before his 26th birthday, in April 1980,
Trevor Francis bought a new home, set in $3\frac{1}{2}$
acres near Newark in rural Nottinghamshire.
The £100,000 house is an investment as well as
a symbol of Trevor's earning power in a
game to which he thoroughly enjoys
dedicating himself.

For Helen Francis it is her fourth house in
$5\frac{1}{2}$ years of marriage; and now Matthew,
already in his second home at four months, is
the centre of attention. If Trevor Francis
stays in Nottingham, you can easily envisage
Matthew's first dog-paddles in the 30ft.
heated indoor swimming pool on the south
side of the house. But, a player's life being
what it is, transient, the boy may well not
graduate to using the sauna, much less the
billiards room upstairs behind double
mahogany doors.

If there is anything that worries the master
of the house, it is that his lifetime's work, and
the achievements he still seeks, are set
against a time clock. The comforts may, with
care and common sense, stretch on, but the
peak of both earnings and ability will extend,
God willing, perhaps six more years.

Key to introductory picture gallery

● Where timing and courage is all ... Francis appears oblivious to the flailing fists of Chelsea goalkeeper Petar Borota.

● A player written into history simply through the price on his head and the signatures of men willing to pay.

● Nottingham Red, England white, Detroit orange ... colours that merge into a single figure of a man most wanted.

● A last fling for Birmingham. Francis attempts a spectacular overhead kick at the end of nine years at St. Andrews.

Picture credits

● At work and play, if Francis is there in Detroit the publicity machinery can never be far away.

● A taste of the good life, but for Helen as well as Trevor Francis everything has to pass the test.

● He shall leap tackles wherever he moves . . . speed and courage override even artistry amidst the lunging boots.

● Back endpaper: The elements of concentration and movement become inseparable as Alan Gowling meets Trevor Francis.